Social History of Africa

TANU WOMEN

uses women's lives to prove her point

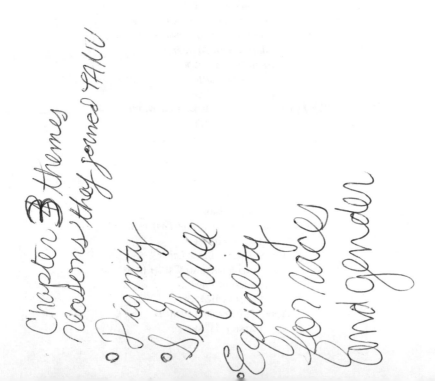

Chapter 3 themes

reasons they joined TANU

o Dignity
o Self rule
o Equality
for races
and gender

Social History of Africa Series

Series Editors: Allen Isaacman and Jean Hay

TANU WOMEN

GENDER AND CULTURE IN THE MAKING OF TANGANYIKAN NATIONALISM, 1955–1965

Susan Geiger

HEINEMANN   JAMES CURREY   E.A.E.P   MKUKI NA NYOTA
Portsmouth, NH   Oxford   Nairobi   Dar es Salaam

Columbia FLI Partnership
HQ1236.5 T34 G45 1997

Heinemann	James Currey Ltd	E.A.E.P.	Mkuki Na Nyota
A division of	73 Botley Road	Kijabe Street	P.O. Box 4246
Reed Elsevier Inc.	Oxford OX2 0BS	P.O. Box 45314	Dar es Salaam
361 Hanover Street	United Kingdom	Nairobi	Tanzania
Portsmouth, NH 03801-3912		Kenya	
Offices and agents throughout the world			

The author and publisher wish to thank those who have generously given permission to reprint borrowed material:

Photo credits: *Daily News/Sunday News* Dar es Salaam, Tanzania, p. 52, 54, 62, 70, and 200. *Government Information Office of Tanzania*, Dar es Salaam, Tanzania, p. 112, 192, and 203.

ISBN 0-435-07254-4 (Heinemann cloth)
ISBN 0-435-07421-0 (Heinemann paper)
ISBN 0-85255-679-9 (James Currey cloth)
ISBN 0-85255-629-2 (James Currey paper)

British Library Cataloguing in Publication Data
Geiger, Susan
    Tanu women: gender and culture in the making of Tanganyikan nationalism, 1955–1965.—(Social history of Africa)
    1. Women—Tanganyika—History 2. Nationalism—Tangyanika I. Title
    967.8'2'03'082
    ISBN 0-85255-629-2 (Paper)
    ISBN 0-85255-679-9 (Cloth)

Library of Congress Cataloging-in-Publication Data
Geiger, Susan.
    TANU women: gender and culture in the making of Tanganyikan nationalism, 1955–1965 / Susan Geiger.
    p.   cm. —(Social history of Africa)
    Includes bibliographical references and index.
    ISBN 0-435-07254-4 (cloth).—ISBN 0-435-07421-0 (paper)
    1. Women in politics—Tanzania. 2. TANU (Organization). Women's Section—History. 3. Umoja wa Wanawake wa Tanzania—History. 4. Women in development—Tanzania. 5. Women—Tanzania—Social conditions. 6. Nationalism—Tanzania. 7. Tanzania—Politics and government—1964– I. Title. II. Series.
    HQ1236.5.T34G45 1998   97–27010
    305.42'06'0678—dc21   CIP

Cover design by Jenny Jensen Greenleaf
Cover photo: Women's March, Dar es Salaam, 1984. Photo by Susan Geiger.

Printed in the United States of America on acid-free paper.
00 99 98 97   DA   1 2 3 4 5 6 7 8 9

For all TANU women, and
For my mother, Susan Geiger, whose
"When will you finish that book?" kept me going, and
For Janet Spector, who never doubted that I would.

CONTENTS

LIST OF MAP
AND PHOTOGRAPHS

GLOSSARY OF SWAHILI TERMS

askari	soldier, guard, policeman
baraza	official meeting
buibui	black head-to-foot garment worn by Muslim women in public
heshima	respect
kanga	cloth wrap
kitenge	patterned cloth rectangles
lelemama	a form of *ngoma* group that originated on Zanzibar
maduka	rural shops
mwali	girl who has come of age, reached puberty
mwami	chief
ngoma	drum; also a musical group involving singing and dancing[a]
pombe	locally produced beer
shehe	Muslim religious leader
sheheratib	lead singer in an *ngoma* group
shamba	farm, plot of land
shoga	close woman friend, a term of endearment or familiarity between women
uhuru	freedom
ujamaa	familyhood, kinship, community
upato	[games]; rotating savings/credit unions
ushoga	friendship between women
ushugi	headcloth
vitumbua	rice flour fritters

---

[a] Each group has a distinctive name, such as "Egyptian," Alwatan," "Bombakusema," "Submarine," or "Good Luck."

ABBREVIATIONS
USED IN THE TEXT

AMNUT	All Muslim National Union of Tanganyika
CCM	Chama cha Mapinduzi
COSATA	Cooperative Societies of Tanganyika
CSR	Congress for the Second Republic of Malawi
DC	District commissioner
IJAHS	International Journal of African Historical Studies
JAH	Journal of African History
KCCU	Kilimanjaro Chagga Citizens Union
NEC	National Executive Council
OAU	Organization of African Unity
PAFMECA	Pan-African Freedom Movement of East and Central Africa
PRO	Public Records Office
RH	Rhodes House
SDO	Social development officer
TAA	Tanganyika African Association
TAGSA	Tanganyika African Government Servants Association
TANU	Tanganyika African National Union
TANUYL	TANU Youth League
TCW	Tanganyika Council of Women
TNA	Tanzania National Archives
UMCA	Universities Mission to Central Africa
UTAFITI	National Scientific Research Council of Tanzania
UTP	United Tanganyika Party
UWT	Umoja wa Wanawake wa Tanzania
WRDP	Women's Research and Documentation Project
WSL	Women's Service League

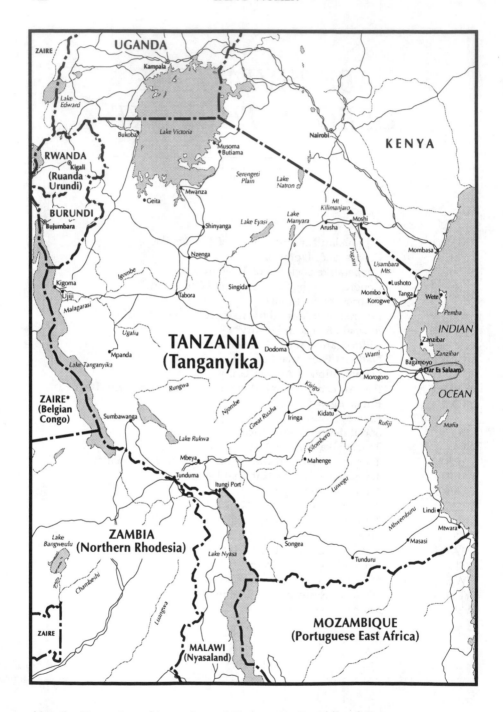

Map 1: Tanzania and its environs. * Democratic Republic of Congo

PREFACE

Time was when I accepted the idea that a book should have sections entitled "Acknowledgements" and "Preface" where an author mentions helpful people and funding agencies, and says something about the origins and context of her research. In the course of researching and writing this book, however, I came to regard such divisions as misleading and forced. Many of the individuals who made my work possible (acknowledgments) and the circumstances under which I worked (preface) were as much a part of the *content* of my research—my understanding of what I was doing and how I was doing it—as the information I was gathering, whether from people or written sources.

In an initial draft of this book, I avoided these divisions by attempting to weave into my introduction material and thoughts usually consigned to pre-introductory and arguably dispensable sections. (Do *you* always read acknowledgements and preface?) But my editors balked; and readers of that draft agreed that the introduction was too long and covered too much.

Fortunately, Gracia Clark, in her 1994 study of Ghanaian market women, *Onions Are My Husband*, provided a model of compromise for me: a preface that includes a narrative acknowledging in more than a perfunctory way the extent to which individuals and her own prior experience and even personality shaped and informed her research and interests and therefore her findings.[1] With thanks to Gracia, I have adapted the model of her preface to provide readers with a picture of this book's genesis and development.

I first became interested in women's participation in Tanzania's nationalist movement in 1979, while conducting research on the extent to which Tanzania's National Women's Organization, Umoja wa Wanawake wa Tanzania (UWT), was able to respond effectively to the needs of poor rural women.[2] In reading documents in the Tanzania National Archives (TNA) and theses in the University of Dar es Salaam's East Africana Collection, I came across references to the UWT's predeces-

---

[1] For example, her explanation that "Diffidence about ethnographic authority encouraged me to plan a specialized study of market relations rather than aiming to understand the total lives of traders in any definitive way." See Gracia Clark, *Onions Are My Husband: Survival and Accumulation by West African Market Women* (Chicago, 1994), xix.

[2] Susan Geiger, "Umoja wa Wanawake and the Needs of the Rural Poor," *African Studies Review* 25, 2/3 (1982): 45–65; Susan Geiger, "Efforts Towards Women's Development in Tanzania: Gender Rhetoric vs. Gender Realities," *Women and Politics* 2, 4 (1982): 23–41 (also published in Kathleen Staudt and Jane Jaquette, eds., *Women in Developing Countries: A Policy Focus* [New York, 1983]).

sor, the Women's Section of the Tanganyika African National Union (TANU), and to Bibi Titi Mohamed, leader of the TANU Women's Section and first chairman of UWT, about whom I knew little beyond her imprisonment for treason in the early 1970s.

During the fall of 1983, with a single-quarter leave and funding from the Graduate School at the University of Minnesota, I spent five weeks in England in search of written documentation concerning Bibi Titi Mohamed and other TANU women activists. While I spent most of that time in the library of the School of Oriental and African Studies, to whose staff I am most grateful, I owe a particular debt to John Iliffe of Cambridge University, who generously provided me with his meticulous notecards on women in TANU, recorded during his own research in the late 1960s.

In important respects, however, July 1984—thirty years to the month from the date of the establishment of TANU—marks the moment of my commitment to this project. In that month, I arrived in Dar es Salaam, hoping to record Bibi Titi Mohamed's life history and the life histories of other TANU women activists. Thus 1984 was the year from which many of the TANU activists interviewed, including Bibi Titi Mohamed, reflected back upon political actions and experiences that had taken place some three decades earlier.

It was purely coincidental but obviously crucial to my work that on October 2, 1984 while I was in Dar es Salaam, President Julius Nyerere appeared in public with Bibi Titi for the first time since her fall from grace. Some six months before arriving in Tanzania, I had applied for research clearance from UTAFITI (the National Scientific Research Council of Tanzania) and sent my research proposal as well to members of the Women's Research and Documentation Project (WRDP) at the University of Dar es Salaam. But as long as Bibi Titi remained *persona non grata*, UTAFITI decision-makers were bound to question my interest in her and in TANU women activists associated with her, as were other Tanzanians.[3]

Bibi Titi's situation was not the only factor shaping my life and research during the months I spent in Tanzania in 1984. Most analysts and most Tanzanians would agree that the country reached a low point in its postcolonial economic decline during that year—a year that also saw the beginning of the end of the government's resistance to International Monetary Fund and World Bank demands for economic restructuring. Public transportation and the roads to support it were among the many casualties of Tanzania's disastrous economic situation. On many occasions, it took over two hours of waiting and bus travel each way to get to the University of Dar es Salaam, some six miles from the town center, to discuss my work with colleagues and use the East Africana research collection. Because the University had long ceased to have money to purchase books or journals, and because students were desperate enough to take books or segments of them in order to study for exams, the main university library was of little use to me. But I could

---

[3] UTAFITI did not provide reasons for granting research clearance; nor did they explain why clearance was delayed, as it was in my case, or denied, which was not uncommon. From the late 1970s and well into the 1980s, foreign researchers were generally regarded with suspicion and Tanzanians were frequently worried about local informers among them. See Donna Kerner, "The Social Uses of Knowledge in Contemporary Tanzania" (Ph.D. dissertation, City University of New York, 1988), viii–ix.

also work in the Tanzania National Archives, a two-mile walk into the city center from where I was living.

The impoverishment of virtually all sectors of the Tanzanian economy affected my sense of what I could reasonably expect to do, and served as a constant reminder of the relative insignificance of my needs as a foreign researcher, and my interest in history. At the same time, as a result of my own adult life history, I received vital assistance in my daily life and work in Tanzania during 1984. For much of that time, I lived in Upanga (Dar es Salaam) in the "middle-class" household of M. W. K. and Natalia Chiume. Natalia Nathanael (Chiume) was a former Tabora Girls' School student whom I had gotten to know while teaching there from 1962 to 1964.[4] Natalia became my younger sister's "pen pal," and a dozen years later, in 1975, the two met when my sister stopped in Dar es Salaam on her way home from two years as a Peace Corps math teacher in Fiji. Four years later, in 1979, our friendship was renewed when I was in Tanzania for three months as advisor to a group of twelve Minnesota college and university students undertaking study projects. At that time, I was accompanied by my son David, who had been born in Arusha in 1966 while I was working on my Ph.D. research on Mount Kilimanjaro. During my 1979 visit, David often played with Natalia's oldest sons, Tasokwe (Tassi) and William (Bossi), and, when they could get money from us, went to Bruce Lee "Kung Fu" movies together.

Natalia, her husband, and their five children, were my family. I lived with them during most of my stay in Dar es Salaam in 1984, eating vegetables and fruits from their garden and sharing the sugar and bread rations to which Natalia was entitled through her place of work, the Tanzania School for the Deaf. For one week following each of two fishing trips to the waters near Mafia Island, we ate some of the miraculous-looking fish Kanyama brought back for the family and to sell in Dar es Salaam. While I lived with them, and when house-sitting for U.S. Embassy employees on vacation, I paid the Chiumes the maintenance portion of my grant money; and I supplied staples (oil, soap, toilet paper, and peanut butter) unavailable in town that I purchased from a friend with American Embassy privileges.

Postmodern critics of all face-to-face relations between privileged Westerners such as myself and nonprivileged persons such as most Tanzanians might misread the above paragraph as a naive claim to parity on my part, if not with the poorest of the poor in Tanzania, at least with urban/suburban, struggling but educated people such as the Chiumes. It is one of the ironies of "self-positioning" that for some academics, scrutinizing the text produced by that act for the researcher's failings has now become a scholarly end in itself.[5] Western feminist scholars have arguably been particularly vulnerable to criticism precisely because they have taken seriously the responsibility to publish not only what they know, but how they think they know it and where they

---

[4]   I was teaching in Tabora as part of the Teachers for East Africa program developed to provide American replacements for the British teachers leaving Tanganyika, Uganda and Kenya at independence.

[5]   See for example, the introduction by Sherna Berger Gluck and Daphne Patai to their edited volume, *Women's Words: The Feminist Practice of Oral History* (New York, 1991); also in that volume, Claudia Salazar, "A Third World Woman's Text: Between the Politics of Criticism and Cultural Politics"; and Daphne Patai, "U.S. Academics and Third World Women: Is Ethical Research Possible?"

were situated in the act of trying to understand.[6] It is, of course, a further irony that most scholars, whether male or female, foreign or indigenous, continue to draw a veil of silence over the subjective aspects and conditions in which they produce their work, thereby escaping scrutiny and dissection.

Foreign researchers working in Tanzania from the late 1960s on will confirm that Tanzanians themselves were raising questions about place, power, and privilege and the use and production of knowledge long before these issues became the stock in trade of postmodern academics. Critical scrutiny and oversight were exercised by the government and came as well from Tanzanian intellectuals working at the University of Dar es Salaam. Government policy stipulated that all research conducted in Tanzania had to be relevant to the needs and priorities of the nation; while critics on "The Hill" (as the University is aptly named) pointed to the differential access of foreign and local scholars to books and journals, to research funds, and to communications systems of all kinds (from conferences to computers, and from reliable phones and mail delivery to fax and publishing outlets). The "help" those of us who were foreign researchers could offer our Tanzanian colleagues, far from eroding the gulf of privilege between us, reinscribed our relative power. We could try to find fellowships for those who wanted to study elsewhere; we could offer conference invitations and hustle funds to enable Tanzanian scholars to attend; we could assist certain individuals in our fields of interest and suggest joint projects. Although it was clear that such acts did little if anything to redistribute power based on institutional placement and location, I met few Western or Tanzanian scholars who misunderstood these acts or dismissed them as insignificant because of their limited nature.

In contrast to the concerns expressed by many Tanzanians, most postmodern critics have focused more directly on the perceived power of Western researchers over the human subjects of their research. Many fail to add that privilege and power are always contextual and relative, underestimating at best and devaluing at worst the intelligence of the "researched" and the extent of control all Africans exercise in their relationships with researchers. Yet multiple kinds of power exist and are exercised and exchanged in a research relationship, and there are many ways in which researchers are dependent upon those with whom they seek such a relationship.[7] Ultimately, of course, a researcher has the final power of "translation."[8]

---

[6]   Examples of feminist scholars who have positioned themselves include Marjorie Shostak, *Nisa: The Life and Words of a !Kung Woman* (Cambridge, 1981); Belinda Bozzoli, with Mmantho Nkotsoe, *Women of Phokeng: Consciousness, Life Strategy, and Migrancy in South Africa, 1900–1983* (Portsmouth, N.H., 1991); Shula Marks, ed., *'Not Either An Experimental Doll'* (Durban, 1987); and Sara Mirza and Margaret Strobel, eds., *Three Swahili Women* (Bloomington, 1989). For a blatant example of critical scrutiny as scholarly product, see Kirk Hoppe, "Whose Life Is It, Anyway? Issues of Representation in Life Narrative Texts of African Women," *International Journal of African Historical Studies[IJAHS]* 26, 3 (1993): 623–36; but see also, Heidi Gengenbach's excellent response, "Truth-Telling and the Politics of Women's Life History in Africa: A Reply to Kirk Hoppe," *IJAHS* 27, 3 (1994): 619–27.

[7]   For telling accounts of the powers wielded by research "subjects" and the dependence of researchers see Carol Spindel, *In the Shadow of the Sacred Grove* (New York, 1989); Margery Wolf, *A Thrice Told Tale: Feminism, Postmodernism and Ethnographic Responsibility* (Stanford, 1992); Kamala Visweswaran, *Fictions of Feminist Ethnography* (Minneapolis,1994).

[8]   The best rendering of the "power exchange" that goes on in a relationship with a "life historian" is contained in Ruth Behar, *Translated Woman: Crossing the Border with Esperanza's Story* (Boston, 1993).

To return to my own circumstances, I state that the Chiumes became "my family," with full knowledge of what that entails in terms of mutual affection and contradictions, understandings and misunderstandings, inequalities and obligations. I talk about eating their food in 1984 well aware that I was consuming scarce resources; and I report that I paid them in money and consumer goods. I remain acutely conscious of the realities of difference between us. Most obviously, I have chosen to be in Tanzania for a variety of reasons over time, and I can leave behind conditions the Chiumes neither chose nor created.

An enjoyable and familial living situation wasn't the only way I benefitted from my twenty-year friendship with Natalia. Natalia's husband, himself a veteran anticolonial nationalist from Malawi, was deeply interested in and personally familiar with TANU's origins and development. A Malawian exile, and former minister of external affairs, Mr. Chiume was first and foremost a politician. Founder and chairman of the anti-Banda, prodemocracy Congress for the Second Republic of Malawi (CSR), he devoted most of his energy and resources to Malawi's liberation—a cause absent from support groups' lists of major African crises in the 1970s and early '80s. Since his escape to Tanzania in 1964, Mr. Chiume had also worked as a journalist, novelist and publisher. However, because of the economic crisis gripping Tanzania in 1984, he barely received enough for his articles to pay the cost of their postage to the journal or newspaper concerned. Moreover, his publishing business had no paper and a major client, the Tanzanian Ministry of Education, had long since stopped paying for the Swahili translations of Nkrumah and other African leaders that Mr. Chiume had written for the nation's secondary schools. Undaunted, he turned his hand to farming and occasional fishing trips to help make ends meet.

It was my good fortune that the constraints Mr. Chiume faced as a publisher and journalist left him in a position to offer me assistance to an extent that would scarcely have been possible in better times. His own secondary schooling in Tanganyika and his early political career had frequently intersected with those of the emerging East and Central African nationalists of the 1950s, and his abiding interest in and passion for African and pan-African politics of the post–World War II era had never dimmed.[9] Indeed, he is a well-known and warmly regarded figure among many TANU veterans, including Bibi Titi Mohamed. Thus it was that Kanyama Chiume made many of the initial inquiries and contacts that enabled me to get started, enthusiastically poured over the list of names I had gleaned from John Iliffe's notes and Swahili histories, worked with me on interview questions, accompanied me on many interviews, and transcribed many interview tapes. It is no exaggeration to say that I could not have accomplished the interviews conducted in 1984, and many other aspects of my research from that point onwards, without his assistance.[10]

The TANU Women's Section was born in Dar es Salaam, the capital, and there were therefore good reasons to begin our interviews with activists in that city and surrounding communities. Had the economic situation been better and transportation

---

[9] See his autobiography, *Kanyama Chiume*, published in the Panaf Great Lives series (London, 1982), a revised version of his earlier book, *Kwacha* (Nairobi, 1975).

[10] In early 1994, Mr. Chiume was finally able to return to Malawi. He was met with a hero's welcome, escorted to his home area, and launched into the newly democratized politics of the country.

less difficult, I might have attempted to extend my 1984 interviews to other parts of Tanzania. As it was, with two exceptions,[11] all of the women we interviewed during the five-month period of research in 1984 lived in Dar es Salaam and its environs. Towards the end of my stay, the funeral of a relative took Mr. Chiume to Dodoma, where he managed to interview three more prominent TANU activists.[12]

By the time a sabbatical leave and funds provided through the University of Minnesota's Bush Sabbatical Program and a Fulbright Senior Research Award from the Africa Program enabled me to return to Tanzania in 1988, travel conditions were somewhat improved and I was able to interview TANU activists in Moshi and Mwanza as well as in Dar es Salaam. Again, Tanzanian friends and colleagues provided me with introductions to individuals in each place who helped me in crucial ways. Eva Pendaeli Sarakikya, with whom I had taught at Tabora Girls' Seconday School, introduced me to the Moshi regional cooperative development officer, Bassilla Urasa of Machame, who helped me locate and interview TANU activists in the Moshi area and whose daughter, Anita, also assisted with interviews and tape transcription and translation. Ruth Meena of the WRDP and the Political Science Department at the University of Dar es Salaam sent me to her sister in Mwanza, while Grace Mesaki helped with additional interviews in Dar es Salaam.

Following my 1988–89 sabbatical, a Rockefeller Humanist in Residence award enabled me to spend the 1989–90 academic year at the Southwestern Institute for Research on Women at the University of Arizona, in Tucson. There, two scholar-activists, Renny Golden and Fran Buss, provided invaluable intellectual and moral support while I wrote; and I presented aspects of my research to a helpful audience of women's studies faculty and students before returning to Minnesota to chair the Women's Studies Department.

By the time of my third and final research trip to Tanzania related to this study (one month in 1992) further change, both political and economic, was altering the focus and shape of national and nationalist political discourse. "Democratization" had led to the end of one-party rule and the formation of new political parties, none of which seemed at that time to be able to garner broad support. Organizations affiliated to TANU and later to its successor, Chama cha Mapinduzi (CCM)—the Party of Revolution—including the UWT, were detaching from party control. Echoed and fed by politicians and an expanded media no longer subject to government sanction, people's anger over economic dislocation and increasing economic disparity focused on convenient targets. Tanzania's Asian population in particular, always vulnerable for their privileged position as "middlemen" during the colonial period, was increasingly subject to verbal and physical attacks, and identified as the sole beneficiaries of "economic liberalization" which they were allegedly using to grab valuable land and dominate commerce. The direct association of particular religious groups and denominations with political programs, demands, and complaints—an association that Nyerere continuously and firmly overrruled both before and after independence—seemed in the as-

---

[11]   These were a trip to Morogoro to interview Hadija Swedi; and to Zanzibar, where the UWT secretary (undoubtedly thinking of my convenience) summoned women activists to UWT headquarters to talk with me. Some fifteen women showed up, creating conditions that were very interesting but precluded open exchange.

[12]   Kijakazi Feruzi, Tabu Athmani, and Fatma Bint Suleman.

cendant. At the same time, members of the Muslim community who believed that Muslims had been erased from nationalist history—in extreme versions of this position, singled out for persecution, imprisonment, and death—were reasserting claims to centrality in the Tanganyika African Association (TAA) and TANU.[13]

My major objective during this brief visit was to provide Bibi Titi Mohamed with the opportunity to hear, correct and add to the Swahili version of her life history,[14] which appears in English as three chapters in this book. But Kanyama Chiume's enthusiasm for contacting individuals I had not seen before continued unabated. Most notable among the former were Teresa Ntare, once *mwami* (chief) of Mbulu and among the few chiefs supportive of TANU in the 1950s, whose death a few months later surprised and saddened me; and Mr. Ally Sykes, himself an early TANU activist, who was seeking to reconstruct a TANU history that accorded the Muslim presence, and particularly his brother, Abdulwahid Sykes, greater prominence. Blantina Ley, whom we had not interviewed previously, had been a teacher at the girls' primary school Bibi Titi Mohamed attended.[15]

In addition to the women I interviewed, then, all of the people mentioned above, the place of Tanzania in my own adult life history, and the circumstances of research in Tanzania between 1984 and 1992 are embedded in the substance of this book. Marjorie Mbilinyi's support and critical responses to my work have always been important to me, while other Tanzanian friends and colleagues, including Grace Mesaki, Suleiman and Neema Ngware, N'nali and Anina Mbilinyi, Judica King'on, Leah Semgaruka and Steven Maloda, and my Minnesota colleague and friend, Ben Pike, helped me with the translations of interviews and Swahili documents. Long-time friend and fellow teacher at Tabora, Gail Baker, read an early version of Bibi Titi Mohammed's life history and her thoughtful questions told me what needed further explanation.

Margaret Strobel's detailed comments on an earlier version of the manuscript were invaluable; and the editorial, bibliographical and substantive assistance of several graduate assistants—Sheryl McCurdy, Helena Pohlandt-McCormick, Amy Kaler, and especially Heidi Gengenbach—got me over humps, sharpened my focus and kept me going at difficult times. Janet Spector carefully read the manuscript at various stages, and Jean Allman's enthusiastic response to the penultimate draft helped me finish the book, as did Jean Hay's superb editing.

Finally, I want to thank Heinemann Social History of Africa series editors Allen Isaacman and Jean Hay for patience and encouragement, for many useful suggestions and incisive comments, for trust in this project, and especially, for waiving some of the requirements of chronology in the interest of history as a living relationship between the present and the past.

---

[13] See Mohamed Said's articles "In Praise of Ancestors," *Africa Events* (March/April 1988), and "Founder of a Political Movement: Abdulwahid K. Sykes (1924–1968)," *Africa Events* (September 1988), and an unpublished manuscript "Ally K. Sykes Remembers." For an example of direct accusations concerning Nyerere's treatment of Muslims, see A. E. Baalawy, "Nyerere and Muslim Tanzania," a pamphlet published by the Zanzibar Organization, 4 Bayfields, Shaftesbury Rd. Southsea, Hants. PO 5 3PJ, Eng. (n.d.). Dr. Baalawy is a former minister of health, Zanzibar.

[14] Kanyama Chiume produced the Swahili version of Bibi Titi's life history from the English version that I compiled and edited from the translated transcriptions of taped interviews conducted with her in 1984 and 1988. Mr. Chiume transcribed and translated these tapes.

[15] Blantina Ley's health did not permit her to talk at length, and she spoke primarily of her regret that as a teacher, she had felt constrained from participation in the nationalist struggle.

1

Introduction

In October 1985, six days before leaving office, Julius Nyerere, whose political leadership of Tanzania spanned three decades, received some 5,000 women on the State House grounds in Dar es Salaam. The occasion was one of numerous ceremonial farewells staged for the 63-year-old TANU founder; yet according to journalist William E. Smith, this one included "one of the most extraordinary events of the whole process of leave-taking...."[1]

The gathering of women, in and of itself, was by no means extraordinary. Thirty years earlier, in 1955, thousands of women from Dar es Salaam had joined the newly established nationalist party within three months, and by the end of that year, more women than men had become card-carrying TANU members.[2] From that time on, the sight of huge, orderly groups of singing, marching women was to become commonplace in a nation which, despite increasing economic stagnation from the mid-1970s onward, could still line streets and roads or fill stadiums and meeting halls for public rituals of party support.

Nor were the exchanges between the women and President Nyerere extraordinary. In response to the women's offering of speeches, chants, and presents, "including a lion skin and three cows," Nyerere replied with the mixture of good-natured wit, solemn reflection, and paternalistic encouragement characteristic of his charismatic leadership style. Linking the history of Tanganyika's freedom struggle and the struggle for women's rights, he reflected disapprovingly on the sexist traditions of his own ethnic group, the Zanaki, urging the women to abolish all discriminatory traditions and to be active in politics in order to maintain the equality that had been gained through legislation.[3] All of this had typified Nyerere's relationship to Tanzanian women as a group and his public pronouncements on the subject of women's equality over the years.

The extraordinary event began when he

> called to the stand a heavy-set old woman, gray-haired and very proud in her bearing. It was Bibi Titi Mohamed, who was once the leader of the national women's organization and had later fallen into disgrace. He said

---

[1]   William E. Smith, "A Reporter At Large: Transition," *New Yorker*, 3 March 1986, 82.

[2]   Susan Geiger, "Women in Nationalist Struggle: TANU Activists in Dar es Salaam," *IJAHS* 20, 1 (1987): 2.

[3]   Smith, "Transition," 82.

1

Photo 1: Bibi Titi Mohamed and Julius Nyerere, first public reunion, October 1984. Courtesy of *Daily News/Sunday News,* Dar es Salaam, Tanzania.

that she had been a true leader of the Party in its early days and a leader of the fight against colonialism, and he congratulated her, and then allowed her to sit down. He smiled and said softly, "After that, she slipped a little. But that's all right, that happens." He started to speak again but changed his mind, and then he, too, sat down.[4]

The following day, Nyerere acknowledged to Smith that his public recognition of Bibi Titi Mohamed had been intended as "an act of forgiveness." A year earlier, he had made a similar but unspoken gesture when Bibi Titi had been among a throng of women gathered on the same grounds to conclude a week of marches and speeches held throughout the numerous sub-areas of Dar es Salaam, Tanzania's capital, to commemorate the work of the women's organization, Umoja wa Wanawake wa Tanzania (UWT). At that time, a special call had gone out to women who had been activists during the struggle for independence from British colonial rule, and Bibi Titi had shared the platform with Nyerere for the first time in nearly twenty years. A picture capturing this moment appeared the following day, October 3, 1984, on the front page of Tanzania's English language paper, the *Daily News,* and on October 6, in the Swahili paper, *Mfanyakazi.*

The extraordinary event, then, was a ritual of forgiveness on Nyerere's part. Bibi Titi, described by Smith as an "old woman," but in fact three years Nyerere's junior, was being forgiven for her alleged participation in a plot to overthrow Nyerere's government in 1969. Although she maintained her innocence throughout Tanzania's first lengthy treason trial of 1970-71, she was convicted with several others, including the self-exiled former cabinet minister, Oscar Kambona, and sen-

_____

Ibid.

tenced to life imprisonment.[5] In February 1972, however, her life sentence was commuted by presidential order and she was released from prison.[6] Whether Nyerere's act reflected clemency, forgiveness, or doubts about her guilt is not clear. Nor is it clear whether the quiet, nonpolitical, nonpublic life Bibi Titi was to lead for a dozen years following her release was self-chosen, or a requirement of her pardon.[7]

Perhaps clemency, forgiveness, and doubt were all at work in Nyerere's decision. Frequently characterized as a leader who has valued above all the bonds created by a shared history of political struggle,[8] he may, with the benefit of hindsight, have begun to doubt the extent of Bibi Titi's involvement in any plot to overthrow his government, and, so the charge read, kill him and several other top officials. Could this woman, who had totally dedicated herself to the task of mobilizing support for TANU and Nyerere's leadership, have plotted treason?[9]

Bibi Titi first expressed disaffection from party policy when she objected to the lack of democratic process accompanying the promulgation of Nyerere's famous African socialist manifesto, the "Arusha Declaration" of February 1967, by the party's National Executive Committee (NEC).[10] Moreover, she disagreed with Section (a) of Part Five of the Declaration, known as the leadership code, which listed restrictions on TANU and Government leaders. In particular, she disagreed with point number five which read, "No TANU or Government leader should own houses which he rents to others."[11] But her disagreement was open, and she resigned from the party's Central Committee, as required by the code, rather than relinquishing her right to income from her rental properties.[12] She had, in any case, lost her parliamentary seat in the 1965 elections, and the shift toward the recruitment of educated individuals for positions in both government and the women's organization

---

[5]   *Nationalist*, 31 January 1971. *Nationalist* newspaper reportage of the trial, for which there is a very useful "Treason Trial" index, is held in the National Library, Dar es Salaam.

[6]   *Nationalist*, 9 February 1972.

[7]   Bibi Titi explained in an interview with Ruth Meena that following her release from prison "she could not freely interact with her friends as many of her colleagues were very cautious in dealing with her. She jokingly remarked: 'One would have thought that I contracted an infectious disease.'" See Ruth Meena, "Bibi Titi: Traitor or Heroine of *Uhuru?*" *Southern Africa Political and Economic Monthly*, April 1992, 48.

[8]   Duggan and Civille conclude that given Oscar Kambona's numerous antagonistic acts toward Nyerere in the early postindependence years, "Only Nyerere's intense loyalty to his long-time associate had kept Kambona in power until [1967]." William Redman Duggan and John R. Civille, *Tanzania and Nyerere: A Study of Ujamaa and Nationhood* (New York, 1976), 94.

[9]   Bibi Titi told Ruth Meena that although her position "was never influenced by Oscar Kambona's political ambition," she believed their close political association implicated her in the alleged coup plans. Meena, "Bibi Titi," 47.

[10]   For a diverse set of analyses of the Arusha Declaration, see Jeannette Hartmann, ed., *Re-Thinking the Arusha Declaration* (Copenhagen, 1991).

[11]   Julius Nyerere, "The Arusha Declaration," in Nyerere, *Freedom and Socialism* (Dar es Salaam, 1968), 249.

[12]   Ali Mazrui reflects the way in which Bibi Titi's resignation was presented for public consumption when he writes, "A well known female leader felt compelled to resign her office ... because she valued her business interests and collection of houses for rent more highly than a political career under TANU" (Ali Mazrui, "Building Socialism Without a Vanguard Party," in *Re-Thinking the Arusha Declaration*, ed. Hartmann, 76). Bibi Titi told Meena that she had sold some of her gold jewelry to purchase one house and had taken out a loan to purchase the other. While she had decided to seek security for herself and her daughter in this way, her colleagues, she added, "had decided to marry more women and drink more beer..." Meena, "Bibi Titi," 48.

seemed to point to the increasing marginalization of anticolonial foot soldiers such as herself—especially those who were female and had minimal formal education.[13]

Although Nyerere was quick to respond angrily to public challenges to his authority—his swift dismissal of the university students who in 1966 protested national service comes to mind[14]—he also distinguished himself among his fellow African heads of state as a man willing to admit his government's failures and, however belatedly, to take personal responsibility for them.[15] Moreover, he has acknowledged misjudgments and errors at a more personal level.[16] So it would not have been out of character for him to decide that a life sentence was too harsh a burden for his own conscience to bear if he doubted the extent of her guilt.

This is where I intended to leave the matter when I concluded my research in 1992. In September 1994, however, Wambui Otieno, an activist in Kenya's nationalist movement now known primarily for her vigorous fight for rights to the body and property of her deceased husband "S.M.," called me unexpectedly, claiming some responsibility for Bibi Titi's release from prison.[17] When I interviewed her that evening, Mrs. Otieno explained that she had first met and greatly admired Bibi Titi in the late 1950s, and had also hosted Nyerere when he had visited the late Kenyan nationalist leader and trade unionist, Tom Mboya. Mrs. Otieno vehemently expressed her opinion that Bibi Titi had been instrumental in paving the way for Nyerere's success, and that upon learning of her imprisonment, she, Mrs. Otieno, had been shocked and appalled at Nyerere's lack of gratitude. She therefore called Nyerere at his mother's house in Butiama to tell him so.

According to Mrs. Otieno, Nyerere listened, asked after her family, and concluded their conversation by saying that nation-building wasn't easy. About two weeks later, however, John Malacela, then Tanzanian foreign minister, came to visit Mrs. Otieno, saying that Nyerere wanted her to know that he had released Bibi Titi.

> I told Malacela to go and thank Nyerere very much. I told him exactly how I felt about Bibi Titi, and now that she is released I'm very happy and I think that Julius has done a good thing, something that can be appreciated by all women who knew Bibi Titi....

That was the last time I talked about her.[18]

---

[13] Often justified as necessary for the bureaucratic requirements of governing, this shift and others reflected the TANU government's need for increased state control and hierarchies of rule, for educated functionaries, and for the "taming" of associations and organizations whose enthusiasms and interests were not easily subsumed into or controlled by party and government directives.

[14] See Chris Peter and Sengodo Mvungi, "The State and the Student Struggles," in *The State and the Working People in Tanzania*, ed. Issa G. Shivji (Dakar, 1986), 155–94.

[15] See Gus Liebenow, "Nyerere of Tanzania: The Legend and the Ledger," Universities Field Staff International [UFSI] Reports 1987/ No. 3 Africa/Middle East, 6.

[16] See Cranford Pratt, *The Critical Phase in Tanzania, 1945–1968: Nyerere and the Emergence of a Socialist Strategy* (Cambridge, 1976). Ali Mazrui notes that "Julius Nyerere was readier to admit that he had not realized his goals than to confess that his goals were wrong in the first place." Mazrui, "Building Socialism," 63.

[17] Mrs. Otieno called me after learning from Jean Hay that I was working on Bibi Titi's life history, and on TANU women activists during the 1950s.

[18] Interview with Mrs. Wambui Otieno, Minneapolis, 22 September 1994.

Bibi Titi herself had little to say about Nyerere's decision to release her during our 1984 interviews in the modestly furnished sitting room of her house in Temeke, an older "suburb" of Dar es Salaam. Tired and in poor health—carrying more weight than was good for her heart—she was supporting herself selling paraffin oil by the Coke bottle out of her home to neighbors. Other family members living in the household undoubtedly contributed in various ways, but life was clearly difficult. Although slightly more critical of Nyerere four years later,[19] Bibi Titi did not have much to add on the subject of her release from prison or the reasons for Nyerere's action when next I saw her in 1988—this time in her large and modern house in the far wealthier section of Dar es Salaam, Upanga. This house, which she was able to reoccupy just days before our first 1988 meeting, was one of two that were taken away from her while she was in prison. Now, she explained with obvious pleasure, both had been returned to her: one by Nyerere, which could be inherited by her daughter; the other, by President Ali Mwinyi, which would revert to the state when she died.

By 1988, perhaps forgiveness and loyalty were working in both directions in the relationship—now over thirty years old—between Nyerere and Bibi Titi. But given the ambiguity of these events and circumstances, why begin the introduction to this book about the nationalism of women in Tanganyika in the 1950s with an "extraordinary event" of the mid-1980s whose reference point is an event fifteen years earlier?

Any attempt to understand the scene between Nyerere and Bibi Titi Mohamed in 1985 must negotiate uneasy terrain between conjecture about Nyerere's conscience and motives and the meaning of Bibi Titi Mohamed's silence about Nyerere's reasons for staging a public reconciliation with her. Whatever Nyerere intended in this act, its symbolic force at the moment of his own departure from political center stage involved confronting and reclaiming the "silenced" past, and bringing that past into the present in the person of Bibi Titi. It is thus a moment of "truth" regarding Tanzanian nationalism as an historical process in which people drew on their social experience to construct a "nation" in which they might experience freedom from colonial overrule and dignity as human beings. It is for this reason that I find this event a compelling place to begin my own exploration of women's experience of, and work for, this construction. As Margaret Somers argues in formulating her concept of "social narrativity,"[20] it is clear that this event can only be understood in relationship to many others, some of which—women's mobilization efforts in 1955, the 1967 Arusha Declaration, and Bibi Titi Mohamed's imprisonment and release—I mentioned briefly above. "It is emplotment of narrative," writes Somers, "that allows us to construct a *significant* network or configuration of relationships."[21]

---

[19] By 1988, Nyerere was no longer president. This may have made it easier for Bibi Titi to criticize him.

[20] Somers writes, "Narrativity demands that we discern the meaning of any single event only in temporal and spatial relationship to other events. Indeed, the chief characteristic of narrative is that it renders understanding only by *connecting* (however unstable) *parts* to a constructed *configuration* or a *social network* (however incoherent or unrealizable). In this respect, narrative becomes an epistemological category." Margaret R. Somers, "Narrativity, Narrative Identity, and Social Action: Rethinking English Working-Class Formation," *Social Science History* 16, 4 (1992): 601.

[21] Ibid., 602.

As the Popular Memory Group reminds us, history is about past-present relationships.[22] It is about present lenses ground and polished by particular contemporary material and cultural conditions focused on and influenced by past events. This is as true for social actors, in this case Nyerere and Bibi Titi, as it is for social researchers. As for the latter, it is true whether the wearer of the lenses is a lone historian in an archive full of fragile manuscripts, or whether she is actively soliciting recollections from participants, trying to understand the past not only as it is subjected to the particular scrutiny of her own present, but as it is seen from the collective present of those participants. As for particular silences, whether those of individuals like Bibi Titi and Nyerere, or the silence of the written record concerning a particular historical period or its actors, these too become historical artifacts, as meaningful for our understanding of historical process as is deafening speech or endless documentation.

In this book, I use the life histories of women participants in TANU to confront the biases, silences, and resulting distortions found in existing histories of the period of Tanzania's nationalist movement. By their nature, life histories represent history as a relationship between the present and the past, and constitute social narratives of events and conditions connected to each other over time. Moreover, TANU women's life histories, as the products of specific economic and social contexts, present different criteria for understanding Tanganyikan nationalism than those employed in nationalist histories of the period 1965–1975, which taken together constitute the country's metanarrative of nationalist triumph. Conceptualizing nationalism as Nyerere's handiwork or as imported ideology, as is typically done, ignores women whose actions and "culture of politics"[23] constructed, performed, and maintained nationalism in Tanzania.

The Metanarrative of Tanzanian Nationalism

Neither a former British protectorate like its northwestern neighbor Uganda, nor a former British colony like Kenya, Tanzania was subjected to German rule from 1885 to World War I, and with Germany's defeat became the British Mandate of Tanganyika under the newly formed League of Nations. With the establishment of the United Nations after World War II, all Mandates, including Tanganyika, became Trust Territories.

From the British standpoint, both Uganda, and Kenya were more valuable and more volatile than Tanganyika. Always the "poor sister," Tanganyika could

---

[22]   Popular Memory Group, "Popular Memory: Theory, Politics, Method," in *Making Histories: Studies in History Writing and Politics*, eds. Richard Johnson et al. (Minneapolis, 1982), 240–41.

[23]   Pearl T. Robinson defines the "culture of politics" as "political practice that is culturally legitimated and societally validated by local knowledge. Rooted in a community's habits, customs and symbols regarding power, authority, participation and representation, its mores are readily accessible to elites and ordinary people alike. Moreover (and this is a critically important point), a culture of politics may be altered over time through a process of political learning. A culture of politics is thus the product of a polity's distant and its more proximate political past." Pearl T. Robinson, "Democratization: Understanding the Relationship between Regime Change and the Culture of Politics," *African Studies Review* 37, 1 (1994): 40.

nevertheless boast a territory-wide African Association by 1929; and in succeeding decades, Tanganyikans established both local and regional quasipolitical associations and cash-crop cooperatives, usually based on what the British understood to be and most Africans accepted as "tribal" affiliation, identity, and location.

As elsewhere on the African continent, discontent with virtually all aspects of colonial rule intensified among Tanganyikans after World War II. By the early 1950s, leaders attempting to revive the floundering Tanganyika Africa Association (TAA) recognized the importance of joining with local organizations challenging everything from unjust marketing regulations to restrictive crop controls, and from cattle-dipping to further European land alienation. It was under these circumstances, and with British imperial decisionmakers simultanously ambivalent about Tanganyika and anxious to avoid the violence of nationalist activity in Kenya, that Julius Nyerere, with the support of the majority of TAA branch leaders, turned the Association into TANU for the openly voiced aim of seeking independence from British overrule.[24]

Most studies of the emergence of the nationalist movement in Tanganyika, as elsewhere in Africa, concentrate on the role of political elites who were conscious of mass aspirations and able to attract a broad following and articulate popular concerns; that is, able to harness numerous disconnected and usually discontinuous popular expressions of anticolonial protest to the wagon of self-government and political independence.[25] The goal of "the nationalists" was, of course, to take power at the center and remove the colonial rulers, thereby transforming colonial "subjects" into national citizens. According to this rendering of African nationalism, it was the Western-educated African male elite which made all this possible, held it together, and made it *nationalism*. This same elite group was also responsible for transporting and translating Western ideas or ideology central to the whole movement.[26]

African nationalism, then, had its past/present narrative reaching back into the earlier part of the twentieth century to explain the evolution of localized anticolonial responses, and to account for the emergence of a particular kind of African elite leadership. Under these circumstances, the job of the historian interested in African nationalist history was to demonstrate how and why particular groups of Africans were "ready" to be ignited by the spark of nationalism introduced by educated male elites. According to a recent formulation of this view:

> The task of nation-builders is to unify all the disparate elements within a state and to *endow* [emphasis mine] the collectivity with a national consciousness.... Nation-builders had to work to transfer loyalty from traditional centres of authority to the state....[27]

---

[24] The most thorough general history of this period remains John Iliffe's *A Modern History of Tanganyika* (Cambridge, 1979).

[25] John Lonsdale, "The Emergence of African Nationalism," in *Emerging Themes of African History*, ed. T.O. Ranger (Nairobi, 1968), 201.

[26] Iliffe, *Modern History*, 486.

[27] Caroline Thomas, *In Search of Security: The Third World in International Relations* (Boulder, 1987), 15–16.

In a local version of this view which appeared in an issue of the *Business Times* of December 9, 1988, an issue marking the 27th anniversary of the nation's independence, Jeanette Hartmann wrote:

> The first challenge that confronted Nyerere and the Political Party, TANU, was to engineer and create out of the ethnically differentiated society a cohesive nation, a nation with a strong national identity. This was achieved not through repression but through the use of ideology that preached equality and social egalitarianism.

Scholars of Africa have been generally unanimous in a positive assessment of Julius Nyerere as "nation-builder," even while divided on the question of his economic and political policies since independence.[28] What is striking, however, is the extent to which Nyerere's accomplishments as a "nationalist" and more recently, the state's relative political stability despite an ever-worsening economy, are subtly minimized by what I call the "lacks and absences theory" of Tanzanian nationalism. This theory attributes Tanzania's ability to become a "nation" and remain a nation-state to (1) the absence, among the 120 "tribes" counted during the colonial period,[29] of a single dominant ethnic group positioned to monopolize power to the detriment of other groups; (2) the absence of a large or nationally unified European settler community able to exercise significant control over the British colonial administration, or to thwart TANU; (3) the lack of significant wealth or resources in the country and of any concentration of economic wealth or advantage in the capital itself; (4) the absence of an entrenched "embryonic African bourgeoisie;" and finally (5) Tanganyika's Mandate, and later Trusteeship, status: that is, as something other than a "real" colony.[30]

A feminist reading would note the ways in which "lacks and absences" theory demasculinizes, if not feminizes, Tanganyika and its nationalist movement as essentially passive and lacking in substance and defining power. I remember well an exchange with a Kenyan journalist visiting Dar es Salaam who asked, "Why would you want to know about women in Tanzania's nationalist movement? Surely this is boring compared to Mau Mau and our fight against white settlers!"

The one *presence* usually identified along with the lacks and absences to explain Tanzanian nationalism is the Swahili language. However, even the importance of Swahili is frequently cast in negative terms as a language untainted by identification with colonial powers or by identification with any particular dominant ethnic group—a language, therefore, that could not serve "as a vehicle for establishing an ethnic hegemony."[31]

Few Tanzanians of the 1950s knew English; many more could understand and speak Swahili, and for those on the coast and in many towns of the inte-

---

[28]   See Liebenow, "Nyerere of Tanzania," 3.

[29]   For the importance of counting and classifying populations in the colonial enterprise, see Benedict Anderson, *Imagined Communities: Reflections on the Origins and Spread of Nationalism*, 2nd ed. (London, 1991), Ch. 10, "Census, Map, Museum."

[30]   John Cartwright, *Political Leadership in Africa* (New York, 1983), 156–58.

[31]   Ibid., 157–58.

rior, Swahili was a first language. Historians and political scientists have pointed to the relevance of Swahili's existence as a widely understood *lingua franca*, and to what Henry Bienen calls "Swahili political culture,"[32] for the success of the nationalist cause. Anthropologist Deborah Amory states that, "By the 1950's, we can talk of an African nationalist Swahili identity that originates in Tanzania...."[33] The contradictory and somewhat ambivalent attitude of historians and political scientists toward connecting Swahili culture and social identity, as distinct from the use of Swahili language, to nationalism is reflected in John Iliffe's assertion, which presents nationalism in the classic way—as an import, even if imported by African intellectuals:

> There were remote areas where little Swahili was spoken. Few Tatoga or Iraqw knew it, and few women in several regions. But only in Usukuma, Mbulu, and Masailand did Nyerere need an interpreter during the nationalist campaign.[34]

A consideration of TANU women activists prompts a reconceptualization of the broad use of Swahili, the relevance of an open Swahili culture, and the significance of a sense of "Swahiliness" in Tanganyika as an epistomological basis for nationalism and nationalist consciousness. This consciousness reflected, accepted, and created inter- and trans-tribal *national* identities.

Where Are the Women?

The relatively brief period of active mass nationalist mobilization of anticolonial sentiment (1955–1960) which resulted in Tanzania's political independence on December 9, 1961, was sufficiently recent during the time of my research to be easily remembered by most Tanzanians over the age of forty, albeit vaguely by some. Those who remember also recall the period as one noted for the presence of women as vocal, often vociferous TANU enthusiasts. Most especially, they remember Bibi Titi Mohamed, either because they heard or saw her address a TANU rally, or because they learned about her through word of mouth, the radio, or the press. According to Iliffe, Bibi Titi Mohamed and Julius Nyerere were probably the only TANU leaders whose names were known throughout the country at independence.[35] Yet, despite her historical prominence, Bibi Titi receives only passing mention in most accounts of Tanzanian nationalism; even less so the thousands of women TANU activists who recognized her leadership.

The marginalization of women in this historiography reflects a now-familiar pattern: the accumulation of androcentric bias in the written record—both primary (produced by colonial officials, missionaries and travellers) and, more recently, secondary (produced by Western as well as African scholars). Women's

---

[32]   Henry Bienen, *Tanzania: Party Transformation and Economic Development* (Princeton, 1970), 43.

[33]   Deborah P. Amory, "Waswahili Ni Nani?: The Politics of Swahili Identity and Culture," unpublished paper presented at the annual meeting of the African Studies Association, Baltimore, Maryland, November 1990, 22.

[34]   Iliffe, *Modern History*, 530.

[35]   Ibid., 572.

political actions and history are "disappeared" in a cumulative process whereby successive written accounts reinforce and echo the silence of previous ones. The erasure of women has been more complete in texts about Tanzanian nationalist history and politics written in English than in the few accounts by Tanzanians, including activists of the period, writing in Swahili.[36]

In another corpus of writing, African women again disappear into the blind spot of Western gender and racial ideologies. These writings are the few accounts produced by women who were engaged in one way or another in the colonial enterprise and witnessed the rise of TANU, typically as wives of colonial officers, settlers, or missionaries. Some of these women were missionaries, social welfare and education officers, or travelers in their own right. A few participated in and wrote about the nationalist struggle.[37] Much of their writing reveals Western gender ideology and even its fissures, the intersections of that ideology and racist imperialism, and the construction of the colonized woman as "the other's other."[38]

To cite an admittedly extreme example, one young wife of a district officer, writing to her parents about life in Shinyanga in 1958, expressed her fear of TANU—a fear that was probably fed by African "disturbances" in the neighboring district of Geita and reinforced by images from the Mau Mau Emergency in Kenya.[39] Perhaps whites in Tanganyika will soon be "sleeping with loaded guns," she worries.[40] Later, reporting on a TANU rally from her vantage point among the invited dignitaries, she describes Bibi Titi Mohamed as "TANU's leading lady, a huge mountain of a woman and a reputed bitch...."[41]

From much of the written record, then, we can extract images, ideologies, fragments, and representations of African women, including TANU women. But such renderings obviously fall far short of Somers' criteria for the production of a social narrative of women's nationalist consciousness and activities, for they fail to reveal a constellation of relationships embedded in time and space and constituted by causal emplotment. Both written and oral historical accounts do, however, converge on one event as pivotal to the beginnings of Bibi Titi

---

[36]   Examples in English include J. Clagett Taylor, *The Political Development of Tanganyika* (Stanford, 1963); William Tordoff, *Government and Politics of Tanzania* (Nairobi, 1967); Bienen, *Tanzania*; A. J. Temu, "The Rise and Triumph of Nationalism," in I. N. Kimambo and A. J. Temu, eds., *A History of Tanzania* (Nairobi, 1969); Andrew Coulson, *Tanzania: A Political Economy* (Oxford, 1982). Swahili accounts include E. B. M. Barongo, *Mkiki wa Siasa Tanganyika* (Dar es Salaam, 1966); S. A. Kandoro, *Mwito wa Uhuru* (Dar es Salaam, 1961); D. Z. Mwaga, B. F. Mrina, and E. F. Lyimo, *Historia ya Chama cha TANU 1954 hadi 1977* (Dar es Salaam, 1981); Abubakar Ulotu, *Historia ya TANU* (Dar es Salaam, 1971).

[37]   Sophia Mustafa, *The Tanganyika Way* (Dar es Salaam, 1961); Judith Listowel, *The Making of Tanganyika* (London, 1965).

[38]   For examples and critiques of such writings, see Nupur Chaudhuri and Margaret Strobel, eds., *Western Women and Imperialism: Complicity and Resistance* (Bloomington, 1992); Patricia W. Romero, ed., *Women's Voices on Africa: A Century of Travel Writings* (Princeton, N.J., 1992); Mary Louise Pratt, *Imperial Eyes: Travel Writing and Transculturation* (New York, 1992).

[39]   White women were among the eager conveyors of "Mau Mau's" horror stories. See, for example, Rehna "Tiny" Cloete, *The Nylon Safari* (London, 1956), 3.

[40]   Family letters of Tanganyika district officer P.L. Birkett's wife, Ursula, 15 March 1958, Rhodes House, Oxford (RH).

[41]   Birkett letters, 5 December 1958.

Mohamed's life as a political actor, and women as a political force in Tanzania's nationalist movement. That event was John Hatch's visit to Dar es Salaam.

Nearly all accounts of women's participation in TANU begin, and many end, with the story of John Hatch's "Where are the women?" query to TANU's all-male Central Committee during his June 1955 visit. Hatch, Commonwealth officer of the British Labour Party and an admirer of the young Nyerere, was touring "British Africa" on behalf of the Labour Party, which was sympathetic to African nationalist aspirations and anxious to play a major role in an orderly decolonization process. Met at the Dar es Salaam airport by a "huge welcoming crowd,"[42] Hatch was even more impressed the next day, June 1, when an attentive and enthusiastic crowd he variously estimated at 15,000[43] and from 20,000 to 40,000[44] gathered at Mnazi Moja, an open, park-like plaza in the central city to listen to TANU speeches even though Nyerere wasn't present and had not been in Dar es Salaam for two months.[45] When he spotted within the "vast sea of dusky faces and white clothes...several rows of black-veiled Muslim women,"[46] Hatch was surprised, and later, speaking to members of TANU's Central Committee, he "happened to mention the lack of women members of TANU, a universal weakness of all African nationalist parties in their early years."[47]

Although the TANU Constitution adopted in 1954 called for a Women's Section, no such section existed. Nevertheless, committee members told Hatch that he could meet the leader of the women the following day. They then sent TANU committee member Sheneda Plantan, Bibi Titi Mohamed's brother-in-law, to persuade her husband to allow her to meet Hatch as the "TANU women's leader." Bibi Titi's husband consented, and she agreed to meet with Hatch if her friend, Tatu Mzee, could come as well. The meeting took place, Hatch was satisfied, and so, the story goes, the Women's Section of TANU was born.

A birth narrative that makes John Hatch the midwife of a TANU women's section conceived by TANU male leaders fits nicely into Tanganyika's nationalist metanarrative. What it doesn't explain is *how* Bibi Titi Mohamed, a 30-year-old lead singer in the popular *ngoma* (musical) group, "Bomba," became an actual rather than fictive TANU leader, and *why* thousands of women became nationalist activists as a result of her political acumen and enthusiastic work.

When Bibi Titi held the first meeting of the TANU Women's Section on July 8, 1955, some 400 women reportedly joined;[48] and in October 1955, just four months after she met with Hatch, Oscar Kambona, then TANU's organizing secretary, wrote to the liberal Fabian Society headquartered in London that Bibi Titi had enrolled 5,000 women members. "Though only semi-literate," he added, she was "inspiring a revolution [in] the role of women in African society." Thus, claimed Kambona

---

[42]   John Hatch, *Two African Statesmen: Kaunda of Zambia and Nyerere of Tanzania* (Chicago, 1976), 104.

[43]   John Hatch, *New from Africa* (London, 1956), 55.

[44]   Hatch, *Two African Statesmen*, 104.

[45]   Ibid., 104.

[46]   Hatch, *New from Africa*, 55.

[47]   Hatch, *Two African Statesmen*, 107; see also Listowel, *The Making of Tanganyika*, 268.

[48]   Mwaga et al., *Historia ya Chama Cha TANU*, 113.

confidently, "The problem of the emancipation of women at a later date has, in this way, been disposed of."[49]

Although Kambona's eagerness to declare women emancipated was premature, his rhetoric captured the sense of astonishment expressed by the fledgling TANU leadership in reaction to the rapidity and extent of women's mobilization behind the nationalist cause. Joan Wicken, who became Nyerere's close advisor, echoed Kambona's views while visiting Tanganyika in 1956–1957. She predicted that the work of over 6,000 TANU women would "undoubtedly have long-term effects on the position of women," that "the leaders of the women's organisation in the capital were every bit the equal of the other members of the Central Committee, and that "the jovial Bibi Titi" would "make as big a mark in the history of Tanganyikan women as Mrs. Pankhurst made in Britain."[50]

Existing accounts of the "rise of TANU" fail to follow the relational connections among events marking the origins of women's politicization. They are not part of the narrative that explains how TANU leaders took nationalism to the countryside, encountering a "readiness" evidenced in organized resistance to unwanted livestock and crop regulations, increasing discontent with local chiefs and their councils, and the desire of the small educated elite for more and better jobs.

Women, "Woman," and Nationalism

I began my research into the history of TANU's women activists with a number of straightforward questions.[51] Why did women respond to TANU so enthusiastically, and how did they organize? Which women were most responsive to political engagement, and how can we account for their interest? Given the social and cultural constraints on women's public activities, what sorts of gender-specific challenges accompanied the emergence of political consciousness among certain segments of Tanzania's female population? These questions were framed in the early 1980s, before the emergence of scholarship focused primarily if not exclusively on the representation, construction and use of women (or more commonly, "woman") as symbol, icon, or protector/repository of the culture in nationalist and other political movements,[52] and on nationalism itself as inher-

---

[49] Oscar Kambona, Organizing Secretary-General of TANU, to Fabian Society, 18 October 1955, FCB Papers 121, Rhodes House (RH).

[50] Joan E. Wicken, "African Contrasts." Submitted to Somerville College, Oxford, 1958. MSS. Afr. s. 1726, Rhodes House, Oxford. I am indebted to Aili Tripp for calling my attention to Wicken's comment.

[51] In 1990, I surveyed studies of African women's involvement in nationalist movements. See Susan Geiger, "Women and African Nationalism," *Journal of Women's History* 2, 1 (1990): 227–44.

[52] See, for example, Anne McClintock, "'No Longer in a Future Heaven': Women and Nationalism in South Africa," *Transition* 51 (1991): 104–23; Lynn A. Hunt, *Eroticism and the Body Politic* (Baltimore, 1991); Partha Chatterjee, "Colonialism, Nationalism and Colonized Women: The Contest in India," *American Ethnologist* 16 (1989): 622–33; Cherifa Bouatta and Doria Cherifati-Merabtine, "The Social Representation of Women in Algeria's Islamist Movement," and Sucheta Mazumdar, "Moving Away from a Secular Vision? Women, Nation, and the Cultural Construction of Hindu India," in *Identity Politics and Women: Cultural Reassertions and Feminisms in International Perspective*, ed. Valentine M. Moghadam (Boulder, 1994); Nira Yuval-Davis, "Gender and Nation," *Ethnic and Racial Studies* 16, 4 (1993): 621–32. For the range and limits of postmodernist approaches, see Andrew Parker et al., eds., *Nationalisms and Sexualities* (New York, 1992).

ently masculine and fundamentally evil.[53] The Eurocentrism in nationalism's historiography has remained a constant.

> [E]thnicity and nationalism are not "givens," but are social and political constructions. They are creations of elites, who draw upon, distort, and sometimes fabricate materials from the cultures of the groups they wish to represent in order to protect their well-being or existence or to gain political and economic advantage for their groups as well as for them-selves.... [E]thnicity and nationalism are modern phenomena inseparably connected with the activities of the modern centralizing state.[54]

Such conceptions of nationalism are simultaneously too narrow in their claim to universal truth about nationalisms, too masculinized (even in their feminist renderings), too Eurocentric, and too elite-centered to illuminate the contours of Tanzanian nationalism, especially when considering the relations between women and nationalism, or when viewing women not simply as recipients or bearers of nationalism, but as among its major progressive creators.

For example, how do we explain the fact that whatever else its characteristics, Tanganyikan nationalism has remained remarkably devoid of the symbolic objectification of women? What are the implications of the fact that much of nationalism's cultural work in Tanganyika was undertaken *by* TANU women? How can we account for the fact that nationalism in Tanzania has not manifested itself as a reactionary impulse or a calculated product of elite control or "the state"? These broader questions, framed in the context of nationalism's general historiography, emerged as fundamental to the larger story in which women's social narratives have been situated.

Past/Present Narratives of Nationalism

At the time of our interviews, the vast majority of political veterans whose personal accounts form the centerpiece of this book were living in modest circumstances. Most were neither extremely impoverished nor particularly affluent relative to the urban standard of living in Tanzania in the 1980s. Like most urban Tanzanians, the women lived in "traditional," "Swahili-type" rather than "Western" houses.[55] With few exceptions, all of the older women (over sixty at the

---

[53] Classic statements of European nationalism's male and homosocial gendering are Anderson, *Imagined Communities*, esp. 16, and George L. Mosse, *Nationalism and Sexuality: Middle-Class Morality and Sexual Norms in Modern Europe* (Madison, 1985), esp. 67. For nationalism as fundamentally and ultimately evil, see, among many others, E.J. Hobsbawm, *Nations and Nationalism Since 1780* (Cambridge, 1991), esp. 164, and "The New Threat to History," *New York Review of Books* XL, 21 (1993): 62–64; Walker Connor, "The Specter of Ethno-Nationalist Movements Today," *PAWSS Perspectives* 1, 3 (1991): 1–13.

[54] Paul R. Brass, *Ethnicity and Nationalism: Theory and Comparison* (Newbury Park, 1991), 8. Drawing his examples primarily from India and secondarily from Eastern Europe and the Soviet Union, Brass divides theorists of both ethnicity and nationalism into two camps: "instrumentalist" and "primordialist" and sees his argument as moderate "instrumentalist" (9).

[55] Swahili houses are rectangular, with three rooms on each long side entered by doors from a central passageway that also leads to a back courtyard at the end of which, in opposite corners, are a kitchen and a lavatory. Unlike European-style houses, Swahili houses frequently accommodate several unrelated individuals or families who rent or occupy one or more rooms each. For a study and diagrams of Swahili-type housing, see Eva Olenmark and Ulla Westerberg, *Tanzania. Kariakoo, a Residential Area in Central Dar es Salaam*, Department of Architecture. University of Lund, Sweden, n.d.

time of the interviews) were Muslim, and two—recently widowed—were observing the requisite forty-day period of seclusion. The predominance of Muslims does not represent a bias or flaw in my "sample." The vast majority of women who distinguished themselves as TANU stalwarts in the 1950s identified as Muslim.

Initially, I regarded the similarities among the most active TANU women in terms of residence, age, and religious identification as important "social facts" relevant for understanding how particular women had become the *audience* for and *transmitters* of nationalism thirty years earlier. This conceptualization was grounded, of course, in a notion of nationalism as fundamentally Western and foreign, whose proponents were the educated (male) modernizers—most notably Nyerere himself—and the World War II veterans analyzed by Iliffe and others.

Only gradually did I come to understand the extent to which women in TANU had in fact been a major force in *constructing, embodying,* and *performing* Tanzanian nationalism. Clues to the limitations of my original framework were already evident in the responses of elderly TANU women activists to the severe economic crisis of 1984. These responses differed markedly from those of most younger and more highly educated working men and women I encountered on a regular basis. Even allowing for the sense of acceptance or resignation that may come with advancing age, it was apparent that a distinctive political and cultural consciousness was operating in the attitudes of TANU veterans. Asha Ngoma's view exemplifies this:

> When I hear this talk, "We have too much trouble now; better colonial rule," I see such a person as my enemy.... When I remember how we suffered.... We were ruled by chiefs but they had no say in government. They were only given orders.[56]

At first, I found it puzzling that a generation of women who had devoted themselves to the nationalist anticolonial struggle were not particularly bitter about the lack of fruits of that struggle to be enjoyed, one might presume, in their old age. Those who were ill and infirm complained about their poor health and about the shortages of staple goods, and the high cost of everything; but they did not attribute economic difficulty to the failures of nationalism, although some complained that Nyerere, "our son," has "forgotten us." Nyerere had promised the women who had been instrumental in his political success and survival that no one would ever suffer any form of deprivation while he was leader. In fact, he had seen to it that many were assisted economically over the years in terms of employment, the provision of building materials and housing plots, and medical attention.

While I assumed that the filter of present socioeconomic conditions and health would shape women's remembrances of past political activities, I had not considered the extent to which women's accounts of their own lives in the past, as well as in the present, expressed what nationalism in Tanzania was most significantly about. Recent scholarship on African nationalism has focused on the fact that the "flag" independence secured by the government-successors to African nationalist move-

---

[56] Interview with Asha Ngoma, Dar es Salaam, 17 October 1984.

ments has frequently been characterized by political upheaval, authoritarian mis-
rule, and devastating economic decline. By the 1970s, most historians and political
scientists had abandoned the study of nationalism in Africa and had turned instead to the formerly taboo concepts of "ethnicity" and/or "class," the latter becoming a powerful component of many analyses from the early 1970s onwards.
According to Crawford Young's lengthy overview, African nationalism had run its
course by the mid-1980s,[57] and Basil Davidson traces why and how that course was
doomed in *The Black Man's Burden.*[58]

Benedict Anderson's definition of nationalism, however, is clearly relevant
to this study of Tanganyikan nationalism centered on women activists and their
narratives. Nationalism, according to Anderson, "has to be understood, by align-
ing it not with self-consciously held political ideologies, but with the large cultural systems that preceded it, out of which—as well as against which—it came
into being."[59] So too is Iliffe's observation that states, especially colonial states,
create subjects, not nations: "The subjects create the nation and they bring into
the process the whole of their historical experience."[60] Unfortunately, Iliffe goes
on to conflate nationalism and nationalist movements such as TANU and offer
the less nuanced but more typical observation that TANU was not a "local in-
vention but a deliberate imitation of earlier nationalist movements elsewhere,"
and that Tanganyikan nationalism was therefore a "late and imitative" one whose
educated leaders, "the imitators ... played a larger part, especially as expound-
ers of nationalist ideas."[61]

Tanzanian women featured in this study provide a very different picture in
their construction of the present and reconstructions of their past political involvement. Their narratives show that in the 1950s, "ordinary" (illiterate, frequently self-
identified as Swahili, Muslim) women created and performed Tanganyikan
nationalism's "culture of politics."

About My Use of Life History Interviews

Anyone who has undertaken research in which the collection of oral narratives
played a large part understands the dilemma of deciding when, where, and how
extensively to quote the persons interviewed. I had to remind myself many times
in the course of writing this book that however problematic the issue of representation, the meaning of personal experience, and the constructed nature of the interview situation, I wanted the words spoken by TANU women activists—Tanzanian
women's nationalist discourse—to push, pull, and in a central way, inform this

---

[57]   In this 53-page review article, there is no mention of gender until the second to the last paragraph,
where Young refers to it as one of three "new cognate fields of inquiry." Crawford Young, "Nationalism,
Ethnicity, and Class in Africa: A Retrospective," *Cahiers d'Etudes Africaines* 103 (1986), 474.

[58]   Perhaps because of its relative success as a nation, Basil Davidson barely mentions Tanzania's nationalist history in his book, *The Black Man's Burden: Africa and the Curse of the Nation-State* (New York, 1992).

[59]   Anderson, *Imagined Communities*, 12.

[60]   Iliffe, *Modern History*, 486.

[61]   Ibid., 486.

study of Tanganyikan/Tanzanian nationalism. It was not enough to preserve the women's words and voices on tape and paper for the exclusive use of other interested researchers. This means that most chapters contain substantial sections of first-person narrative from what I term modified or directed life history interviews.[62] The narratives themselves, prompted by our presence as interviewers and our questions, were obviously not spontaneous, any more than the women interviewed were randomly selected. In some cases, women spoke to us solely within the framework of and in response to the questions asked. Often, however, women went beyond our questions to add information they thought we should have, or to tell stories and express feelings provoked by, though not directly responsive to our questions, or even necessarily to our presence as "audience."

It is important to distinguish between a simplistic and in my view, overly egotistical notion that one's research questions *shape* the responses, and especially the recollections of the person being interviewed, and a more comprehensive understanding of the role of questions in determining the terrain and framework of interview exchanges. While some of my questions (e.g., "When and how did you first hear about TANU?") were intended to secure information about how women's mobilization began and spread, other questions (e.g., "Do you think women's and men's problems were the same or different during the colonial period?") were clearly intended to solicit opinions and perceptions.

Most interviews lasted an hour to an hour and a half, and interview tapes were handled as follows. First, I employed Swahili-speaking assistants fluent in English to write complete transcriptions, including repetitions, common inflections, religious references or exclamations, side-comments and questions, and equally complete English translations of the tapes. My assistants and I then met to discuss questions or problems arising in the context of this process and tried to address as many as possible. Then, I constructed narrative "life histories" from the English translation, removing my questions and comments and creating a text that we then re-translated back into Swahili. Although not all of the "life historians" were interested, they were offered copies of their life histories to hear or read, correct if necessary, and keep. The result of this process is five versions of each interview: the tape, a tape transcription, an English translation of that transcription, an English rendering of the life history narrative from the translation, and a Swahili translation of the English narrative. In incorporating long segments of interviews in this book, I have usually drawn from the English translations of the tape transcriptions. For the most part, I have referred only occasionally and, more often than not, indirectly, to the questions—usually my questions—that prompted the discourse presented. Furthermore, I have frequently chosen not to interrupt the re-presentation of TANU women's narratives with my analysis or comments, reserving these for footnotes and introductory or concluding commentary. Although this decision on my part is problematic, producing as it does seamlessness that did not exist, so too are all the

---

[62]   I qualify the basic definition of a life history as "an extensive record of a person's life told to and recorded by another, who then edits and writes the life as though it were autobiography" (L.L. Langess, *The Life History in Anthropological Science* [New York, 1965], 4–5) to indicate the extent to which my interest in women's participation in politics and TANU in the 1950s shaped which aspects and period of a person's life I wanted to know about. The women I interviewed were fully aware of my central interests.

alternatives. Although the women themselves are the best judges of whether or not I have been "true" to their words and meaning in the book, they are unfortunately least likely to be able to pass judgment on my work.

Based on the ways they responded to my questions about their participation in TANU, I believe the women I interviewed saw themselves as political actors who shaped TANU and Tanganyikan history through their actions. Moreover, with the exception of several women whose clarity and comprehensive recall were impeded by advanced age and poor health, women related the most public period in their lives—the period of their political activities in the 1950s—with considerable attention to chronology. Other aspects of their narratives were chronologized, so to speak, by my questions, answers to which were linked to "before" and "after" the period of activism.[63]

My interviews with TANU activists suggest to me, then, that a sense of oneself as an historical actor depends crucially and critically on political conditions and context—the intersection of one's life and life course with a heightened "political moment," whether and how extensively one is able to participate in that moment, and finally, whether one has a sense of collective agency within the context of historical action.

The Construction of Bibi Titi Mohamed's Life History

My presentation in this book of a three-part "life history" of Bibi Titi Mohamed raises some of the most pressing and serious questions about my use of personal narrative. I have already provided a brief chronology of our 1984, 1988, and 1992 interviews, but because of the centrality of her story to this book, I need to say more about my "authorial" and editing role, Bibi Titi's interest and placement in this project, and the relative degrees of power and influence each of us exercised in representing her political story and nationalist discourse.

Unquestionably the best known and most centrally positioned of all TANU women activists, Bibi Titi Mohamed enjoyed both vast popularity and a basically admiring and positive press for the decade during and immediately following Tanganyika's nationalist struggle for independence (1954–1964). Often photographed in that period next to Nyerere in parades, meetings, or public gatherings, or pictured addressing large audiences of enthusiastic supporters, Bibi Titi had a well-developed public *persona* long before we met. By the time of our first interview in 1984, she had given dozens, and had provided the basic outline of her personal and political story (with surprisingly few variations) to many journalists and authors, Tanzanian and foreign.[64]

---

[63] In comparing the life history narratives of Kaje wa Mwenye Matano, Mishi wa Abdala, and Shamsa Muhamad Muhashamy, Sarah Mirza and Margaret Strobel, editors of *Three Swahili Women*, conclude that Muhashamy's clear sense of herself as an historical actor and her attention to chronology, as compared with the others, came from her class background, education, and experience. While these structural factors were no doubt important, the twenty- and thirty-year age differences between Muhashamy and the others must surely be considered as well.

[64] Barongo, *Mkiki wa Siasa Tanganyika*; Listowel, *The Making of Tanganyika*; Kandoro, *Mwito wa Uhuru*; Interview with Bibi Titi by Henry Morganthau, 28 August 1965, Indiana University Archives of Traditional Music (OT 2162.71–017–F Tanzania).

The years from 1965 to 1973, however, were to prove as difficult for Bibi Titi as the earlier years had been triumphant. During these years, she lost her parliamentary seat in the 1965 elections, was rejected as UWT's national candidate, and resigned from the TANU leadership in response to the Arusha Declaration of 1967 and its leadership code. By the end of the decade, she had been convicted of treason and sentenced to life in prison. Despite Nyerere's pardon early in 1972, the accusations of treason and the notoriety and pain of trial and imprisonment shattered any possibility that Bibi Titi could achieve a seamless political story or unambiguous place in Tanganyika's nationalist history.

Because both my introduction to and relationship with Bibi Titi Mohamed were mediated by her longstanding friendship with Kanyama Chiume, any notion of intersubjectivity must be triangulated to include him. With the exception of our first meeting, during which I remember feeling overwhelmed and excited by the fact that it was finally happening, I always felt welcomed by Bibi Titi—in a sense "included" in her well-established warm and joking relationship with Mr. Chiume. It was on my return visit in 1988 that Bibi Titi first called me her *shoga* (close woman friend), and that was her term thereafter. Although at one level, the friendship between us could only be regarded as superficial—after all, we have been together seven times, over a period of eight years—at another level, I feel, and felt at the time, that the term was appropriate to our genuine liking for each other. I responded immediately and positively to Bibi Titi's humor, her intelligence, her toughness and refusal to cast herself as a victim, and her command of the terms of our engagement. I responded, in fact, to her charisma as so many others have.

Our interview sessions were intense and usually lasted the better part of a day, always ending in a delicious meal she insisted on providing for Mr. Chiume and myself, and sometimes others whom she had invited. Steadily improving living conditions and prospects, and her own increasing reintegration into the public/political life of the country over the time of our interviews, account for the most significant changes in our relationship over time. Despite her ever-improving situation, however, I believe Bibi Titi's interest in talking to me remained the same: she wanted TANU women's political efforts documented and published. She wanted "the record" acknowledged and in that way set straight. Her acceptance of me as someone who might do that, especially in 1984, was based on her trust in Kanyama Chiume's judgment *and* the fact that no one else was showing any particular interest.

By the late 1980s this had changed, and Bibi Titi was in a position to simultaneously scold Tanzanian women (through Ruth Meena) for neglecting her, while strategically "questioning the legitimacy of White feminists ... [who were] turning African women into their objects of study for their own interests at a time when Africa had its own female intellectuals."[65] While the content and phrasing of this concern seemed to reflect most centrally the concerns of African women scholars, insofar as the views expressed were those of Bibi Titi, I could only marvel at what appeared to me to be her political acumen in dealing simultaneously with foreign and Tanzanian women academics. First, of course,

---

[65] Meena, "Bibi Titi," 45.

I had to stop wincing at the criticism of "white Western feminist academics" like myself, even as I knew that I was an intended object.

Initially, I asked Bibi Titi the same questions that I asked all other women interviewed. Because she has repeated parts of her story many times, there is a real sense in which what she told us is little more than an elaborated version of *the story*. In fact, after the first interview, it was often our "Can you tell us more about..." kinds of questions that prompted the elaborations. Always, however, Bibi Titi reinforced and reiterated common themes—most notably, a commitment to identifying others by name and additional commentary, and a refusal to provide details regarding personal controversy or her life and activities just prior to her arrest for treason.

A comprehensive biography of Bibi Titi remains to be written. In writing this book I have tried to reflect the view of Bibi Titi and other women activists interviewed that the task of creating and performing nationalism during the 1950s was not one woman's work, it was *women's* work. Chapter 2, an overview and comparison of the lives of colonial Tanganyika's rural and urban women, provides a context for understanding the mobilization of *particular* women into the nationalist movement. Chapter 3 comprises the segment of Bibi Titi's life history that covers her early years and the beginnings of her political life in Dar es Salaam. Chapter 4 concerns the mobilization of Dar es Salaam women more broadly, and is followed by the second segment of Bibi Titi's life history (Chapter 5), detailing her work in the countryside. Chapters 6 and 7 draw on the life histories of women activists from Moshi and Mwanza, where colonial conditions created substantially different contexts for TANU and nationalism. Chapter 8 returns to Bibi Titi's narrative of her life after independence, while Chapter 9, a postscript, takes the women's nationalist narrative into the early postcolonial years to reflect on the changing focus of women's movement activism and continuities in nationalist consciousness.

In this book, Bibi Titi's life is the "thread" that extends and connects the narratives of TANU women's activities and nationalism and moves the larger narrative forward chronologically and conceptually. It is also a metaphor for the strengths and limitations of women's political participation and the continuing gender constraints facing Tanzanian women. Steven Feierman argues persuasively for the significance and power of peasant discourse despite its declining salience in the context of a postcolonial government controlled and dominated by a bureaucratic elite.[66] Peasants did not prevail during the first three decades of political independence in Tanzania; nor did workers, trade unions, marketing cooperatives, religious communities, or chiefs. Yet their failure to do so does not negate the significance of their social histories, nor, in some cases, their profound engagement in the construction and expression of nationalism. Similarly, although TANU women did not make a revolution in the future lives of Tanzanian women, this does not negate the importance of their collective biography or their importance to Tanzanian nationalism.

---

[66] Steven Feierman, *Peasant Intellectuals: Anthropology and History in Tanzania* (Madison, 1990).

2

Women in Dar es Salaam: Colonial Ideologies vs. Urban Realities

Do you live alone or with a wife? Who cooks for you? Did you leave your wife behind?[1]

European colonialists in sub-Saharan Africa never liked the idea of Africans living in towns and cities, except in those places in West Africa where urbanization had long preceded their arrival. The fear of losing control was paramount in shaping this colonial attitude,[2] yet was frequently expressed as a concern for the damaged psyche of the "detribalized" African. In the parlance of colonial ideology, all African town dwellers were thought to be torn loose from a rural umbilical cord which provided the only nutrients for healthy African life.[3] The management of African urban anomie was in this sense a metaphor for the greater difficulties colonial administrations faced in maintaining order and exercising control over diverse and ever-changing African urban populations.

This chapter examines the ways colonial actors perceived and constructed African men and women, and the effect of these gendered constructions on African women in Tanganyika's capital, Dar es Salaam. I argue that colonial administrators experienced particular difficulties in conceptualizing and therefore actually "seeing" urban African women, except when events or circumstances involving them demanded attention. I then consider the lives of women in Dar es Salaam in the

---

[1]   J.A.K. Leslie, "Original Report," 29 December 1957, 313–17.

[2]   Frederick Cooper, "Urban Space, Industrial Time, and Wage Labor in Africa," in *Struggle for the City: Migrant Labor, Capital, and the State in Urban Africa*, ed. Frederick Cooper (Beverley Hills, 1983), 20.

[3]   Marjorie Mbilinyi, "'City' and 'Countryside' in Colonial Tanganyika," *Economic and Political Weekly* XX, 43, Review of Women's Studies, 26 October 1985, 83–96. British colonial biomedical theory also saw "deculturalization" through urbanization as a central factor explaining African "insanity, sexually transmitted disease, leprosy, and industrial disease." See Megan Vaughan, *Curing Their Ills: Colonial Power and African Illness* (Stanford, 1991), 202.

1950s, identifying the material and social conditions that underlay the political activism of some women and the relative silence of others.

Constructing Gendered African Labor in Colonial Tanzania

In Tanganyika, as elsewhere in colonized Africa, Europeans viewed African urban dwellers, and especially the stream of migrants from the rural areas, as a necessary evil—and adjusted to them as one adjusts to the inevitability of drought or floods in season. During the 1920s and 1930s, however, most Tanganyikan migrants, men forced to leave their home areas in order to seek money for taxes and other requirements, headed for sisal and other plantations, where they worked for the European settler population, which was small relative to those of Kenya and Southern Rhodesia, and concentrated in the rich southern and northern highland areas.[4]

Nevertheless, the colonial state needed *some* workers in Dar es Salaam, the administrative and commercial capital, as well as in the other towns scattered throughout the territory. Africans and immigrants from India were the solution.

Racial segregation and discrimination were firmly entrenched in Dar es Salaam and throughout Tanganyika from the earliest days of colonial rule, dividing the European, East Asian, and African populations hierarchically in all spheres of life: residential areas were racially exclusive; schools were separate, and types and grades of employment were racially categorized.[5] African men performed virtually all forms of unskilled and skilled manual labor, including dockwork at Dar es Salaam's active deep water harbor, street repair and maintenance, office cleaning, and domestic service.[6] Of the nearly 400,000 African workers registered in 1953, 15,500 or just over 6 percent were salaried workers in low-level civil service and administrative jobs.[7] While a few had managed to establish themselves in business or transport, competition with Asians, who dominated business from small shopkeeping to large-scale commercial enterprise, was both formidable and stacked against Africans, who lacked training; access to apprenticeships, capital, and goods; and the mutually supportive networks enjoyed by many Asian businessmen. The vast majority of urban Africans—men and women—tried to meet their needs for cash by selling one thing or another in the streets and markets.

[4] Deborah Fahy Bryceson, "A Century of Food Supply in Dar es Salaam," in *Feeding African Cities*, ed. Jane Guyer (Bloomington, 1987), 163. For Kilimanjaro, see Susan (Geiger) Rogers, "The Search for Political Focus on Kilimanjaro: A History of Chagga Politics, 1916–1952" (Ph.D. dissertation, University of Dar es Salaam, 1973); N.N. Luanda, "European Commercial Farming and Its Impact on the Meru and Arusha Peoples of Tanzania, 1920–1955" (Ph.D. dissertation, Cambridge University, 1986).

[5] R. Sabot, *Economic Development and Urban Migration: Tanzania 1900–1971* (Oxford, 1979); Allen Green, "A Socio-economic History of Moshi Town" (Ph.D. dissertation, University of Dar es Salaam, 1979); Thomas J. Trebon, "Development of the Pre-independence Educational System in Tanganyika, with Special Emphasis on the Role of Missionaries" (Ph.D. dissertation, University of Denver, 1980).

[6] Table 6.5, "Occupational Status of African Adult Male Population, 1953," *Tanganyika Statistical Abstracts 1954* (Dar es Salaam, 1955).

[7] Ibid. The 1957 census of African population recorded 276,362 Africans living in urban areas, accounting for 3.2 percent of the total African population. Government of Tanganyika, "The 1957 Census of African Population," in Hadley Smith, ed., *Readings on Economic Development and Administration in Tanzania* (Dar es Salaam, 1966).

Apart from a few female teachers, hospital and social welfare staff, the colonial state needed and wanted male labor in Dar es Salaam. And it was usually migrant men who were periodically judged by authorities to be "too many" and for whom colonial vagrancy and "undesirable persons" regulations were created to "clean out" those who could claim no reason (i.e., waged work) for being there. The city, then, was a place where African men did or did not belong depending on colonial labor requirements, and where African women were shadow figures—anomalous creatures inhabiting invisible spaces in a male domain. The dominance of this view among European colonizers helps to explain the androcentric framing of the questions for J. A. K. Leslie's 1956 survey of Dar es Salaam,[8] while an acceptance of this colonial construction by Western scholars whose research relied primarily on European writings helps to explain why, for example, historian John Iliffe entitled his chapter on changing urban patterns in colonial Tanganyika, "Townsmen and Workers."[9]

Even more profoundly, this representation of Dar es Salaam and other urban areas as male spaces necessarily obscures many important aspects of colonial ideology regarding urban African women, and it seriously obscures urban African women's lives.[10] Colonial constructions of colonized African women were (mis)informed by basic assumptions about African women in their "natural," that is, rural, "tribal" setting, and as with men, furthered by an ideology in which problems of control and extraction figured centrally.

Moreover, the colonial state's interest in control and extraction was also deeply gendered. In the case of "the African man," authorities assumed that the twin requirements of control and extraction had to cover all aspects of his life, from how and where he might work, to what crops he could produce; and from what associations he could form, to how many cattle he could own.

In contrast, the colonial state's interest in controlling and extracting from African women was narrowly focused on their sexuality and their role in social and biological reproduction. The matters taken up in documents devoted to women in the Tanzania National Archives (TNA) illustrate this focus. These "women's files" are replete with ponderous exchanges among colonial officers and reports of exchanges between colonial officials and native authorities on the "problem" of women's sexuality and the "rights" of particular males (fathers, husbands) to regulate or to have exclusive access to women's sexual services and reproductive potential.[11] Subtopics include *adultery* (seen as an injury,

---

[8]   Leslie's work is based on a questionnaire administered to a sample of 5 percent of the houses in predominantly African parts of Dar es Salaam during 1956 (see Appendix C, 311, "Original Report," for Leslie's methodology). Early sections on "the African" and why "he" comes to Dar es Salaam, etc., are uniformly androcentric.

[9]   Iliffe, *Modern History*, 381–404. "Each section of Dar es Salaam," writes Iliffe, "housed certain categories of men" (p. 387).

[10]   Sheryl McCurdy's recent research on women in Ujiji and Kigoma in western Tanzania provides an important correction. See "The 1932 'War' Between Rival Ujiji (Tanganyika) Associations: Understanding Women's Motivations for Inciting Political Unrest," *Canadian Journal of African Studies* 30, 1(1996): 10–31.

[11]   Cf. Martin Chanock, *Law, Custom, and Social Order: The Colonial Experience in Malawi and Zambia* (Cambridge, 1985); Margot Lovett, "Gender Relations, Class Formation, and the Colonial State in Africa," in *Women and the State in Africa*, eds. Jane L. Parpart and Kathleen A. Staudt (Boulder, 1989), 23–46; Elizabeth Schmidt, "Patriarchy, Capitalism, and the Colonial State in Zimbabwe," *Signs* 16, 4 (1991): 732–56.

originally civil and later criminal, to the "owner-husband"), including whether and how severely women should be punished, forced to pay or even imprisoned for their presumed complicity in an adulterous union;[12] *bride price* (the exchange of money or goods between the groom and the bride's family to legitimate marriage), including its monetization and/or increase, with almost exclusive attention to the consequences for men of the changing nature of the transaction;[13] *fines for impregnating unmarried girls*, viewed as punishment "for having stolen something to which he was not entitled;"[14] *marriage/divorce law and custom* and appropriate court jurisdiction over same;[15] *control of prostitutes*, alleged or known;[16] and *beating and desertion*, especially complaints from wives concerning their husbands,[17] but also the desertion of husbands by wives. In the latter case, district officers appear to have assisted husbands in securing the return of wives on the sole grounds of a husband's request for help.[18]

Even when the issue was whether women should pay hut or poll tax,[19] or the appropriate posting and differential pay scales of African women teachers,[20] the rights, needs, and responsibilities of men in relationship to their dependents are the focus of concern against which the "problem of women" is posed. In 1943, for example, the European headmistress of the African Girls' School in Dar es Salaam sought permission to sack a teacher, Josephine A., for shirking her work and claiming to be sick all the time. According to the headmistress, Josephine's "bad state of health" was caused by "loose living," which had in turn caused a government teacher to leave "his young wife and four children under seven completely unprovided for."[21] As late as 1956, the provincial education officer for Bagamoyo objected strongly "to sending new [female] teachers to places away from their homes unless they are either married or of mature years."[22]

Two aspects of the ideology concerning control over African women's sexuality and reproductive functions are especially important for understanding the structural situation of colonized women. First, both African men and colonial officials understood women to be essentially and appropriately subordinate to

12   TNA 20411; 156/1/Vol. V.

13   TNA A2/13; L5/7.

14   Minutes of Dodoma District Council Meeting, 9 February, 1953, in TNA L5/7.

15   TNA 29536.

16   TNA 3/14, Vol. VIII.

17   TNA 16.

18   DC, Dar es Salaam to DC, Kilwa, 3/14/1326, 9 July, 1955, TNA 3/14, Vol. VIII. Missionaries and settlers did not necessarily share the administration's position on restoring women to the "right place." For a discussion of German missionary responses to women's situations, see Marcia Wright, *Strategies of Slaves and Women: Life Stories from East/Central Africa* (New York, 1993). Birgitta Larsson, *Conversion to Greater Freedom?: Women, Church and Social Change in North-Western Tanzania Under Colonial Rule* (Stockholm, 1991) examines the interaction between missionaries and Haya women in northwestern Tanzania.

19   TNA 10690.

20   TNA 1/8.

21   Elsie Vatcher, Headmistress, African Girls' School, DSM, to Director of Education, DSM, Ref. 2/a/44 of 22 November, TNA 1/8.

22   Provincial Education Officer to D.C., Bagamoyo, E.1101/160, 7 March 1956, TNA 1/8 Bagamoyo. African Staff: Women.

men.[23] British authorities found some African practices for securing control and ensuring the dependence of girls and women repugnant. Child marriages, excessive beating, arbitrary abandonment of wives, and belated claims to ownership of daughters were among these practices. Some Haya men, on the other hand, were incensed by the British administration's refusal to prevent the freedom of movement of Haya women and criminalize prostitution.[24] But there was no disagreement about the fundamental need to control women.

The notion of a shared interest in the control of African women among African and European men in Tanganyika was never collectively challenged as it was in neighboring Kenya. There, the missionary-led attack on the practice of clitoridectomy among the Kikuyu during the 1920s, while dividing the Kikuyu population, destroyed any sense of a shared agenda with respect to African women's place among colonial and colonized men,[25] and reinforced among many Kikuyu men and women alike a refusal to succumb to forced westernization. Moreover, Kikuyu women's emergence as a force for nationalism in their own right can be traced to this struggle among others.[26]

In Tanganyika, however, British attempts in 1930 to raise an alarm over the physical damages of clitoridectomy and the alleged "near-slavery" of African women never caught on. Emanating from the Colonial Office and reinforced by the views of an unofficial parliamentary committee,[27] the alarm was countered by the report of Dr. J. O. Shircore, director of medical and sanitary service in Tanganyika, who stated: "during 22 years [of] divided service in Nyasaland, Uganda, Kenya and Tanganyika ... no suggestion of what might be construed as slavery of the African wife has come to my knowledge." To this Governor Cameron added, "Women are by no means slaves in Tanganyika; they have their rights in their own social order."[28]

A second aspect of the colonial state's gendered approach to control and extraction concerned the presumed source of authority with respect to African women. Whereas designated European and African colonial functionaries were held responsible for controlling African male labor, migration, and cash-crop production, the control of African women was invariably left to colonized men—to fathers, husbands, brothers, or uncles. Its legal parameters were defined and redefined by colonial officials, including the Africans designated "native authorities" by the colonial administration. The safari notes of a local court adviser touring Musoma District in northeastern Tanganyika in 1951 illustrate several key aspects of gender ideology during the last decade of colonial rule. He writes that:

---

[23] Cf. Cora Ann Presley, *Kikuyu Women, the Mau Mau Rebellion, and Social Change in Kenya* (Boulder, 1992).

[24] D.C. Mwanza to Bahaya Union, Ref. 103/8/149, 14 November 1949, TNA A6/6.

[25] For a nuanced study of the language and meaning of the controversy over clitoridectomy, see Susan Pedersen, "National Bodies, Unspeakable Acts: The Sexual Politics of Colonial Policy-Making," *Journal of Modern History* 63 (December 1991): 647–80.

[26] Presley, *Kikuyu Women*, Chs. VI–VII.

[27] Col. Sec. Passfield to Gov. Cameron, 8 March 1930; Memo to Lord Passfield from "Committee for the Protection of Coloured Women in the Crown Colonies," n.d. but sent to Cameron 10 April 1930, TNA 18881.

[28] Dr. J. O. Shircore, "Memorandum on the Improvement of Physique of Native," 5 May 1920; Governor Cameron to Passfield, 22 May 1930, TNA 18881.

The men complain that the women are difficult, disobedient and out of hand, the women that they are badly treated. These of course are usual complaints, but in this district...it seems that women have just cause for complaint and that the men have made little or no attempt to make life easier for them.... The young women of the tribe are now adopting an attitude which is considered "uppish" by the men and the latter naturally tend to resist any measures designed to improve women's status.[29]

The particulars which made the situation of Musoma women seem especially difficult included child and other "forced" marriages; easy divorce, but only for men; various disadvantages in connection with rules governing the return of marriage cattle; and ex-husbands' belated claims to child custody, especially to custody of marriageable daughters. But the court adviser's statement also makes it clear that he believed that men controlled women and were "naturally" reluctant to raise their status, and that without caution, interfering could "make things worse."

The colonial administration's stake in the sexual and reproductive control men exercised over women was directly related to its desire to maintain a virtually cost-free system of subsistence agriculture in the territory.[30] As the primary food producers, women supported households and families, feeding workers and future workers who were thereby "freed" to enter the wage labor economy or to grow cash crops so long as women continued to shoulder responsibilities for subsistence.[31] Marriage determined not only with whom a woman was permitted to have sex and conceive children, but for whom she would farm and provide all other domestic labor services.[32] This was true whether or not women controlled a portion of what they produced, and whether or not they also had additional labor obligations to other kin group or community members or, as in the case of Shambaa women, to the chief.[33] It was also true even when husbands were away from their wives for extended periods of time. Since these norms dovetailed neatly with the colonial reliance on African women to bear all the costs of subsistence and reproduction of the male labor force, officials had no reason to undermine existing gender relations.

To maintain this ideal, however, district commissioners (DCs) had to spend a great deal of time trying to get "deserting" wives to return to their husbands.[34] By the 1950s the colonial administration was alarmed about growing "marital instability" in rural areas with high rates of male labor migration,[35] and it was clear that both cases of desertion and of domestic and extra-domestic violence against women were on the rise.

What, then, was to be done, conceptually speaking, with women who were born in or migrated to towns and cities, including Dar es Salaam, where subsis-

[29]   TNA 1/2/6 Vol. 1.

[30]   Marjorie Mbilinyi, "'Runaway Wives' in Colonial Tanganyika: Forced Labour and Forced Marriage in Rungwe District, 1919–1961," *International Journal of the Sociology of Law* 16 (1988): 1–29.

[31]   Deborah Fahy Bryceson, "Women's Proletarianization and the Family Wage in Tanzania," in *Women, Work and Ideology in the Third World*, ed. Haleh Afshar (London, 1985), 133.

[32]   Deborah Fahy Bryceson, "The Proletarianization of Women in Tanzania," *ROAPE* 17 (1980), 6.

[33]   Feierman, *Peasant Intellectuals*, 51–52.

[34]   See passim, TNA 5/25/14, Native Affairs General, Moshi, Vol. VII.

[35]   Bryceson, "Women's Proletarianization," 134–35.

tence agriculture was not the most salient factor in social reproduction, where neither extraction from nor control of women seemed quite so simple, and where African women were, in the colonial mind, simply not "supposed" to be? In order to address these questions and to analyze the permutations of colonial and African gender ideology under urban conditions, we must first consider the nature of those conditions in Dar es Salaam, especially during the decade following World War II.

Dar es Salaam:
A Legacy of Hierarchy, Racism, and Neglect

Established in 1866 to advance the mercantile interests of Sultan Sayyid Majid of Zanzibar, Dar es Salaam, with its excellent natural harbor, was initially populated mostly by local Zaramo people, by Indians, and by Arab traders. As Bryceson notes, "a hierarchy of slave and master relations characterized this community."[36] In 1887 the Germans replaced the sultan's power with their own and in three years made the city the capital of German East Africa. During the period of German rule the slave economy was ended, a dichotomized peasant/rural : wage-earning/urban economy was established—in theory if not reality—and race became the major criterion for employment, with a consequent development of differential living standards.[37] Historians Iliffe and Depelchin use the terms "misery" and "disaster" respectively to describe African living conditions in Dar es Salaam in the 1930s and during World War II.[38]

A parallel and related process of African Islamization, begun on the East African coast in the nineteenth century, continued without German interference. Because it proved advantageous to do so, many migrants from the interior sought to adapt and assimilate—to become "civilized," according to coastal norms—by speaking Kiswahili, adopting relevant items of dress, and becoming Muslims. As Glassman notes of the coast and its urban centers in the late nineteenth century,

> This was a time when slave, urban plebeians, and rural people, both Swahili speakers from coastal villages and non-Swahili speakers from the further hinterland, all sought enhanced roles within the expanding trade economy. The greatest number of opportunities were present in the urban centers.... thus, there was an ongoing struggle as hinterland people sought to become members of the urban community.[39]

Dar es Salaam's African population grew very slowly prior to World War II, from 19,000 in 1913 to 33,000 by 1943. By 1948, however, it had increased to

---

[36] Bryceson, "A Century of Food Supply," 158.

[37] Ibid., 158.

[38] Cited in Mbilinyi, "'City' and 'Countryside,'" 89.

[39] Jonathon Glassman, "Social Rebellion and Swahili Culture: The Response to the German Conquest of the Northern Mrima" (Ph.D. dissertation, University of Wisconsin, 1988), 16. Glassman's thesis has been revised and published as *Feasts and Riot: Revelry, Rebellion, and Popular Consciousness on the Swahili Coast, 1856–1888* (Portsmouth, NH, 1995). See also David Henry Anthony, "Culture and Society in a Town in Transition: A People's History of Dar es Salaam, 1865–1939" (Ph.D. dissertation, University of Wisconsin, 1983), 232.

50,765,[40] and by 1956, the African population of the city was just over 101,000, a figure which represented an increase of 29,000 residents in the years 1952–1956.[41] Meanwhile, the ratio of adult males to females in Dar es Salaam declined from 141:100 to 131:100 between 1948 and 1958, as more women left the rural areas for the cities.[42]

In response to mounting labor unrest manifested in the country's first general strike in 1947, the colonial administration began, belatedly, to address pressing urban problems. African housing in Dar es Salaam was totally inadequate and overcrowded, and the city lacked the most basic urban amenities—sanitation, piped water, street lights, a minimal public transportation system—and industrial development.[43]

Even in the mid-1950s, when government expenditure on housing, sewage work, and street repair had ameliorated the worst manifestations of neglect, African areas of the city could still be characterized as slums, especially in contrast to those set aside for Europeans. John Hatch described what he saw during his brief visit to Dar es Salaam in 1955:

> here again is a picture of slums inhabited by most urban Africans.... When I was told that the first African District Officer had been refused admission to a European hospital after a car accident I realized that racial discrimination has not by any means been entirely destroyed in this country.[44]

Social Engineering and Political Anxieties

If World War I was "both the culmination of European imperialism and the beginning of its decline,"[45] World War II forced the waning colonial power to exploit whatever additional resources it could from its Trust Territory. Following the war, Britain also faced increased pressure for political and economic rights from colonized peoples throughout its possessions, and especially from African troops returning home with an expanded understanding and resentment of their colonized existence. In Tanganyika, the administration sought to forestall radical political change by instituting gradual political reform and social development as cheaply as possible. Since African men were considered most likely to cause trouble, social development efforts were primarily designed to channel their energies into "appropriate" activities. As the social welfare officer for Dar es Salaam explained:

> In small towns and rural areas ... it is hoped that the availability of social amenities will decrease the drift of individuals to the towns in search of pleasure.[46]

---

[40] Bryceson, "A Century of Food Supply," Appendix I, 195.

[41] Monthly Report of the DO, Dar es Salaam to the PC, Eastern Province, September 1956, TNA 540/A/14.

[42] Coulson, *Tanzania*, 101; Bryceson, "The Proletarianization of Women," 19.

[43] John Campbell, "Urbanization of Dar es Salaam," seminar presentation, Women's Resource and Documentation Project, University of Dar es Salaam, September 17, 1984.

[44] Hatch, *New from Africa*, 54.

[45] Iliffe, *Modern History*, 240.

[46] SWO, Notes on Social Welfare Centres, Dar es Salaam, October 1945, Ref. 2/46, TNA 540 3/70.

Although men, and especially ex-servicemen, were to be the target popula-tion for an African social center for Dar es Salaam, the assistant district officer thought women should be included in adult education and cultural activities. However, because the majority population in Dar es Salaam was Muslim, he felt it would be best to start with a "special 'ladies night,' say one night a week ... and a separate reading room for the ladies."[47] In 1946, the center committee decided to allow women to use the facility between 2:00 and 4:30 p.m daily—a decision that was reported to be "extremely popular"—and unlike the social welfare officer's suggestion of a "ladies night," agreeable to African men who were willing to "allow their womenfolk to become members provided their doing so does not interfere with the evening meal...."[48] By the end of the decade, the Social Welfare Department's Ilala Social Club, located in an African housing estate where many tenants were said to be well educated and in the "higher income group," was being used regularly for women's sewing classes, a nurs-ery school and a weekly mother-child clinic. Although English and literacy classes were poorly attended by men, women were taking advantage of the adult education facilities to learn to read and write in Swahili and to borrow Swahili books.

Meanwhile, at Alexandra Hall, where the Social Welfare Department main-tained a large "open club," dancing and cinema were most popular and by early 1952, dances and "government backing" were keeping the club going.[49] There was, however, little interest in "general community work,"[50] and as Social Wel-fare Officer E. C. Baker had earlier observed, the popularity of Western dance could not be

> viewed with unreserved approval until such time as a man can dance with his wife and allow her to dance in public with other men. This is not the case at present ... and the necessity of inviting spinsters to provide part-ners for the men is to be deplored....[51]

The above reports and observations suggest that African recipients of the programs and amenities newly offered as "development" accepted what inter-ested them and rejected European attempts at social engineering. Deprived as girls of the opportunity to learn to read, write and sew, women jumped at the chance to do so in adult education classes. Meanwhile, men had little interest in literacy classes or community service, but were extremely enthusiastic about doing the foxtrot, waltz, swing, tango, and rumba (*dansi*) in European clothes; but that didn't mean they wanted to see their wives dance with other men, or even in public.[52]

---

47   Memo from Ass't DO, DSM, 18 June 1945, TNA 540 3/70.

48   E.C. Baker, SWO, DSM, Report on Social Welfare, 1946 (Dar es Salaam, 1948), TNA 540 8/70.

49   Annual Report of the Social Development Department, 1949–1950 (Dar es Salaam, 1951); memo frag-ment, DC, Dar es Salaam, 24 January 1952, TNA 540 3/70.

50   Memo fragment, DC, Dar es Salaam, 24 January 1952, TNA 540 3/70.

51   E.C. Baker, SWO, DSM, Report on Social Welfare, 1946 (DSM, 1948), TNA 540 3/70; see also Anthony, "Culture and Society," 154–55.

52   For the popularity of *dansi* in Zanzibar after World War II, see Laura Fair, "Pastimes and Politics: A Social History of Zanzibar's Ng'ambo Community 1890–1950" (Ph.D. dissertation, University of Minne-sota, 1994), 316–19.

By the late 1940s, the European Women's Service League, previously focused on the war effort,[53] was also turning its attention to African women. Through an African Women's Welfare Section, European women offered African women sewing and knitting classes, tea parties, and jumble sales. Once again, African women expressed particular interest in learning to read and write Swahili, which was a problem because instructors were reportedly hard to find. Towards the end of 1948, the first woman welfare officer, Miss Elwes, was appointed and by 1949, there were fifteen African women's branches of the Women's Service League scattered throughout most of the country. Summarizing the achievements of a three-year period, the author of the Women's Service League Report for 1948 noted that African women were "cleaner, friendlier, and more co-operative."[54]

By 1951, the African Women's Section of the Women's Service League numbered twenty-six branches and three centers in Dar es Salaam, and plans were under way to establish separate African women's clubs.[55] In the same year, a Tanganyika Council of Women (TCW) under the patronage of Lady Twining, the governor's wife, was forming to promote unity among the women of Tanganyika, improve community and child welfare, share information, and link with other councils through the International Council of Women.[56]

In a letter requesting government funding, Lady Twining called it "the only interracial women's society in the Territory" and stated that although it only had about 150 members, mainly in Dar es Salaam, those members intended to study and work on nursery schools, mothercraft and welfare, child health and hygiene, and homemaking— "in fact the general raising of the standard and status of women...."[57] Not surprisingly, the administration responded positively to Lady Twining's request for support.[58] By March 1953, the TCW claimed 700 members in Dar es Salaam and ten upcountry centers; members paid a two-shilling subscription each year. Working closely with the Social Development Department, the TCW "gradually [took] over African women's sewing classes up-country," and began to help with rural women's clubs and the organization of small handicraft shops. Plans for a women's news sheet in Swahili and English were also under way.[59] The government continued to approve Lady Twining's requests for funding, and membership increased steadily, from 1100 members by early 1954, to 1500 members in 20 groups shortly thereafter. By

---

53   File notes, Women's Service League, TNA 21217; HRH The Duke of Gloucester's Red Cross and St. John Fund, TNA Secretariat 29430, Vol. II.

54   Women's Service League Report, Appendix A, Annual Report on Social Welfare, 1948 (DSM, 1950), TNA 540 3/70.

55   Ibid.

56   Constitution of the TCW, TNA 42226. The International Council of Women was a nongovernmental body founded by Susan B. Anthony in 1888. It favored "the opening of all institutions of learning to women, equal pay for equal work, and ... an identical standard of morality for the sexes." Lisa Tuttle, *Encyclopedia of Feminism* (New York, 1986), 155.

57   H.M. Twining, President, TCW, to Chief Secretary, 21 February 1952.

58   The TCW received a grant of £200 a year for 1952 and 1953, and £500 at 5 percent interest for ten years in loans, half of which the TCW accepted. Acting Member for Local Government to TCW, Ref. 42226/21, 12 May 1952, TNA 42226.

59   Short notes on the TCW, 11 March 1953, TNA 42226.

this time, with the Mau Mau emergency in neighboring Kenya, better race relations had become the Council's chief objective.[60]

Meanwhile, the Twining administration worried that social welfare activities in Tanganyika were insufficient to prevent Africans from erupting into Mau
Mau–like behaviors. Twining himself was especially impressed by white settler
and author Elspeth Huxley's notion of "rural jollification,"[61] and borrowed the
concept for the title of his confidential file on the subject. Huxley considered
Mau Mau a psychological disease and set of "pathological symptoms" resulting
from the failure of British colonialism to provide Africans with the sense of
wellbeing and/or excitement and interest in their lives that was once provided
by festivals, hunts, cattle raids, sacrifices, ceremonies, and swift and clear punishment.[62] Neither social welfare, with its emphasis on "ladies' sewing classes"
and hygiene, nor the churches, which refused to replace the paganism they
abhored with "substitute rituals," were addressing African boredom and discontent. The younger generation in particular, warned Huxley, had no outlet
for excitement and passions, and "young toughs" were especially susceptable
to Mau Mau. Huxley's answer was "rural jollification":

> It comes back, of course to bread and circuses. Should the Government,
> then, have a Department of Rural Jollification and aim at a Circus State
> rather than a Welfare one? With travelling fairs and cinemas, massed danc-
> ing, pageants and tattoos, bullfights and prizefights—and on the reverse
> side, public executions and floggings? The answer is probably yes.... But
> at the very least, things could be brightened up to provide a counter-at-
> traction to Mau Mau.[63]

Despite Governor Twining's enthusiasm for Huxley's ideas,[64] the chief secretary wondered how "healthy relaxation" could be imposed on Africans when
the only attraction welfare centers seemed to be providing was a "level floor
for European-style dancing (to which they do not bring their own wives)."[65]
But the main stumbling blocks impeding the introduction of rural jollification—
including organized sport, traditional and modern dance contests, agricultural
shows, bike races, fireworks, and tennis courts for African clerks and school
teachers—were the apathy of local officials, perceived staff shortages, and dis-
agreements over which administrators had the time to organize and oversee
such projects.[66] While some administrators blamed missionaries for stamping

---

[60] Secretary of TCW, Myra Murray, to Miss Tate, Social Development, DSM, 2 February 1954; H.M. Twin-
ing, President TCW, to J. P. Moffett, CSD, DSM, 27 March 1954, TNA 42226. See also Presley, *Kikuyu
Women*; and Audrey Wipper, "The Maendeleo ya Wanawake Movement in the Colonial Period," *Rural
Africana* 29 (1975–76): 195–213.

[61] Elspeth Huxley, "The Lion Needs the Jungle," *Time and Tide*, 10 October 1952.

[62] Huxley, "The Lion Needs the Jungle," "Rural Jollification," TNA 50424 (Confidential).

[63] Huxley, "The Lion Needs The Jungle."

[64] Twining to CS, MLG., and MS.S., confidential file note 1, 2/11/52, TNA 50424 (Confidential) "Rural
Jollification."

[65] Chief Secretary, DSM, to MLG, File Note 6, TNA 50424.

[66] File note, 30; F.H. Page-Jones, MLG, Memorandum 9, for PCs Conference, June 1953: Extract from
minutes of PCs conference, June 1953; Dir. Education to Hon. Member for Social Services, Ref. G/111/42,
Dec. 2, 1953, TNA 50424.

out *ngomas*, others noted that only a small minority of people seemed attracted to existing programs, and that women were especially neglected. Perhaps in self-defense, one administrator noted that he always had *ngomas* during "annual dry-season post-harvest *barazas* [official meetings]" and that women attended too."[67] The PC for local government concluded that if the district commissioners were given responsibility for the organization of arts and crafts, they should be told how to "pass on the routine work involved to their wives, their cousins and their aunts—not forgetting their departmental colleagues and Native Authorities...."[68]

With anxious eyes fixed on Kenya, administrators attempted to fend off African-initiated political change with sports (especially football), dancing competitions, and agricultural shows. Nevertheless, by 1955 the "40 such so-called 'welfare centres' existing in the territory were generally moribund [and] there were plans to turn them into attractive community centres with beer gardens attached."[69] Meanwhile, in 1954, Arnautoglu Centre in Dar es Salaam made a profit of £1,000 after all overhead expenses were paid.[70] Clearly, Africans with the time and interest to participate enjoyed football and dancing, sewing and literacy classes; but colonial authorities who thought such activities could prevent or substitute for nationalist movement were fooling themselves.

Women in Dar es Salaam

[handwritten: rural vs urban women]

J. A. K. Leslie, a district officer who later became commissioner for social development, conducted his survey of Dar es Salaam's population in 1956, the first detailed information collected about the city's inhabitants. From this survey, it is possible to construct a picture, albeit tentative and incomplete, of the adult female population in the mid-1950s.[71] This picture is complex and, clearly, individual women's lives varied depending on a number of interrelated factors—most notably age, marital status, access to economic resources, and length of residence in the city. Moreover, the direct relevance of each of these factors, and the nature of their interrelationship, differed for the vast majority of women who were Muslim (90 percent) and illiterate (88 percent), and for the tiny minority of educated women, primarily Christians. By the mid-1950s this latter group included women with sufficient educational training to be employed in teaching, hospital work or social services in the city.

The lives of Muslim women born in Dar es Salaam were most likely to reflect the blend of Islamic and regional/ethnic values and traditions indigenous to coastal culture that permeated urban life.[72] Most were secluded as *wali* ("young

---

[67]   File note 30, TNA 50424.

[68]   PCLG, 29.12.53, to CS, Dar es Salaam, TNA 50424 (Conf.).

[69]   Extract from Minutes of PCs Conference, June 1955, TNA 50424.

[70]   Extract from Minutes of PCs Conf., June 1955, TNA 50424.

[71]   Leslie's *Survey of Dar es Salaam* (London, 1963) first appeared as a lengthy report dated 29 December 1957. My references to this original report are so specified. Where I refer to *Survey*, my reference is to the book.

[72]   Anthony, "Culture and Society."

TABLE I
Some Statistics on Women and Men in Dar es Salaam, 1956*

	% of women	% of men
Population between the ages 16–45	42	58
Born in Dar es Salaam	35.5	25.8
Self-identified as Muslim	90	?
Illiteracy rate**	88	59
Age 6 and over, no formal education	82	48
Literate in Swahili (Roman)	12	41
Literate in Swahili (Arabic)	4	15
Literate in English	2	8
Attended only Koranic School	5	11
Completed Primary School	6	18
Completed Middle School	1	5
Completed Standard X	0	2

Notes: *Numbers reconstructed from Leslie, "Original Report," 1957.
**Literacy was defined as the "ability to read and write a few words."

maidens in closest purdah") from the age of puberty until their first, arranged marriages, usually to men much older than they.[73] As young wives, many quickly re-entered a state of confinement to the house if their husbands were financially able to uphold this "ideal." It was common, then, for an adolescent girl to spend most of her teenage years in seclusion, though it is important to note that even in the extreme form, seclusion did not involve isolation, but rather gender segregation. Custom, youthful inexperience, and the absence of alternatives meant that few girls thought to resist either seclusion or this first marriage.[74]

While the seclusion of pubescent girls was practiced widely throughout Tanganyika, it was probably most fully realized among coastal peoples who adopted Islam. Young and first-married women in Dar es Salaam were therefore likely to experience greater restriction than their rural sisters at this point in their lives. But if seclusion was common, divorce was an equally common outcome of first marriages. Childlessness was the most widely recognized reason for divorce, but other reasons were acceptable, and divorce itself was considered neither unusual nor immoral within the context of Islamic law.[75] Thus, it was considered perfectly normal for a young woman to look forward "eagerly" to "her first divorce," and with it, the chance to marry by choice.[76]

[73] Leslie, "Original Report," 2N, 220; cf. Margaret Strobel, *Muslim Women in Mombasa, 1890–1975* (New Haven, 1979); Mirza and Strobel, *Three Swahili Women*; Pamela Landberg, "Widows and Divorced Women in Swahili Society," in *Widows in African Societies: Choices and Constraints*, ed. Betty Potash (Stanford, 1986), 107–30.

[74] Marja-Liisa Swantz, *Women in Development: A Creative Role Denied?* (New York, 1985), 34.

[75] Landberg, "Widows and Divorced Women," 114.

[76] Leslie, "Original Report," 221.

A divorced woman was free to remarry without a dowry—to "send herself," as Swahili-speakers put it, to the husband of her choice, perhaps "in the hope of bearing children, or she [might be] attracted to the racy town life of some women...."[77] Once remarried, the children of this union belonged legally to her new husband; if she did not remarry, and bore children, they were hers by Islamic law.

According to what the men interviewed told Leslie, the disadvantage of second marriages was that women who were "taken with town life" and who became "true town women" were "less easy to please, more liable to demand that water be carried by a servant ... wanting to be well-dressed and fed and to go to cinemas and dances"—in sum, less subservient.[78] For a woman, there appeared to be considerable advantage in not being married at all, since her "price as a mistress" was "higher than it would be as a wife," and she could not be forced to do menial wifely tasks.[79]

Leslie reports that in the 14 to 45 age group, 15 percent of the men and 36 percent of the women had been divorced. Among women in this age group, of the 90 percent who were or had been married, 57 percent had been married once; 25 percent twice; 6 percent three times; and 2 percent more than three times.[80] Had the target group been further restricted to adult females over the age of 19, the percentage married more than once would have certainly been much higher. Eleven percent of the women and 39 percent of the men surveyed stated that they were either single or in a "free marriage;" but Leslie found both men and women reluctant to acknowledge the latter status, and assumed that the real figures were probably considerably higher. On this assumption, and somewhat confusingly, Leslie decided that "free marriage" (*kinyumba* or *kimada* in Swahili) was "believed to be the rule" in Dar es Salaam.[81] In summarizing the range of marital and sexual arrangements, he concluded that "full" or "formal" marriages with the consent of both sets of parents as well as religious sanction and/or the payment of brideprice were difficult to arrange in Dar, and in the minority.[82] But while the relative dearth of formal marriages in Dar es Salaam may have been due to the geographical and psychological separation of some urban residents from parental influence, marriage "instability" in general was as much a coastal as an urban/migrant phenomenon.[83]

Leslie details other arrangements including remarriage without parental consent or brideprice, living together (sometimes semipermanently, but with no formal bonds), and prostitution. What is clear is that women's marital and sexual

---

77   Ibid., 20, 221.

78   Ibid., 221.

79   Ibid., 222.

80   Ibid., 268.

81   For innovative marriage forms in urban colonial Zimbabwe and Zambia, see Teresa Barnes, "The Fight for Control of African Women's Mobility in Colonial Zimbabwe, 1900–1939," *Signs* 17, 3 (1992): 576–608, especially 598; and Jane Parpart, "Sexuality and Power on the Zambian Copperbelt: 1926–1964," in *Patriarchy and Class: African Women at Home and in the Workforce*, eds. Sharon Stichter and Jane Parpart (Boulder, 1988), 118.

82   Leslie, "Original Report," 215–16.

83   Ibid., 2M.

options increased substantially once they were freed from a first, arranged marriage. But it is also clear that the degree of freedom women might exercise in "middle age" depended upon their ability to generate economic self-sufficiency.

By the mid-1950s, prostitution ranked with beer-brewing and selling fish as the most lucrative economic activities available to Dar es Salaam women.[84] But there were several other ways to earn money, including the splitting and sale of firewood and the production and sale of cakes, fritters, beans, and coconut ice— i.e., affordable "fast food" for poor workers. Such jobs provided women with income and the Dar es Salaam population with services that helped to make urban life more tolerable. Women who had access to land also grew food. Although Leslie reports that only 7 percent of Dar es Salaam households had *shamba* (farms) for cultivation, this figure was probably low, given the number of urban dwellers with continuing ties to land adjacent to the city. Among those interviewed for the 1950 Survey of African Labourers in Dar es Salaam, 14 percent grew subsistence crops, especially rice, beyond the city perimeter.[85]

Meanwhile, very few women held jobs in Dar es Salaam's formal employment sector, where the few positions available required literacy, specialized training, or both. In its Annual Report for 1953, the administration reported the employment of some twenty African women in the Binding Department of the Government Press, "the first African women to be employed in light industrial activities by the Government."[86] As late as 1952, African women constituted only 6 percent of the regular labor force and 3 percent of the casual labor force, and 39 percent of all women workers in Tanganyika came from neighboring colonies, most notably from Portuguese East Africa (Mozambique) and the Belgian Congo (Zaire). Most (82 percent) were employed in agriculture, forestries, and fishing, a combined sector that constituted just over half (56 percent) of the total paid workforce, and was 8 percent female. Although 87 percent of the female agricultural workers were regular rather than casual laborers, there was greater wage disparity between them and their male counterparts than in any other sector. Virtually the entire female agricultural workforce (99.98 percent) earned less than Shs.70/ per month, compared with 88 percent of male workers.

Out of all employed women, only 4 percent worked in the public sector, which paid the highest wages. Constituting only 1.4 percent of the total, women in this sector enjoyed the closest approximation of wage parity. Sixty-six percent of women public servants earned more than Shs.40/ per month, compared with 73 percent of men, although the wage gap became more apparent at the high end of the wage scale, where 7 percent of the males as compared with 0.4 percent of females earned more than Shs.150/ per month.

The experience and pay of most employed women paralleled that of juveniles more closely than that of adult men. Roughly comparable in size at 21,446 and

---

[84]   Ibid., 90, 227.

[85]   Tanganyika 1951, 63, cited in Bryceson, "Century of Food Supply," 189.

[86]   Tanganyika, *Report for the Year 1953* (London, 1954): picture caption, facing 103. In an essay detailing Nigerian women's slow progress and unequal treatment relative to men, LaRay Denzer nonetheless makes it clear that Nigerian women had more employment opportunities much earlier than women in Tanganyika. See LaRay Denzer, "Women in Government Service in Colonial Nigeria, 1862–1945," *Boston University African Studies Working Papers*, No. 136 (Boston, 1989).

30,824 respectively, the female and juvenile paid labor forces clustered at the low end of the wage scale, earning less than Shs. 40/ per month. Agriculture, forestry, and fisheries accounted for 82 percent and 85 percent of the female and juvenile workforce respectively, but only 49 percent of the male workforce.[87]

In 1956, women still constituted only five and a half percent of the wage labor force, and of the 22,334 women employed throughout Tanganyika, nearly 80 percent continued to be concentrated in agriculture.[88] Overall, adult women wage workers earned 30 percent less than their male counterparts,[89] and the few women who by the early 1950s had completed the necessary eight years of schooling to qualify for teacher training and a teaching job suffered similar discrimination.[90] In 1957, minimum wage regulations established for Dar es Salaam municipality fixed adult female wages at 32 cents per hour—10 cents per hour less than adult males.[91] Even at independence in 1961, women constituted only 4 percent of Dar es Salaam's enumerated wage labor force.[92] Without idealizing women's situation in the tenuous and unpredictable sphere of urban small-scale production and trade, it is difficult to see why women would choose wage and especially factory labor over self-employment given the harshly exploitative terms and conditions of wage labor in general in Tanganyika, and specific wage discrimination against women. With the female hourly wage fixed at 32 cents, even the "lowest grade prostitute" could make three times that for one transaction.[93]

Although it posed a fundamental challenge to colonial and African gender ideologies, which linked male control of female sexuality through marriage to rights in women's productive capacity, the administration considered limited prostitution a "necessary safety valve" for men in Dar es Salaam.[94] Indeed, if prostitutes were reasonably discreet in their behavior, the colonial administration accepted their presence for obvious reasons. Thirty-nine percent of Dar es Salaam's adult male population was unmarried. Moreover, the majority of migrant men interviewed for Leslie's survey stated a preference for marrying

---

[87] Similarities between women and juveniles were evident in the tabulation format for the East African Statistical Department, which juxtaposed figures pertaining to women and juveniles and set off adult male figures in a separate section. Report on the Enumeration of African Employees, July 1952, East African Statistical Department, 1953, 10–24.

[88] Bryceson, "Women's Proletarianization," 137; Tanganyika, *Report for the Year 1956* (London, 1957), 92–93.

[89] Issa G. Shivji, "Development of Wage-Labour and Labour Laws in Tanzania: Circa 1920–1964" (Ph.D. dissertation, University of Dar es Salaam, 1982), 268, 310–13.

[90] Until 1952, women could only qualify for a Women Teacher's Certificate, which required two years of practice teaching after completing Standard VIII. In 1953, this category of teacher earned between Shs.84/ and Shs. 128/ per month. In 1953, women received 8 of 60 Grade I teaching certificates, and 1 of 16 Grade 1 licenses. In the same year, 91 women and 571 men obtained Grade II certificates and a further 28 men and 3 women students received teaching licenses. Men who became Grade I or Grade II teachers earned Shs. 226/ to Shs. 400/, and Shs. 110/ to Shs. 160/ per month respectively. Teachers trained at Makerere in Uganda, East Africa's only university—all men—received diplomas in education and earned Shs. 425/ to Shs. 750/ per month. *Tanganyika Report for the Year 1953*, 89–90.

[91] Shivji, "Development of Wage-Labour"; Bryceson, "Women's Proletarianization," 138.

[92] Bryceson, "A Century of Food Supply," 172.

[93] Leslie, "Original Report," 225.

[94] Ibid., 2N. Unfortunately, there is no equivalent work on Dar es Salaam to Luise White's comprehensive historical work on Nairobi, *The Comforts of Home: Prostitution in Colonial Nairobi* (Chicago, 1990).

women from their home villages who would secure their lineage-based land rights and grow food for themselves and their children—an arrangement that conformed to colonial expectations as well.[95] But whereas men experienced sex with a prostitute as "the most casual of relationships,"[96] women engaged in prostitution were often making a significant and, in some cases, pivotal socio-economic decision.[97]

My concern here, however, is not with the lives or earnings of prostitutes in Dar es Salaam or elsewhere. Rather, it is to suggest how prostitutes' behavior came to be characterized in such a way that virtually any urban unmarried woman became a "suspected" prostitute. For example, since Haya women in Dar es Salaam constituted a "huge preponderance" in Leslie's taxonomy of "professional" prostitutes, any unmarried Haya woman was obviously suspect.[98] Similarly, with "amateur" prostitutes from the coast referred to in a "slightly derogatory" way as "Swahili women," unmarried coastal women were equally suspect.[99] Since only a few women actually told Leslie they were prostitutes, he employed the following "rule of thumb" for his Survey:

> where three or more single women in one house paid each her own rent, then all were prostitutes; sign[s] which can be added as confirmation are a preponderance of Haya, and a habit of cooking on primus stoves in the central passage (obviously for fear of missing customer[s] by being in the back premises when they call)....[100]

Prostitutes did frequently live together, renting all six rooms of a "Swahili-type" six-room house with shared central passageway and courtyard for cooking and washing. Because prostitutes had a reputation for paying on time and could afford higher rents, landlords in general, who were occasionally "madames" living in one of the courtyard rooms,[101] generally liked to rent to them. Houses "containing the trade" were scattered widely throughout the city, but were concentrated in Kisutu, which was regarded as a "red-light" area.[102] In fact, any unmarried woman living in such a house or in Kisutu was assumed to be a prostitute.

---

[95] Leslie, "Original Report," 220.

[96] Leslie's phrase, ibid., 224.

[97] White, *Comforts of Home*. For Nairobi, see also Janet Bujra, "Women 'Entrepreneurs' of Early Nairobi," *CJAS* 9, 2 (1975): 213–34. For one of the few studies which deals with the circumstances of prostitutes through the lens of their home area, see Larsson, *Conversion to Greater Freedom?*, especially Ch. III, 38–143.

[98] Leslie, "Original Report," 224. See also Larsson, *Conversion to Greater Freedom?*

[99] Leslie, "Original Report," 224.

[100] Ibid. Cf. Luise White, "A Colonial State and an African Petty Bourgeoisie: Prostitution, Property, and Class Struggle in Nairobi, 1936–1940," in *Struggle for the City*, ed. Cooper, 186–90; Luise White, "Prostitution, Identity and Class Consciousness During World War II," *Signs* 11, 2 (1986), 258; and Larsson, *Conversion to Greater Freedom?*, on Haya prostitution in Nairobi.

[101] Leslie determined that when a "madame" owned the house, each tenant was nevertheless entirely independent, paying no more than the agreed rent from her earnings. He therefore concluded that prostitution in Dar es Salaam was neither organized nor exploitative, and simply reflected the "very widespread amorality or immorality" which, in his view, characterized the sexual behavior of the city's African population. Leslie, "Original Report," 229.

[102] Ibid., 224–25.

Although the municipal administration in Dar es Salaam took few measures to control prostitution,[103] women could be arrested if they were found
"loitering" in certain streets after dark without flashlights (or "torches"). Although the charge would be "using streets without light," the target was prostitutes and "suspected" prostitutes.[104] Therefore, women on the street after dark
without a flashlight were suspected of prostitution.

Leslie's own survey reveals the contradictions confronted in attempting to
situate African women in Dar es Salaam within the prevailing colonial gender
ideology. According to his male informants, the urban woman was an "economic liability," in contrast to the rural wife "at home," who was an "investment" and an "economic asset."[105] Leslie clearly sympathized with the men who
had to supply "a constant succession of new *khanga* (cloth wraps), earrings, [and]
plastic sandals" to keep their wives or female companions from running off
with "smooth operators" offering them a good time.[106] Yet Leslie also reported
that Dar es Salaam women were hardworking, resourceful, and astute at business—far more adept at saving and investing earnings than their male counterparts.[107] Some women in Dar es Salaam were reputed to be both extremely
wealthy and very influential. But Leslie was no more successful than women's
husbands or lovers in finding out their total worth or earnings. Nor was it easy
to determine a woman's wealth by her street dress:

> In the daytime ... western dresses are hidden, all but a glimpse to prove
> they are there, by the ever present *buibui*.... And some of the richest women
> in town, the widows and *pombe*-brewers, the landladies and fish-sellers
> are so well established that they can afford, like country ladies in the *Tatler*
> in their tweeds, to wear the old-fashioned *khanga*, cheap and serviceable,
> and wear it with finality.[108]

For a substantial minority of women, financial independence appears to
have been complemented by social independence.[109] Women headed 11.2 percent
of all households in Dar es Salaam in 1956; for some ethnic groups, this figure
was considerably higher. Among the Manyema, for example, the figure was 35
percent (the highest), and among the Nyasa, 19 percent (next highest). The lowest figure was for the Matumbi (2 percent).[110] Not surprisingly, Manyema women
were also prominent among female house owners, holding nearly one-fifth of
the titles to some 12,000 of the city's African-owned houses. According to a 1956
rent register for Kisutu, a predominantly Manyema area, 51 of 113 houses (45

---

[103] Tanganyika, *Report for the Year 1955* (London, 1956), 122–23.

[104] Memo from Central Police Station, DSM, to Chief Inspector, TNA 3/14 Vol. VIII, Dar District Office.

[105] Leslie, "Original Report," 220.

[106] Ibid.

[107] Ibid., 94.

[108] Ibid., 90.

[109] We cannot assume, of course, that women household heads in Dar es Salaam in the 1950s were necessarily wealthy; nor can we assume that all women house owners were necessarily household heads. At
the same time, it is important to refrain from imposing a contemporary view of female heads of household in Africa, which relates this status to the increased impoverishment of women.

[110] Ibid., 9 (survey tables).

percent) were registered to women.[111] Of 59 houseowners sampled in the Kariakoo and Ilala areas, 16 (27 percent) were women.[112]

The phenomenon of female urban house ownership was not limited to Dar es Salaam. Throughout Tanganyika, as elsewhere in colonized Africa, urban women built or bought houses as an economic investment.[113] One did not need to be literate to own houses and rent rooms, and landlords, whether male or female, were likely to be among the wealthiest individuals in the city's African population. Invariably, then, house ownership ensured women a degree of economic independence and security that was unlikely to be achieved by any other means.

Breaking through the mists of colonially produced gender ideology which shrouded the lives of Dar es Salaam's female population in the mid-1950s, it is possible to offer the following tentative conclusions. Generally speaking, the range and flexibility of marital and other sexual relationships in Dar es Salaam appear to have offered all but the youngest adult women more choice and self-control in both sexual and reproductive matters than rural women were likely to experience, a fact deplored by colonial authorities, religious leaders, and some African men. In addition, women in Dar es Salaam had opportunities for earning independent incomes that were largely unavailable in rural areas. For these reasons, unmarried urban women, and even married urban women whose "behaviors" seemed "suspect" were, for all practical purposes, assumed to be prostitutes unless proven otherwise—a factor that had important implications for women's nationalist mobilizing in the 1950s.

There were, however, stark differences between Muslim or Swahili women and women migrants to the city who lacked education and may or may not have been Christian, and the small minority of educated women, mostly young and Christian. These differences separated women from each other and the educated minority from the nationalist movement.

Class, Religion, and the Construction of Urban African Women: Domesticity vs. "Bad Habits"

By the 1950s, a colonial system that required migratory male labor and the continued involvement of women in food production was clearly manifested in the sexual politics of Dar es Salaam. Prior to 1952, 42 percent of Tanganyika's urban male migrants and 87 percent of all female migrants were married when they arrived in Dar es Salaam, figures that are probably representative of other urban populations in Tanganyika.[114] While the number of unmarried female migrants in-

---

[111] Ibid., 155.

[112] Leslie cautions that "people" could build houses in the name of a wife or daughter. But he doesn't substantiate this practice with any evidence, and indeed, explains in his survey that women acquired houses through "lucrative small trades;" inheritance from a deceased husband, parent, or brother; prostitution; and government compensation for compulsory relocation. Ibid. 155, 227, Appendices 2H, 2I.

[113] See, for example, White, *Comforts of Home*, 119–24. See also Larsson, *Conversion to Greater Freedom*; and Caroline Bledsoe, *Women and Marriage in Kpelle Society* (Stanford, 1980).

[114] Nwanganga Shields, "Women in the Urban Labor Markets of Africa: The Case of Tanzania," *World Bank Staff Papers*, 380 (April 1980), Table 2.8, 23, derived from 1971 Tanzanian National Urban Mobility, Employment and Income Survey.

creased during the 1950s, the majority of women who moved into Dar es Salaam in 1956 (64 percent) were married when they arrived, having either accompanied or followed husbands to the city.[115] With no access to land, women could not be expected to cultivate food for themselves and their children; but this was only half the problem. At the root of urban men's stated preference for a wife who stayed "at home," as well as Leslie's contradictory stereotypes of urban women, lay the issue of men's apparent loss of access to an urban wife's labor or income. The husbands of women who found a way to earn money had no idea how much their wives made and no enforceable claims to their earnings. Quarrels over these issues produced "marital instability," because the very fact of having independent earning power reduced a woman's need to suffer a husband who demanded access to it. In this view, the real difference between rural and urban women had less to do with relative productivity than with the increased control that urban women might exercise over their own production and earnings, and hence over their lives.

Thus women in Dar es Salaam who were able to exercise a degree of choice in sexual matters and to reinforce their positions through independent money-making activities found a more reliable path to social and economic self-determination than that offered by the government's attempts to "improve the status of African women" after World War II by bringing them into "contact with the manner and customs of other races...."[116] These programs, whether run by voluntary agencies or the administration, were shaped by an ideology of Western-style "domesticity" and an awareness of the emerging class differences among Africans in Dar es Salaam—differences that were clearly exposed in the state's dual administrative approach to the wives of workers and the wives of "middle-class" men.

Provincial Commissioner M. J. B. Molohan argued in 1957 that the way to "stabilize" African working-class families was to open up domestic service jobs to women. As Molohan put it,

> it is ludicrous that domestic service in Tanganyika should be the perquisite [sic] of the male. The Territory cannot afford for much longer the luxury of locking up so many [c. 30,000 in 1956] able bodied men in this unproductive sphere of employment for which women are far better suited and equipped.[117]

Molohan's ideal African worker's family contained two wage earners, including a wife with two domestic service jobs, one free and one paid. [118] Molohan's solution for middle-class Africans (such as higher-paid clerical workers, small-scale entrepreneurs, and traders) also emphasized female domestic labor but differed with respect to how that domesticity functioned. What the "aspiring African" needed in order to advance was a better-educated wife, since her "backwardness" was one of his "greatest handicaps" and "a major chal-

---

[115] Ibid.

[116] *Tanganyika Report for the Year 1953*, 59.

[117] M.J.B. Molohan, *Detribalisation* (Dar es Salaam, 1957), 42.

[118] Molohan's concern to "free" African male labour for other, productive jobs had been echoed elsewhere and earlier in British-controlled Africa. See Elizabeth Schmidt, "Race, Sex and Domestic Labour: The Question of African Female Servants in Southern Rhodesia, 1900–1939," in *African Encounters with Domesticity*, ed. Karen Tranberg Hansen (New Brunswick, 1992), 221–41.

lenge for both the educationalist and the social worker."[119] What Dar es Salaam needed was "female education" modeled on that provided by the "foyer school" in Elizabethville in the Belgian Congo, where women learned "sewing, simple domestic science, cooking and child welfare."[120]

Molohan's views both reflected and reinforced trends in class differentiation among Africans that were already in evidence in Dar es Salaam.[121] Yet class was not all that divided the city's African population. By the early 1950s, there were distinct differences between the lifestyles of women in the majority Muslim, nonliterate population and those in the Christian minority who had learned some English at school. These differences clearly illustrate the distinctive features of gender ideology embedded in emerging class assumptions and aspirations.[122]

Anthony dates the beginning of residential separation of Christians from Muslims in Dar es Salaam to the 1920s and '30s when Muslim landlords refused to rent accommodations to members of Dar es Salaam's fledgling Christian community, noting that non-Muslims continued to feel excluded from Muslim areas even in the 1980s.[123] But if, as Anthony asserts, Muslims viewed African Christians "with a somewhat jaundiced eye,"[124] it is also clear that Christian women returned a similarly jaundiced gaze, especially toward Muslim women. Many Christian immigrants to Dar es Salaam were not prepared to assimilate into a coastal culture that required even nominal acceptance of Islam, and housing discrimination necessitated the establishment of specifically Christian settlements.

Residential separation and differences in housing styles marked social, physical, and psychological boundaries between Christian and Muslim women and illuminated the differing gender ideologies brought to bear on them. Whereas the Mission Quarter to which many Christians gravitated contained houses designed for a husband, his wife, and their children, the ubiquitous six-room Swahili-type house was generally occupied by several families or individuals, each of whom rented a room and shared the common passageway and enclosed or open courtyard at the back. This type of dwelling provided and still provides resident women with ready-made female companionship and common space in which to socialize, take morning tea, and undertake various tasks together.[125]

Among Swahili women, those who engaged in trade or brewed and sold *pombe* (beer) extended household cooperative relationships into working arrange-

---

[119] Molohan, *Detribalisation*, 49–55.

[120] See Nancy Hunt, "Domesticity and Colonialism in Belgian Africa: Usumbura's *Foyer Social*, 1946–1960," *Signs* 15, 3 (1990): 447–74.

[121] Bujra has noted the class dimensions overriding the gendered nature of household labor. See Janet M. Bujra, "Men at Work in the Tanzanian Home: How Did They Ever Learn?" in *African Encounters with Domesticity*, ed. Hansen, 242–65.

[122] For a more thoroughly class-based analysis of women's urban situation, see Marjorie Mbilinyi, "'This Is an Unforgettable Business': Colonial State Intervention in Urban Tanzania," in *Women and the State*, eds. Parpart and Staudt, 111–29.

[123] Anthony, "Culture and Society," 225–28.

[124] Ibid., 228.

[125] Leslie, "Original Report," 95.

ments outside the household. These arrangements were sometimes structured, as among *pombe* brewers, but more often they were based on informal social networks. Rotating savings and credit unions called *upato* (games)[126] were common, and "traditional" forms of mutual assistance were brought to bear for major events such as births, marriages, illness, or death. The Swahili household, then, was a major cultural force, integrating migrant women and men into an urban environment in which Muslims and "pagans" mixed freely, while Christians (13.7 percent of Dar es Salaam males and 10 percent of the females) held themselves apart.[127]

Leslie suggests that by the 1950s, the desire *not* to "mix freely" was more an expression of Christian separatism and attitudes toward "coastal women" than a reflection of Muslim-initiated discrimination.

> Christians feel themselves so much a class apart, with their higher education, their different taboos, their strict canons of divorce, that they prefer to be physically separated.... and often give the "immorality" of the coastal women as a reason for wishing to live in self-contained or semi-detached flats in a mainly Christian area....[128]

For the Christian woman who aspired, with her husband, to a "modern," "progressive" lifestyle, the package of required behaviors included separation from other women, subservience to a husband in a monogamous, lifetime marriage, and adoption of a Western model of domesticity, preferably in a house which shielded her and her nuclear family from unwanted outside influence. Consider, for example, the daily schedule and attitudes of the following professional woman from the Mission Quarter, recorded by Leslie. She and her husband are both teachers. She gets up at 5:00 a.m. to clean, heat water, sweep, and make tea. At 6:40, she wakes her husband and while he washes, she cleans the bedroom and then washes and dresses. They eat breakfast together and go to work. In the afternoon, when she returns from work, she washes clothes, irons, gardens, prepares the meal, and gets water from the standpipe. She accepts the "traditional" division of labor that finds her at work long before her husband awakens and long after he completes his job. In addition, she accepts the new confinement appropriate to their "modern" status:

> When my husband is out I have no permission to go out anywhere except to the [Girl] Guides or the Police, or if I am called away urgently, I must leave my husband a note to show where I have gone and why.... We prefer to live in [the Mission] Quarters rather than a Swahili house, because there is room to spread yourself, and you don't get into bad habits from the other women; there is no noise or jostling, and you can keep the place clean.[129]

Women's acceptance of a particular form of domestic propriety based on a "proper marriage" and wifely subservience extended into the public realm as a

---

[126] Aili Mari Tripp, "The Urban Informal Economy and the State in Tanzania" (Ph.D. dissertation, Northwestern University, 1990), 189–90. Revised and published as *Changing the Rules: The Politics of Liberalization and the Urban Informal Economy in Tanzania* (Berkely and Los Angeles, 1997).

[127] Leslie, "Original Report," 260.

[128] Ibid., 209.

[129] Ibid., 102–103.

preference for the kind of entertainment that reinforced correct behavior and conservative values. Thus, the "professional woman" quoted above preferred to attend dances

> danced by people of the same tribe, not just anyone.... [A]s they are traditional anybody who is an outsider will be unable to create a disturbance; the elders will be there too, to see that everything is done properly. I prefer *ngomas* because they are danced in an orderly and organized manner.[130]

This teacher's disdain for public dance performances reveals much about the class and gender consciousness and ideology of the urban, educated Christian minority. Yet her testimony also expresses important truths about the importance of public performances for Dar es Salaam's Muslim women, for whom urban life with its associated material conditions and cultural norms tended to erode ethnic and class divisions, creating a sense of solidarity as "Swahili women." This solidarity found public expression in the very trans-tribal, open dance organizations and performances that were avoided by the "professional woman" quoted here.[131]

It is important to address the particular situation of Tanganyika's Western-educated female population more generally to understand their relationship to the nationalist mobilization process. In contrast to Nigeria, Kenya, Sierra Leone, and South Africa, where African women from the educated elite were among the early nationalist activists,[132] their counterparts in Tanganyika were not. The Tanganyikan situation, therefore, requires specific explanation to understand the particular construction of its nationalism.

The provision of Western education for girls in Tanzania was remarkably slow in coming and largely provided by Christian missions rather than the government. In 1938, only 4.34 percent of the 520,000 school age girls attended school, almost all in mission schools. Muslim girls constituted only a small part of the 3 percent (171 girls) in government schools.[133]

As late as 1946, there were *no* girls among the 917 secondary school students in Tanganyika,[134] and it was not until the early 1950s that a handful of girls—5 in 1951, 7 in 1952, and 25 in 1954—passed the entrance exam for secondary school. No girls received Cambridge Overseas School Certificates (to advance to higher secondary school and thus preparation for university) until 1953, when 3 girls were among the 86 students who passed. The figures for 1954 were 4 girls and 94 boys.[135]

---

[130] Ibid., 103.

[131] Cf. Strobel, *Muslim Women in Mombasa*.

[132] See LaRay Denzer, "Yoruba Women: A Historiographical Study," *IJAHS* 27, 1 (1994), 32. For Nigeria, see also Nina Mba, *Nigerian Women Mobilized* (Berkeley, 1982); Cheryl Johnson, "Grassroots Organizing: Women in Anti-Colonial Activity in Southwestern Nigeria," *African Studies Review* 25, 2 (1982); LaRay Denzer, "Towards a Study of the History of West African Women's Participation in Nationalist Politics," *Africana Research Bulletin* 6, 4 (1976): 65–85; for Sierra Leone, LaRay Denzer, "Constance A. Cummings-John: Her Early Political Career in Freetown," *Tarikh* 7, 1 (1981): 20–32; for Kenya, Presley, *Kikuyu Women*; for South Africa, Cherryl Walker, *Women and Resistance in South Africa* (London, 1982).

[133] Trebon, "Development of the Pre-Independence Educational System," 156, 172.

[134] Marjorie Mbilinyi, "African Education in the British Colonial Period," in *Tanzania Under Colonial Rule*, ed. M. Kaniki (London, 1980), 265.

[135] "Franchise and Representation in East and Central Africa," Buscot Conference, 8–9 December, 1956, from the section on proposals, Tanganyikan eligibility for voting.

By 1956, 204 girls and 2,409 boys were attending secondary school.[136] Even in 1962, the first year of independence, there were only six girls in the Sixth Form at Tabora Girls Secondary School, therefore six girls in the entire country preparing for university entrance exams.

The coastal region—Eastern Province in administrative terms—was among the most poorly served with respect to education in general and girls' education in particular.[137] Although education authorities attributed the low percentage of girls to "the backwardness of the coastal areas,"[138] the government provided only one-third of the 328 primary school streams in the province while Catholic, Protestant, and private agencies offered the rest. Of the middle schools, two were run by the Catholics and a "parochial" girls' middle school was also Catholic, leaving non-Catholic girls who passed Std. IV exams no school to advance to.[139]

With respect to Western education beyond primary school, then, women in Tanganyika were at least two full generations behind their male counterparts. Julius Nyerere himself went from the elite Tabora Boys' Secondary School to Makerere College in 1943. His was the last generation of Tanganyikan male students without a female component;[140] but as late as 1955, only four of the 150 Tanganyikans at Makerere were women.[141]

Educated women in Dar es Salaam in the 1950s were doubly if not triply isolated: by their small numbers, their religion, and their unusual level of education. Associations and organizations existed for their male counterparts from the 1920s: the Tanganyika Territory African Civil Service Association (1922) which became the African Association (1929); the African Welfare and Commercial Association (1936); and a vast number of ethnically based associations, all of which were in some respects political. In contrast, the Women's Club Movement designed for educated girls and women from the early 1950s was not only *not* a creation of Tanganyikan women; its purpose was, at least in part, to counter women's politicization.[142]

Once again, then, we find that a statement presumed to apply to all Tanganyikans—in this case, Andrew Coulson's conclusion that "the growth of nationalist consciousness was a consequence of the provision of education"[143]— turns out to be primarily about men's nationalist consciousness. Although there were important exceptions,[144] educated women in Tanganyika in the mid-1950s were unlikely to become nationalist activists either as a consequence of their education or, to complete Coulson's generalization, as a result of their urban residence.

For a variety of interrelated reasons, it was primariliy unschooled, "middle-aged" Muslim women in Dar es Salaam whose activism both reflected and infused

[136] Mbilinyi, "African Education," 267.

[137] See enrollment figures in the Annual Report of the Education Department, Eastern Province, 1956, 3.

[138] Ibid., 3.

[139] Ibid., TNA 1/3.

[140] Coulson, *Tanzania*, 103–104.

[141] Iliffe, *Modern History*, 446.

[142] C.F. Wipper, "The Maendeleo ya Wanawake Movement."

[143] Coulson, *Tanzania*, 101.

[144] Lucy Lameck of Kilimanjaro is the most notable of these.

Tanganyika's "nationalist consciousness."[145] Urban existence, "Swahili" cultural norms, greater flexibility of marital/sexual relationships in the city, access to independent yet collaborative income-earning activities and associations facilitated women's relationship to TANU, and in turn, TANU's access to the organizing skills of urban women. Despite colonial and African ideologies about women's proper roles, most urban women activists experienced less surveillance, whether imposed by the colonial regime, by "traditional" authorities, or by husbands or other sexual partners than did rural women, educated women, younger women, or women married to wealthy men. But why were these women interested in mass nationalist politics? What did they hope to accomplish or gain? What did they contribute to nationalism's and TANU's growth and development? These questions form the core of my interviews with Tanzanian women activists.

---

[145] Compare the chapters in *Women and Class in Africa*, eds. Claire Robertson and Iris Berger (New York, 1986) by Janet M. Bujra, Cheryl Johnson, Christine Obbo, and Claire Robertson.

3

Bibi Titi Mohamed: Dar es Salaam

Story of Bibi Titi

Bibi Titi Mohamed, one of Tanzania's most forceful, dynamic, and significant nationalist leaders, had much in common with the "typical Muslim townswomen" of Leslie's survey. Although she was born in Dar es Salaam, her mother and father came from Rufiji, and Iliffe refers to her as a "Matumbi townswoman of formidable energy."[1] Bibi Titi's father, a successful businessman, was probably better off than the average city dweller, and as her relationships with several of Dar es Salaam's local notables suggest, the family was well connected.

Bibi Titi had four years of primary school education, unusual for a Muslim girl in the 1930s. While many women of her generation and background participated in dance associations, only a few would have become lead singers—a position that demanded not only outstanding musical ability but a charismatic personality and performing talent. Thus, while Bibi Titi shared many characteristics with her fellow townswomen—characteristics that enabled her to identify with, relate to, and therefore mobilize other women—she was also exceptional in ways that help to explain her emergence as a leader.

Because of her political prominence and later notoriety, Bibi Titi Mohamed has given many interviews over the years. In particular, she has recounted the story of how and when she obtained her TANU card, and of her meeting with John Hatch many times, though in less detail than presented here. Her narrative reveals major themes in the history of Tanganyikan nationalism, including the importance of women's dance associations; the ways in which TANU women became hardworking political activists who risked censure to move beyond the "normal" boundaries and public spaces established for women; and the ways women activists articulated forms of gender inequality and oppression in the context of TANU's message of equality for all.

---

[1] Iliffe, *Modern History*, 518. Historically, the Matumbi were known for their fierce resistance to outside interference and control. The Maji Maji Rebellion of 1905–1907 began among the Matumbi and their neighbors, for example. When the British administration later sought to introduce indirect rule, the Matumbi refused to "produce any native authority" (ibid., 331).

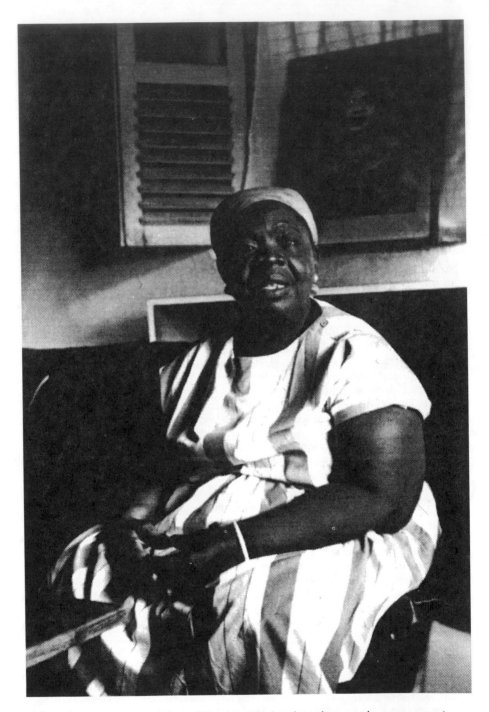

Photo 2: Bibi Titi in Temeke in 1984 seated before her photograph as a young singer. Courtesy of Adarsh Navar, photographer.

I was born here in Dar es Salaam in 1926. My father Mohamed Bin Salim was a businessman and my mother Hadija Binti Salim was a farmer and housewife. *Both my parents came from Rufiji.[2] Luckily they both came from there before they had any children. My father came while he was still a young man—before the [First] World War. He came to Dar es Salaam and lived here and got married to a local woman and had one child, a boy, born in 1911. At that time, he had not married my mother. But eventually my mother came from home, he married her, and I was born. They come from the same district—same place. I had only one brother from the same father, that half-brother of mine, Abdallah, whose mother died. When she died, my father married my mother.

My brother Abdallah died in 1974. He had several children. My mother was the one who brought him up.*

When I was a child I read Koran, and then I went to Uhuru [Government] Girls School, Uhuru [then Kichwele] Street.[3] We were the first students to attend that school and I studied there up to Standard Four. Then I had to stop because I had reached puberty and couldn't leave the house. I stayed inside for one and a half years. *It was the traditional thing for a *mwali* [girl who has come of age], ehe! You are not allowed to go outside. You aren't supposed to meet men or anybody who doesn't know you— even women—unless you have your parents' permission. Your sisters and brothers and other relatives are allowed to see you, except for your father and your eldest brother, who is the heir to your father. Your grandfather can see you because he is *mtani* [kin with whom you can be on familiar terms; joke mate] to you.

Inside, we were taught to cook, sweep, make the bed, wash dishes, because as children, we mostly just played and went to school. We didn't really work. But when you are kept inside during this period, you have to learn all the housework. There are no games anymore. You stay in as if it were a prison. And you are just like a prisoner. You can't even peep through the window. It is strictly forbidden. Windows like these [gesturing to the window behind where she sat] were all shuttered.

It is difficult to explain how I felt about this. Since it is our tradition, I had to tolerate it—that is, just get used to being inside. I wasn't tortured, and I wasn't really a prisoner. It was just the same as when a Muslim woman is kept inside [for four months and ten days] after the death of her husband. She has no worries and I had no worries. This is our religion and I knew these were our customs. Being imprisoned is different from being confined inside in this way. Eehe....*

Anyhow, I stayed inside until I was fourteen years old and married to Mzee bin Haji. *Because my father had died long before, when I was still very young, my older brother made all the arrangements for my marriage. Of course, I

[handwritten margin note: Zenana / separate part of house]

---

2   Sections beginning and ending with * are inserted from later interviews.

3   Bibi Titi uses the postindependence names for both the school and the street.

4   The verbal expression I transcribe variously as eheee, ehee, eehe, etc., is so ubiquitous among older Swahili-speaking women that to leave it out is to fail to convey the emphasis intended by its use. Sometimes, the speaker inflects the expression with a question mark, as in "eheee?" which conveys, "do you understand the importance of what I just said?" And sometimes the expression is more emphatic, so that an exclamation point would better serve to convey the meaning. In conversation, it is not so much accompanied by particular facial expressions or hand gestures; rather the meaning is conveyed by the tone, the length of the sound made, and the inflection at the end.

had never met my future husband. Our Ndengereko[5] traditions are such that no small girl is allowed to talk to a man. You only find out later that those who want to marry you come to your parents to express their intentions. Your parents consider the person's family and decide if they are acceptable. Then dowry is paid and immediately they start making arrangements. Because you are at home, you hear that so and so will come to marry at a certain date, and you also see how you are being prepared for the marriage. At that point, you realize that you are the one who is supposed to get married, but you don't know who your husband is to be. You meet him for the first time when you get married, only to find out that he is an elderly person and you are a little girl! You can't even talk to him.

Nowadays, children meet in school and in the streets. They talk to each other by themselves, and if they decide they love each other, they inform their parents about their intentions. But during those days, when I was young, this was impossible. It was the parents who chose a husband for you, and if you were ever to bring a husband to them, you would be looked upon as a spoiled child. It was not the tradition of the country to bring your own husband.

When Mzee Haji married me, he was about forty; I was fourteen. Was I happy about this marriage? Children of that time were supposed to like what your parents liked. You were happy if your parents were happy. So if they liked someone, then you had to like him too. If there were problems, these would appear later.*

My first husband was a mechanic for the P.W.D. [Public Works Department] transport section here in Dar es Salaam. I was just a housewife. I didn't do any other work. I had one child, a daughter [Halima Mzee]. Now I have nine grandchildren. *We were together for some three or four years and then he divorced me. After all, I was just a child, and he regarded me as childish. So he tolerated me for several years but he preferred older women who knew how to handle him, worship him, and love him the way he wanted. I was very young and inexperienced. I couldn't handle him the way he wanted and he left me.

Then I got married to another man, Buku bin Athmani,[6] and we stayed together for a long time. He was chief clerk at the Water Supply Department. But unfortunately, he died. This marriage was not like my first. We fell in love, me and him. We loved each other. But he died.*

When I was still quite young, there was a political association here in Dar es Salaam called the Tanganyika African Association[7] but I was not involved. In the past, in those days, each tribe had its own organization and its own association. But our organization was just to read *Maulidi*.[8] We women took part in *Maulidi*, but later on we formed "Roho Ni Mgeni"

---

5   Bibi Titi identifies herself variously as Ndengereko, Matumbi, Swahili, and Rufiji depending upon the circumstances and the point she is trying to make. Iliffe pointed out that "Tanganyika was not composed of tribes" but rather, that "its groups and identities were formed in other ways" (*Modern History*, 9), a decade before most scholars of Africa began to note that "tribes" were often colonial creations.

6   Buku bin Athmani is not mentioned in any other interviews with Bibi Titi that I am aware of. In these interviews, Bibi Titi speaks of three husbands: Mzee Haji, Boi Selemani and Micki Mdoe. See, for example, John Bwire interview in *Rai*, 5–11 January 1995.

7   Founded in 1929 by civil servants, clerks, and teachers.

8   Tanzanian Muslims celebrate the Prophet Mohammed's birth by reading, and sometimes performing, a poem based on the Koran describing that event. See Glassman, *Feasts and Riot*, 139–40. For a description of how Swahili women in Mombasa celebrated *Maulidi*, see *Three Swahili Women*, eds. Mirza and Strobel, 43–44.

[Heart is a Stranger]. You could say that "Roho Ni Mgeni" originated from *Maulidi*.

I was a singer—*sheheratib* [lead singer]. In *Maulidi* there were six periods of fasting. We read the *Maulidi* of Prophet Mohamed (Peace be upon him) each year. We read *Maulidi* one time. This was a big event, not small. It was for the Prophet's birthday. After the big *Maulidi* of the community then each group had its own small *Maulidi*. This still happens with us today. Eeeh! That *Maulidi* continues sometimes up to the month of Shaabani [month of feasting preceding Ramadhan]. This was not political in any way.

*Our group ["Roho Ni Mgeni"] was an *ngoma* [a dancing and musical group] and its members were mainly older women. Actually, I was the youngest member in this group when I joined. There were also a few men—about three or four.[9] One of them was the husband of Binti [Tatu] Mzee, Mohamed Maskini. We gave him the title "governor" of our group.[10] And there was also Ismail, Ismail Mwinyimvua, he was our "chief secretary." He is dead now. His wife was our "agent." Aaah, it was a silly name! Agent of what, I don't know. [probably from the military title, adjutant]. And Tatu, daughter of Mzee, was the "resident" of our *ngoma* group. And another man, Juma Salum, was the "kingi," and his wife, Mtoro Binti Khalufani, became "queen."

The "chief secretary" was like the owner of the *ngoma*. He was the organizer and all the planning was generally done by him—for example, where the *ngoma* would be held and so forth. The "governor" and the "kingi" followed these plans. "Kingi" was the first in the hierarchy, but all of the organization was in the hands of the "chief secretary." It is like the system in the U.K. where you have the queen and the prime minister. There is the queen, but Mrs. Thatcher is the one who organizes everything and although she has assistance, she is the head of the government.

All of the *ngoma* groups had this kind of structure, and if you invited a person from another group, you had to give him the same rank he had in the former group. The only qualification for a position of leadership was money. All of the men in the leadership had contributed a lot of money for food and drinks and putting up lights for performances. Everybody else contributed according to their pockets. So if I contributed, say, one shilling, then you, as "chief secretary" or "resident" had to contribute about twenty shillings.*

Unfortunately, all of the leaders of this group have died. You see, they were already adults at the time, and had inherited this *ngoma* "Roho Ni Mgeni" from our forefathers. It was going when I was a small child about three years old, and it was later revived when I was an adult and married to my husband who died.

---

9   Although the member-performers in these *ngoma* groups were women, men held "titles" to ensure community acceptance of the organizations and to secure financial and other forms of sponsorship from the "titled" men, who were often prominent in the community.

10   The conferring of titles drawn from the colonial administrative and military apparatuses characterized both men's and women's dance and related associations from the end of the nineteenth century and throughout the colonial period. See T.O. Ranger, *Dance and Society in Eastern Africa, 1890–1970: The Beni Ngoma* (Berkeley, 1975); Strobel, *Muslim Women in Mombasa*; Mirza and Strobel, eds., *Three Swahili Women*. Prior to that time, ranks and titles were drawn from powerful political positions identified with Shirazi, Zanzibar and other ruling groups. See Glassman, *Feasts and Riot*, 76–77.

There were many *ngoma* groups at that time [from late 1940s]. "Good Luck," eehe? "Safina" [ship, or Noah's Ark], "Submarine," "Snow White," "Ratusudan" [Pleasure of the Blacks], "Ratulail" [Pleasure of the Night], "British Empire." These were *lelemama* groups.[11] They were organized. On Saturdays, they dressed in *sare* [uniforms made of similar cloth, usually matching *kanga*]. They had their own dances and they sang and had their own arrangements and order of singing. The leader would sing and the rest would dance. Do you understand? It was like this: groups competed with each other. I found myself coming into the world.

*These groups started before I was born. There was *changani*, and after *changani* came *lelemama*.[12] The groups derived from these. I close my eyes and I see *changani* changing later on to *lelemana*.[13] All these are Swahili *ngomas* from the coast. "Gombe Sugu" [Stubborn Bull] produced "Mdundiko" [The Beat]. "Gombe Sugu" was known as "Mganda" in the olden days. It was "Mganda" [a band] that was the dance which brought me outside [as a *mwali*] and led the procession when I was taken to my [first] husband to be married. It is an *ngoma* of the Kutus, who live in Morogoro—between Morogoro and the Zaramo area [Dar es Salaam], near Ngerengere.

A lot of these people have died. Prominent members of "British Empire," Bi Maunda, Mwamvita Gumbezi, Bi Mwamvita Mjinga, sister of Khamis Mjinga later married to Maneno Kilongola—all have died. People like Mwanaidi Chapatahivi of "Ratulail" are no longer with us.*

"Roho Ni Mgeni's" objective was unity. To cooperate. To do burial ceremonies together. To participate in weddings and in festivals together, and to help the people concerned. And when it was the time of *Maulidi* we just read *Maulidi*, that's all. We were together with the men.

We Swahili women sing in groups in whatever circumstances, in festivals. This person can sing and I respond. And I can sing and she responds and the others would help. Of course, it was not the singing of Siti Binti Saad![14]

I suppose in a way you could say that singing helped me to get involved in politics because I used to be an expert at composing songs and leading the singing at *ngomas*. But what really helped me was to

---

[11] Glassman describes *lelemama* as a "competitive dance performed primarily by women" (Glassman, *Feasts and Riots*, 144). Strobel notes that in Mombasa, *lelemama* was the female equivalent of men's groups, variously called *beni*, *bwaride* and *gwaride* (Strobel, *Three Swahili Women*, 12). But it is Iliffe who notes, significantly, that while men working away from their home areas in the German colonial period became identified by tribal names and their dances became similarly designated as to tribal origin, "*lelemama* was the most popular women's dance, the dance of towns and caravan routes, the dance of 'emancipated' women." Iliffe, *Modern History*, 238.

[12] *Changani, Mchangani*. Described by Anthony in "Culture and Society" as an East African musical club "primarily concerned with promoting Kiswahili songs" (131). Anthony goes on to say that "in other clubs, particularly the Changani clubs such as Silver Day and Golden Night, rivalry was as much a part of the tradition as was true in competitive dancing" (131–32).

[13] Nasra Mohamed Hilal expressed these changes in a strikingly similar way to Laura Fair: "all *ngoma* come in waves. There came *changani, unyago, lelemama, ndege*, there were all kinds of *ngoma*. Their days passed and *tarab* came. It is only natural that after a period the steam that drives an *ngoma* dies out." Laura Fair, "Pastimes and Politics," 256.

[14] Renowned Zanzibari singer of *tarabu* music. For details on Siti Binti Saad, see Fair, "Pastimes and Politics," Ch. 4.

become well-known. Because I couldn't start anything by myself unless I had support from other people. In that time [1954–55] it was difficult. Nobody knew anything about independence or what it was. People were afraid. Old people like Binti Makabuli of "Warumba" were afraid of the British. Bibi binti Swaleh Kibuyu of "Bomba Kusema"—she saw the Germans. They [people her age] saw the German War and they were really very frightened. They couldn't get involved in a fight with the British just like that. But we approached them slowly and tactfully, explaining what it meant, and where we were going, and the meaning of what we were doing. And they accepted. But my position was helped by these people of the organizations.

The *ngoma* groups weren't tribal organizations. They united people and included people from different tribes, Wanyamwezi and whoever and whoever.[15] Even our Rufiji organization—other people joined. You couldn't restrict. Anyone with interest could join, since we all speak Swahili. We don't speak Kinyamwezi. Ah! I am a Mhaya, she is a Mudengereko. I don't know Kinyamwezi, but we speak the same language which is used in Tanganyika. Now there is no difficulty. All the people are mixed up together, just like this.

The TAA didn't have women's groups; otherwise there would have been no need to mobilize us [for the nationalist struggle of the 1950s]! My first husband, the father of my child, was a member of TAA and every month he left me with fifty cents to pay his monthly dues. He would go away and leave me with a fifty-cent piece to give to the person who would come from TANU every month. He didn't want to be seen and to be known to give money to TANU every month. He was a member of TAA itself; but when TAA became TANU, he used to tell me, "When you see that man with a bicycle calling here, give him this fifty cents." But there were no women members.

To speak the truth, when TAA was dissolved and TANU established [July 7, 1954] in its place, many people resigned. The men resigned. Many deserted TANU, as an organization fighting for freedom of this country. This was the time [1953–54] when even people like Abdul [Abdulwahid] Sykes[16] left the leadership.* He was the president of TAA. Abdul and Sheneda [Plantan][17] were committee members. There were others also at that time, like the late Selemani Mwanjisi

---

[15]   For the tradition of access to dance societies, see Glassman, *Feasts and Riot*, 76–77. In Ujiji in the early 1930s, women of rival dance associations "fought" a serious political and economic battle through the lyrics of ngoma performances. See McCurdy, "The 1932 War."

[16]   Abdul Wahid Sykes was among twenty-one "leading personalities" associated with TAA or TANU, whose brief "pen pictures" were included in a secret memo of 26 November 1955, from R de S. Stapledon to W.L. Gorell Barnes, Colonial Office, No. ABJ.22. EAF 46/7/01, SECRET (closed to 1987) PRO. I use these descriptions of the men mentioned by Bibi Titi to suggest what administrative officers knew and considered important about these men. Thus, Abdulwahid Sykes (Zulu, about 35) is described as an important TANU member "not holding office," educated to Standard Ten, and employed as an assistant market master in Dar. Ex-secretary and territorial vice-president of TAA, Sykes served in World War II in both East Africa and India. Considered "well in with the leaders," Sykes was seen as "a link between TANU and Muslim organizations."

[17]   Schneider Ahmed Plantan (67), self-employed as owner of a taxi, fishing boat. and letter-writing agency, expelled from Dar es Salaam in 1940 for expressing pro-German views; he lived in Lake Province until 1945. He attended all the meetings of the Central Committee. His brother Machado Plantan edited the Dar es Salaam Swahili newspaper, *Zuhra*.

Photo 3: Bibi Titi in front of TANU office, Dar es Salaam in 1956. Courtesy of *Daily News/Sunday News* Dar es Salaam, Tanzania.

[Takidiri?],[18] Thomas Fulandani Plantan[19] and many others. Many were here. Now on that day, Abdul resigned and he himself introduced the young man [Julius Nyerere] to be elected.[20] [Representatives from] the whole country met—because TAA was known throughout the whole country. He [Nyerere] was elected from Mwakanga. He was TAA secretary in Tabora. He came from Mwakanga,[21] so Abdul said, "I am no longer the president of this changed organization. Give this youth a chance."

You know, here where we live there was some sort of "lordship," ehee! [Bibi Titi goes on to recreate the scene:] "Where is he from?" asked Abdul. "The youth is polite, sensible, he has an M.A. I don't. You know where I studied so I agree with him; he will help us with everything in this organization." *When we reached the stage of TAA becoming TANU and the British made it clear that whoever joined this organization would be sacked,[22] that's the time when people like Abdul washed their hands. The reason: fear of losing their jobs. Haven't you heard Ally Sykes saying that he was the first secretary of TANU? But they were all civil servants and feared losing their jobs. There were those who wanted to preserve their jobs; but they had their hearts in TANU. Then there were others who really hated TANU for fear of getting imprisoned or being killed by the British.*

I first heard about TANU right here in Dar es Salaam. My brother-in-law, Sheneda [Plantan] stayed in Dar es Salaam. *He was a business man, not a civil servant. He had left the civil service a long time before and had a lorry which he used to conduct his businesses— like carrying sand and soil to the builders. He had been a member of TAA and was a member at the time when TAA became TANU.* This Sheneda is the one who came to give us cards and to tell us about Nyerere

---

[18] Here, Bibi Titi may have collapsed the names of Selemani Takidiri and Warte Bertie Mwanjisi. Takidiri (Manyema, 60–65) was an auctioneer in 1955, a strong TANU supporter, and a "staunch Muslim" who "strongly resents the Arab claim to superiority in Muslim affairs...." A former *akida* (person in charge) of Bagamoyo District, and a PWD clerk, Takidiri had "no education." Mwanjisi (Nyakyusa, 34) obtained a medical diploma from Makerere College and was employed at Sewa Haji Hospital in Dar es Salaam until 1954, when he resigned after being suspended for failing to return to work after an illness. A psychiatrist at Mirembe Hospital in Dodoma described him as suffering from an "almost unshakable attitude of racial hatred." In 1955, Mwanjiji was running a trading business and was believed to be practicing medicine illegally. He first "came to notice" in 1951 when he was elected president of the Tanganyika African Government Servants Assocation; he was elected provincial representative for the Southern Highland Province at the 1955 TANU annual meeting.

[19] Not profiled by the administration in the 1955 report, Thomas Plantan became president of TAA in late 1951. Iliffe describes him as "a former askari [soldier] with little education." Iliffe, *Modern History*, 508.

[20] Nyerere (Zanaki, 35) formed the "Action Group" of TAA and became TAA president in 1953, and president of TANU in 1954 (Iliffe, *Modern History*, 510). He received his B.A. from Makerere College and an M.A. from Edinburgh University in 1952. Appointed to teach at St. Francis' College, Pugu, he resigned under pressure at the end of March 1955. According to British officials, "his education and overseas experience" contributed to his influence. "He is sometimes extreme in his public utterances but, in counsel, appears usually to be on the side of moderation."

[21] Mwakanga: location of Pugu Secondary School, where Nyerere was teaching.

[22] Government Circular No. 6 of 1954, from R. de S. Stapledon, Chief Secretary, 16 September 1954, states that TANU and all branches will henceforth be regarded as a political association, and all junior and senior officers who wish to continue in government service must resign from TANU. S.M.P. 16797. EAF 46/7/01. PRO.

Photo 4: Bibi Titi Mohamed and Dossa Aziz in 1991. Courtesy of *Daily News/Sunday News*, Dar es Salaam, Tanzania.

and UNO [United Nations Organization].[23] Afterwards, we were given cards, which cost two and a half shillings in those days.[24] My card was number sixteen. My husband's [Boi Suleiman, a taxi driver] card was number fifteen. The card of my child's father [first husband]—fortunately, he had come to visit us—was number thirteen. Who had card number fourteen? Wasn't it Ali? They say Ali has it—TANU card number fourteen.

Many people resigned from the organization after he [Nyerere] became president and they had no government jobs. I saw John [Rupia][25] being harassed [by the government]. They harassed him until 1955 and 1956. Then John agreed. He joined the organization and became vice president. Dossa Aziz [Ali][26] was treasurer, and his assistant was Abbas Sykes.[27] Selemani Majisu [Takidiri?] and Thomas Plantan said no [to joining TANU] because everybody wanted to be the leader.

But Abdul [Abdulwahid Sykes] agreed with the youth being elected. He saw him as a wise man and very polite. They used to meet. He came from Mwakanga to Abdul's place. Even Dossa [Aziz] agreed, and Abbas agreed too. Sheneda collected some money so that he [Nyerere] could be sent to UNO; but UNO brought its members here [in 1954].

Now [when the UN Visiting Mission arrived] they [the TANU people] were wondering who would speak, who knows this country? We were all young. So Chamwenyewe, who was eighty years old at the time, agreed to speak. They called him from Kisiju [seaside town, Rufiji District] and he came here.[28] He told the UNO, "I wasn't born during German rule; I was born during the Arab period. When the German came, I fought him. And our elders fought against the Germans because they didn't want to be ruled. You know, we were ruled by force, due to lack of weapons. The Germans fought the British, who took over the country. Now we are prepared to rule ourselves. We are ready. We elders of this country are prepared to rule ourselves."[29]

---

[23] Nyerere's plans to take Tanganyika's case for independence to the United Nations.

[24] Two shillings entry fee and fifty cents each month.

[25] Rupia (Sukuma, c. 50), vice president of TANU in 1955 was educated at the German School in Dar es Salaam and first worked as a clerk in the Provincial Administration. He then became a successful transporter and contractor with three lorries, and was owner (with Dossa Aziz) of the popular Blue Bar. A "wealthy man" (with holdings of over Shs. 100,000/), he was "a very influential member of the inner circle"—in the administration's view, because of his wealth. "Intelligent" and "shrewd," he "seldom takes an active part in public meetings."

[26] Dossa Aziz (Digo, 32) and TANU treasurer in 1955, was Rupia's business partner. Educated at Government Secondary School, Dar es Salaam, where he was dismissed for striking a teacher, Aziz later obtained a diploma through private tuition. Not thought to be influential, he was in trouble with the TANU Central Committee over the loss of some Shs. 4,000/. His accounts were rejected at the annual conference in October 1955 and he was told to prepare a correct statement.

[27] Twenty-six years old and educated at Government Schools in Dar es Salaam and Tabora, Abbas Kleis Sykes was self-employed and managing a petrol station at Ilala in partnership with his brother, Abdulwahid. He was also ward councillor for Kariakoo Ward, Dar es Salaam.

[28] Saidi Chamwenyewe was, in Iliffe's words, "a TANU pioneer" in Rufiji district (Bibi Titi's district), which in turn established the strongest TANU branch outside of Dar es Salaam in 1955. An elder and "moving spirit in Coast Region," Chamwenyewe presented TANU demands to the UNO Commission of 1954. Iliffe, *Modern History*, 519.

[29] At this and several other points in her account, Bibi Titi represents the words of the person about whom she is speaking as if she remembers and quotes directly from what he or she said.

The [UNO] members took this report and they left. The collection of money [for TANU] continued and we had to pay two shillings, you know. So Bwana Mkubwa [literally, "Big Man", i.e., Nyerere][30] left, and the chief secretary, accompanied by Justin Mponda from Songea, also flew to UNO [Headquarters, New York] to oppose Nyerere. He [Mponda] argued that Nyerere was the only person [in Tanganyika] who wanted independence. [He said] "We aren't ready to govern ourselves." The chief secretary said 75,000 Indians had property [to worry about]; and there were 25,000 [Europeans] besides—people who had farms and businesses. Bwana Mkubwa [Nyerere] phoned the TANU office and said "I have been stopped!" These people [Nyerere and Mponda] had been friends a long time. But the Rattansey people[31] met and said "We of the Indian Association"—they used the name Asian Association at that time—"we are ready and we want our independence. We have children, we have property, and this is where we belong. We don't know anything about India. We want our independence with these people. We have faith in independence."

So this saved him [Nyerere]. It was decided that we could have our independence in twenty or twenty-five years. And so Bwana Nyerere returned. It was announced that he had returned. It was the first day for the people in Dar es Salaam to see Nyerere [meeting held March 20, 1955], because the plan was to organize Dar first. If we could do that, other people would come, because everybody was fed up by that time. So when Nyerere arrived, someone translated [from English to Swahili] for him. I've forgotten who. That's correct. Nyerere didn't know [Swahili]. I say in this matter I was his teacher. I'm not afraid to say I was his teacher. He didn't know [how to talk to the people in] Swahili. He only knew his language and English, and he gave his first speech [in Dar es Salaam] in English. This was his first meeting with the people of Dar es Salaam.

Anyway, Sheneda is the one who really recruited me. Then there was John Hatch's visit. We heard John Hatch was coming. "I say! John Hatch is coming to a meeting! Where will it be?" "Mnazi Moja." Our representative was Sheneda and he was a member of the TANU Central Committee. We went to Mnazi Mmoja. John Hatch came, and Ali Mwinyi was his interpreter. I remember that.[32] I have forgotten who translated Bwana Nyerere's speech, but it was Ali Mwinyi [Haloua?] who translated into English for John Hatch. John Hatch gave a lot of confidence to

---

[30] Throughout his political career, Nyerere has been most commonly referred to as Mwalimu, "Teacher"—although Bibi Titi more often refers to him as "Bwana Mkubwa." Nyerere had been a secondary school teacher by profession, i.e., a teacher (*mwalimu*) in the Western, modern sense. His manner also "fit" this title. But it is seldom noted that *mwalimu* is also an honorific and high-ranking title, equal to *imam* in Muslim society (see Anthony, "Culture and Society," 208, for Muslim/Swahili meaning). In other words, "Mwalimu," as a title of respect, held equally important meanings for Muslim and Christian Tanganyikans.

[31] Mohamed Rattansey, a prominent Asian lawyer who backed TANU throughout the struggle for independence.

[32] Mwinyi (Comoro Islands, 37) was educated in Zanzibar and employed in the Lands and Mines Department in 1952. As TAA's Mwanza representative, he had been critical of the Tanganyanyika European Council during an interview with Lennox-Boyd, and also "an outspoken opponent" of the liwali ("headman" in charge of Muslim community affairs) of Dar es Salaam and of Nassoro Kiruka, MLC, Dar. "The Comorian community would like to see him expelled." Although the administration considered him "an unstable character" who was unlikely to go far "because of his non-African origin," Mwinyi became a junior minister of foreign affairs after independence, and was stationed in Zanzibar for some time.

Tanganyikans. He said, "You have the right to govern yourselves. You are a Trust Territory, not a colony. Any day you are ready, you have the right to govern yourselves. But ask for your independence peacefully, not through violence. Let me not talk nonsense, you will get your independence. If you use violence, you won't defeat the English. Just ask, because it is your legal right; you will get it."

From that day, people knew that it was true that Nyerere had been to the United Nations and that this country was a Trusteeship [i.e., not a colony]. Then [following Hatch's speech] there was a party for John Hatch at the TANU office—it was a small house [40 New Street]. It was at that time that I became a leader. Before the party, at his hotel, John Hatch said, "I see there were a lot of people at Nyerere's meeting today. About 25,000 people." Bwana Nyerere wasn't there then; he was at his home in Butiama. Hatch continued, "I saw that a lot of people came, but do you have a women's section? Or are the women just called to listen and then to leave?" Well, the TANU leaders replied, "Oh yes, we have a women's section," and Hatch said, "I want to meet their leader." "Ah," they said, "you will be able to meet her tomorrow. We will organize a party for you at the TANU office so that you can see her."[33]

But the truth is, they didn't have a woman then! You understand? Everyone had locked their wives away [in the house]. No one wanted to take his wife and say "This is my wife, this is the one," or even to say, "She's not my wife." Everybody refused. "Then what shall we do?" they asked themselves. Then Sheneda said, "I will go and collect Titi." "Bwana, ha! Titi is married," they said. "But her husband is my friend. I'll talk to him and she will come."

So Sheneda came to me. He met with Boi, my husband. And he said, "Tomorrow, John Hatch, the person who spoke yesterday will be invited to the TANU office. He wants to see some of the women. I have come to ask you if your wife can meet John Hatch." Boi said, "Take her, she is there. At what time will you come to collect her?" Sheneda said, "John Hatch is coming at four. I will come at three for Titi."

Well, I told Sheneda that he should go and collect Tatu Binti Mzee as well so that there would be two of us, and he agreed. *Tatu and I are related because she shared the same grandmother with my half-brother. Tatu Mzee's mother and my half-brother's mother were sisters. They had the same father. So I'm related to Tatu through my half-brother.* Sheneda went to Binti Mzee and spoke to her and she agreed, so he came back and told me. So tomorrow we were going! I prepared myself, and when it was three, Sheneda came. He collected me in his car and also Binti Mzee. I'm sorry I can't show you the picture that was taken. I don't know where I have put it.

Well, we were taken to the TANU office. At four exactly, Dossa [Aziz] arrived. We didn't know him. Perhaps he was one of the leaders, we thought, because before I had gone to the other women, the beginning was like that [i.e., Bibi Titi didn't know many of the TANU leaders]. Anyway, he introduced us to John Hatch, saying, "This is Bibi Titi binti Mohamed, leader of the women's section." But I was not a leader of that section—not even the "vice!" Do you hear? Ohoo! John Hatch took my hand and said, "I pray to God that you will be able to undertake this

---

[33]   This is Bibi Titi's recollection of what Sheneda Plantan told her John Hatch said.

work without problems. You know, if women wanted to cause a riot, they could do so. You should be polite." He spoke like this and like that.

John Hatch talked a lot. Then he took hold of my friend's hand. So I sat there. We had a little tea party. Then he went away, and from then on, I was told that I would be the chairman of the women. How could this be possible, to be elected chairman of the women just here? They said that the committee would meet, and it met. They held discussions and decided to write a letter to my husband asking him to allow me to be part of the TANU Committee so that I could encourage the other women. And my husband gave his written permission. That's how I joined the TANU leadership.

To mobilize the women, I went to the *ngoma* groups. First of all, I went to their leaders. The leaders got together in a meeting, and after I spoke to them, they told me that on a certain day at a certain time they would call all their people so that I could come and talk to them about TANU—what it does, what it wants, where it is going. For example, I talked to Mama Salehe Kibuyu, leader of the "Bombakusema," and she called together all of the "Bombakusema" women. I met them at Livingstone Street at the corner of Kariokoo Street where Mama Binti Salehe Kibuyu stayed. She said, "Titi is calling you, and I have called you for the sake of Titi. Here she is and she will tell you what she wants."

Then I spoke: "I am telling you that we want independence. And we can't get independence if you don't want to join the party. We have given birth to all these men. Women are the power in this world. We are the ones who give birth to the world. I am telling you that we have to join the party first." So they went and joined the party.

Then I went to Mama binti Makabuli. She was a leader of "Warumba." She lives in Narumg'ombe Street near Lumumba Street. She is still alive, but very old. She called the "Warumba." And that's how I went to "British Empire" and to "Ratusudan" and to the "Safina" group, "Submarine," and "Ratulail." I went to all these groups. What helped us a lot was the language. Swahili helped us because we could understand each other and know what we were talking about.

The first public building I visited to recruit women was a *pombe* [local beer] shop. I hadn't been in one before, ever! For sure, in my day we Swahili children were not allowed to go to *pombe* shops, or even to the market. It isn't surprising now to see people going to the market. But at that time, the question I was asking myself was, "Where shall I get women? How can I approach them so suddenly?" I went to the *pombe* shop, and I got the women from the club. It was just where the DDC [District Development Corporation] building stands. It was a *pombe* shop there, ehee. Some of the women I recruited there are still alive. Bi [abbreviation for Bibi] Kimavi is still alive [1988]. She is living along Tandamuti Street. But many of them have died. Like Binti Mohamed who was the wife of Kijogoo. I wonder where she is.

We reached thirty women at the *pombe* shop. I didn't know what to say so far. We took them to the TANU office. The first secretary for Dar es Salaam was Msumba. At that time, [Oscar] Kambona and Bwana Mkubwa [Nyerere] weren't around. They traveled together to different places. Kambona was with Nyerere. They traveled to Butiama, as far as Masaailand, Moshi and Arusha. When I went to the TANU office, they weren't even there. Only Msumba and Sheneda, who took me, and John Rupia and

Bwana [Stephen Mohamed Clement] Mtamila[34] who was the first chairman of the TANU Central Committee. Abbas Sykes was there, and [Dossa] Aziz. Abbas was assistant treasurer and Dossa [Aziz] was the treasurer.

*The women were the first to join TANU in Dar es Salaam. The men listened to Nyerere's speeches, but they were frightened. They were really afraid; you understand? So the women joined. And they could be seen lining up at the TANU office for cards. Many men would send their wives to get cards for them. I myself had about three hundred and fifty cards that I was keeping for people who were afraid to keep them in their houses.

Women were not afraid. They had no fear at all. Women didn't have office jobs as many do today. In those days there were no such jobs for women. If someone had two or three years of education she would just stay at home and read the newspaper. Jobs for women have only come since independence. Those who had jobs were primarily from upcountry or from Zimbabwe and Malawi. They were mostly teachers.*

Then Kambona[35] returned. After he arrived, I started organizing the women [into active subsections of the Women's Section]. We began meeting in the TANU office yard but it wasn't big enough so we met at Arnautoglu Community Centre. We elected our leaders. The leader from Temeke was Bi Kaundime. Asha Ngoma came later. There was Asha Binti Waziri [Temeke] and there is one Binti Kaundime. Another, Saada binti Kipara. These are the women who were there. Then, in Kinondoni there were others, and in Magomeni, Buguruni and Kigamboni—before the town expanded—and in the center of the town. Then we were asked to hold a meeting to brief the women of Dar es Salaam at Arnautoglu Hall. So, for Kambona's organization, we had to go from house to house, day and night, waiting at the door, asking them to come to the meeting the next day. In those days we had to walk everywhere. Those from Temeke had to walk, also those from Kichwele and from the town center. Binti Mzee, Mwamvita binti Mnyamani—we walked from the town to Ilala to meet there at Arnautoglu, understand?

I didn't say anything at Arnautoglu. Mtamila and Kambona involved themselves in a conversation, asking themselves what they should do to make the men meet with the women. They said, "We should write letters to Kisarawe and Rufiji. We should write first to Chamwenyewe, who introduced TANU to Rufiji, Kisarawe, Bagamoyo, sections of Rufiji, sections of Mjimwema, and nearby areas. We should meet [again] at Arnautoglu on Saturday."

Then they asked me why I had collected the women for them if I wouldn't speak. "What sort of chairman are you who doesn't speak even

---

[34] Matamila (Yao, 45) had been educated in government schools in Dar and Mpwapwa and was later employed as a teaacher at UMCA School, Minaki, and as a railway administration clerk in Dar. As a shopkeeper and ex-municipal councillor in 1955, he was considered "not much in the public eye but by no means a nonentity."

[35] Oscar Salathiel Kambona (Nyasa, 27) became full-time organizing secretary for TANU in January 1955. Kambona was educated at Alliance Secondary School in Dodoma, Tabora Boys, and St. Paul College, Liuli (Southern Highlands), where he obtained a Grade One teacher's certificate. He returned to Alliance as a teacher but resigned in 1954 after "inciting the students to strike for improved living conditions." Held responsible for the reorganization of TANU and a sharp increas in membership, he was considered "a staunch nationalist" who was "against any form of multi-racial Government," and wanted "self-government as soon as possible.

a single word? We want you to speak on behalf of the women." But it was really a problem in those days. Ehee! Our secretary, Halima binti Hamisi, was a teacher. At that time, she was teaching at Habibu Punja School, and was the wife of Mohamed Shineni. I was the chairman, and Tatu binti Mzee was vice-chairman. Halima and I were elected to give speeches at the meeting because my vice [Tatu Mzee] was not a good speaker. But we didn't know how to give speeches, you see? So we said, "Are you going to write for us? Write our speeches for us so that on Thursday and Friday, we can study the words and read by ourselves."

And they agreed to write for us. Bwana Mkubwa [Nyerere] still hadn't returned. He didn't know us yet. We had [only] seen him once on the platform. They wrote those papers [speeches] but they were late and didn't give them to us until Friday. On Friday morning, I took the papers from the office and went to collect my friend at Mission Quarter, Stanley Street [Aggrey Street, today]. She was at home and I left the paper [her speech]. She didn't go to the college. Then I went to Ilala. We kept reading and repeating so that when we had to speak at the meeting, we would have something to say.

Late in the afternoon, my mother arrived. She had heard that I had joined politics. Allahu Waakibaru! [God is Great!] She was angry! She had called the sheikhs and imams, blaming my husband because he had allowed me to join [politics]. She was asking why he had allowed me to join. "Does he want my daughter to be lost? Does he know the white people? I know the power of the white people. The Germans were cruel but the British chased them away. If a bomb was dropped here all the houses in Buguruni would be destroyed. Yalaa! Why do you want to kill my daughter? If it weren't for you, she wouldn't have joined."

Now when, by bad luck, my mother came here to see me, the sheikhs and imams she had called told her that there was nothing wrong with TANU. But they didn't leave until around ten at night. La! I read the paper over again. But whenever I read it, I got lost. So I read it over again, until one a.m. when I was feeling sleepy; so I went to bed saying, "Ah, I'll read it over again in the morning." I tried again in the morning, but I failed. I couldn't get [memorize] the speech from reading. Poor me, I am not blessed by God.

Around one p.m. on Saturday, many people started going to Arnautoglu. They had already heard about Titi but they were not going in order to listen to me. They wanted to listen to TANU. We [women] were house people. We had gone from house to house calling people, but we weren't expected to speak in public. Crowds of people came, and the place was full. Many had to sit outside. We had arranged an inside meeting because it is difficult to pay attention outside. But so many people came that the hall overflowed. It wasn't easy to pass, even outside, and we had to push our way through to go in.

Loudspeakers had been connected inside and outside, so the chairman, Mr. Mtamila, gave his speech opening the meeting and explaining why the people had been called. Then John Rupia took over but didn't speak for very long. The poor man was not good at making speeches, so he just greeted the people and sat down. After that, Kambona stood up and spoke about why we had organized TANU from TAA. He explained what TANU meant and what it was doing for the Tanganyikan—who was an African in this country, and what TANU would do until we achieved our independence. He spoke for a long time.

By this time, Halima was feeling sick and so was I. Then Kambona said, "Now I want you to meet a woman—the chairman of women, Bibi Titi Mohamed." It was the first day I was ever called Bibi Titi Mohamed! [*Bibi* is a respectful Swahili way to refer to a woman.] My name was just Titi. Kambona said, "Bibi Titi binti Mohamed will give a speech to the women to tell them what to do, the meaning of our organization and the power they will have if they join."

Bwana, eeeh! I was in shock. I stood up, as if God had caused me to rise. I didn't look at the people. I looked up so that I wouldn't feel ashamed. It was the first day, my historic day. I spoke well, and all the people listened attentively. They listened. I went through the chairman's words and Kambona's words, encouraging the women to join TANU and explaining why we should struggle for independence. I said: "Who are we in the world? What authority is God giving us? He has given us authority! We shouldn't feel inferior because of our womanhood. God has planted a seed in the women. It has been in us. It has grown. Ehee! We have given birth. All the men have fallen down. Those whom you see with their coats and caps, they are from here [pointing to her stomach]! They didn't come to our backs direct from their fathers. Yalaa! God has given us this power. He did not do a silly thing; he did a good thing and he knew that he did it so that you can bring children into the world. Without our cooperation, we won't achieve our country's freedom. So we must join. I say that it is necessary for us to join. There is nothing else."

I spoke for a long time, and the people were very happy. When they left, lo-lo-lo-lo-lo-lo! People expected us to be caught by the government but nothing happened. Some newspaper reports on the meeting were sent to Bwana Mkubwa [Nyerere] at his home. Then another women's meeting was called. I talked to ordinary women. I had a meeting on Wednesday. At that time, we were meeting every Thursday. Bwana Mkubwa returned on Wednesday and we went to meet him at Pugu.

It was in 1955, around October, when Mwalimu arrived from Musoma and we went to meet him—I and John Rupia and Dossa Aziz and some other the members of the executive committee. There, we joined him on the train and went with him into Dar es Salaam. We told Nyerere that we had heard that he had come to Dar es Salaam after reading in the newspapers about the good work we had done. He said that he had been doing the same work elsewhere and that now, the women had called him. "The women have got a meeting on Thursday. Now, Bibi Titi, what do you say? We are inviting you on Friday so that we can be together."

On Thursday, the women came in great numbers and Bwana Nyerere asked me if we could have a mass meeting on Saturday. In those days you could get a permit to hold a meeting within twenty-four hours. Before that time, you needed seven days. Nowadays you can get permission on the same day.

So we prepared ourselves, hiring a car and a loudspeaker and went everywhere telling the people that Nyerere would speak on Saturday. Nearly 40,000 people came. I have a picture of that day, taken from a plane, of Mnazi Mmoja. I talked to Nyerere and this was really the beginning of our journey.

Photo 5: Bibi Titi Mohamed, leader of the Women's Section of TANU, with Julius Nyerere, TANU President, 1956. Courtesy of *Daily News/Sunday News,* Dar es Salaam, Tanzania.

Bibi Titi's story of her life before TANU and her early association with formal nationalist politics and the men involved present a narrative of Tanganyikan nationalism that intersects with but diverges in important ways from the existing nationalist metanarrative. If the goals of nationalism include a sense of larger community beyond parochial groups, whether "tribes" or other presumably bounded entities, women in Dar es Salaam, through their *ngoma* and other dance/singing organizations, were already engaged in a form of nationalism. As Bibi Titi recalls, these groups were open to all, regardless of tribe or place of organzation. "All people are mixed up together just like this"; and all learned to speak Swahili if they didn't already know it—so a common language reinforced a sense of community beyond previous affiliations.

Helpful to nationalist organizing, if less significant for a sense of nationalism per se, were aspects of structure, leadership, and discipline inherent in the dance groups. Women participants understood hierarchies of authority and the need for coordinated action and discipline. Women responded actively to Bibi Titi's call for mobilization behind TANU. Men listened to Nyerere's speeches, and were afraid.

In Bibi Titi's view, the problem was partly a question of language. In speaking of her early association with Nyerere, then a young Catholic politician with an M.A. from Edinburgh and the first Tanganyikan to pursue higher education, Bibi Titi claims to have taught him Swahili. False modesty has never been one of Bibi Titi's problems, but I remember thinking at the time that with this assertion she was going too far, since among the many books Nyerere has authored are Swahili translations of Shakespeare, including *Mabepari wa Venisi* (*The Merchant of Venice*) and *Juliasi Kaizari* (*Julius Caesar*).

Yet in claiming to have taught Swahili to Nyerere, Bibi Titi was articulating an important social fact. Nyerere received both his secondary school and his college/university education in the English language. His early schooling was in his local language, Zanaki, and secondarily in English. His knowledge of Swahili, then, was "by the book"—correct and fluent, but lacking familiarity with or appreciation of popular idiom—forms of delivery as expressions of particular meaning, ways of manipulating words and phrases to make people laugh, and so forth. In other words, Nyerere needed to learn how to talk to people; and Bibi Titi was a superb teacher.[36]

Finally, Bibi Titi's story of John Hatch's visit is particularly important. As Bibi Titi makes clear, John Hatch's appearance at the TANU meeting gave credibility to the organization, and his question about the lack of women committee members embarrassed the central committee into action. Yet as Bibi Titi points out, neither Hatch nor the TANU central committee could make her a leader or create an active Women's Section. If Bibi Titi became "leader of the women," it was through her own ability to attract an enthusiastic and dedicated following. And if the Women's Section flourished, it was because in 1955, through the work of Bibi Titi and others, women in Dar es Salaam began to devote their energies and passions to nationalist organizing.

---

[36] Cf. Meena, "Bibi Titi," 46.

4

Activists and Political Mobilization

We were furious when the Government said that we could not wear *sare* [matching cloths, as uniforms] the day Mwalimu returned from UNO. He pacified us by telling us that the *buibui* [full-length black garment worn by Muslim women as head to foot covering] we had put on for the occasion was a uniform itself.[1]

When intentionality is marked by consciousness, women's subjectivity is political [emphasis in text]. To the extent that women reclaim their history through their own intentionality, their history will be socially constructed and self-determined.[2]

[C]enterwomen [are] women who initiate and sustain informal ... social networks, and who are often keystones of family and kinship networks as well. They tend to initiate activities that maintain group cohesiveness. People expect them to know the events, opinions, and needs of those in the network, and to use that information for their shared wellbeing.[3]

The thousands of women in black *buibui* whose public presence, attentiveness, and enthusiasm amazed John Hatch in 1955 are captured as an impressive but undifferentiated mass in newspaper photos and in eyewitness accounts.[4] Anonymity with respect to major historical events is, of course, the lot of most people, and unless interrupted, it is reinforced by the passage of time.

This chapter interrupts the anonymity of women who created TANU, and gives voice to several of the many who helped shape the content of Tanganyikan nationalism. It does so by focusing on the recollections of eight TANU activists, as expressed in life history narratives recounted to Kanyama Chiume and myself in interviews conducted in their homes in 1984. As historians, we are continuously

---

[1]   Halima Hamisi, Amani St., Dar es Salaam, 23 October 1984.

[2]   Kathleen Barry, "Biography and the Search for Women's Subjectivity," *Women's Studies International Forum* 12, 6 (1989), 569.

[3]   Karen Brodkin Sacks, "What's a Life Story Got To Do with It?," in *Interpreting Women's Lives: Feminist Theory and Personal Narratives*, ed. Personal Narratives Group (Bloomington, 1989), 91.

[4]   See John Hatch, *Tanzania, A Profile* (New York, 1972), 115.

confronted with the necessity to make choices concerning how much or how little to present of the oral and written "primary" information and evidence we have collected—how much to summarize to make larger generalizations, how much to put aside despite the hours spent in its acquisition. With respect to the dozens of life histories collected in the course of my research, my choice to present some, not all, in more rather than less extensive "first person" form, requires explanation.

My intention here is to confront the anonymity to which most TANU women activists of the 1950s have been consigned in the history of Tanganyikan nationalism. Any insistence on human particularity challenges anonymity; but the presentation of a lengthy string of life history narratives tends to produce a kind of mental blur, with one woman's story eventually indistinguishable from the next, especially in retrospect.

The women whose stories constitute the substance of this chapter were, in the 1950s as in the 1980s, enmeshed in relationships with other TANU women: those we interviewed and many we did not interview; those who were still living in the 1980s and, through the act of remembrance, those deceased. Because of this relatedness and connectedness, the reconstructed experiences of the few serve to strip away the anonymity of the many.

The problem of anonymity is only one of several issues of concern to me. I am also interested in demonstrating how TANU women's subjectivities, in Kathleen Barry's terms, were marked by an intentionality that reflected a nationalist political consciousness. This consciousness simultaneously created and responded to TANU's ability to organize a nationalist movement. TANU women's actions, relationships, and networks, in this analysis, constructed and shaped Tanzanian nationalism. If Julius Nyerere was instrumental in convincing the UNO and much of the Western world that Tanganyikan people were a "nation-in-the-making," women activists were largely responsible for establishing and reconfiguring the grounds for this assertion.

Nearly forty years have passed since the women of Dar es Salaam first came together and listened, told each other about TANU, marched, organized, and gathered again with dedication and regularity. "Anonymous" in history texts, these activists were anything but anonymous to each other. Indeed, they consciously used their shared social identity and pre-existing networks to spread TANU's message. "So many have died" was the most frequently repeated phrase of the women we interviewed; but this lament was invariably followed by a litany of the names of remembered women, now deceased. Gradually, it became clear to me that TANU activists constituted what Halbwachs has called "affective community,"[5] that is, a group that aids each other's memories because its members remain in harmony with each other.

> There must be enough points of contact so that any remembrance they recall...can be reconstructed on a common foundation. [The] reconstruction [of past events] must start from shared data or conceptions. Shared data or conceptions ... are present ... because all have been and still are members of the same group.[6]

---

5   Maurice Halbwachs, *The Collective Memory* (New York, 1980), 31.

6   Ibid., 31.

Shared information and conceptions resonate throughout TANU women's recollections of the nationalist movement supported and advanced through their concerted efforts. Something like Halbwach's "collective memory" exists and is expressed and reconstituted[7] in the life histories of these activists. From their life histories it is therefore possible to construct a collective biography[8] of the larger whole—the thousands of women who by October 1955 had become card-carrying TANU members.[9] The women whose life histories are presented here were among the many active TANU mobilizers in the larger group and were identified as such by other activists. They were "organic"leaders—Karen Sacks's "centerwomen"—who emerged out of Dar es Salaam's Muslim community to assume political roles for which they had no overtly political training.[10]

This absence of political training, however, does not imply a lack of political consciousness. The women who assumed responsibility for TANU mobilization readily grasped what needed to be done and drew on their extensive social resources to develop methods for doing it. In transforming existing urban women's informal networks and associations into trans-tribal entities capable of advancing the cause of independence, women activists put their own socially constituted "nationalism" to the service of independence politics.

Women and the Construction of Nationalist Consciousness

A striking commonality in the life histories of the TANU women activists of Dar es Salaam is the extent to which the women expressed a sense of personal and collective identity that encompassed far more than tribal or ethnic affiliation. For many, a trans-ethnic identity was the product of cumulative life experiences and shifting conditions: "mixed" parentage, rural-urban migration at a relatively early age, and marriages to men of different ethnic backgrounds.

This is not to say that ethnicity was unimportant. Place of origin and ethnic identification often facilitated kin-based self-help and neighborhood groups, belying the "urban anomie" about which colonial officials fretted. Yet claims and rela-

---

[7]   The terms "expressed" and "reconstituted" are used to point to the ways in which in the act of producing a life history, narrators simultaneously voiced and in so doing brought into being the discourse of collective memory.

[8]   The term I use, "collective biography," shares with Richard Werbner's "social biography" a desire to place personal narratives "at the very centre of the description, interpretation and analysis" and to pay "close attention not only to the said but also to the suppressed and the implicit, the taken for granted yet unsaid." Richard Werbner, *Tears of the Dead: The Social Biography of an African Family* (Washington, D.C., 1991), 4–5. To return to Pearl Robinson's useful phrase, my focus is on the "culture of politics" constituted by TANU women's shared political actions and activities.

[9]   Oscar Kambona, Organizing Secretary-General of TANU, to Fabian Society, 18 Oct. 1955, FCB papers 121 RH.

[10]   In identifying these women as "organic" leaders, I follow Steven Feierman's discussion of, and departure from, the Gramscian term "organic intellectual" to establish a context for understanding the Shambaa "peasant intellectuals" whose discourse he analyzes (Feierman, *Peasant Intellectuals*, 18–20). TANU's "organic" women leaders were bound to and embedded in the "original terrain"—the social and cultural networks and associations within which they lived, organized and constructed their daily lives. They were not created, "planted," or produced by TANU, though they became bound as well to the nationalist party.

tionships associated with one level of identity, for example those that entitled new arrivals to the city to expect "relatives" to solve their immediate housing needs, did not limit the continuing development of broader trans-ethnic consciousness. The essentialism attached to "tribal" affiliation, which was the flip side of African urban anomie in the colonial imagination, did not manifest itself in these women's political lives.

Musical and dance groups—extremely popular in Dar es Salaam by the early 1950s—exemplified the easy relationship between women's ethnic and trans-ethnic identities and activities. Although *ngoma* or dance groups usually began with a preponderance of women and dances associated with a particular place or ethnic group, they were invariably open to any women who wanted to join. With the opening of Arnautoglu Community Centre in December 1952, women's "entertainments" became a regular and popular feature of Center activities, which led in turn to a further proliferation of dance and music clubs. By 1954, no fewer than forty associations used Arnautoglu for their activities. Of the twelve "entertainment" groups performing there, four—"Egyptian," "Alwatan," "Lelemama," and "Bombakusema"—were women's musical clubs attracting participants from all ethnic groups, and thereby reinforcing a sense of commonality among women participants.[11] Not incidentally, these four groups became directly involved in TANU mobilization.[12]

Swahili, the language of song in all the popular *ngoma* groups, was also the language of everyday urban interaction, of the non-English media, and of poetry. If they did not speak it before their arrival, women became fluent in Swahili once resident in Dar es Salaam. Facility in Swahili gave urban women a great political advantage relative to rural women, who for the most part spoke and understood only their local language. Swahili-speaking women quickly became familiar with the debates surrounding independence politics, and could create and incorporate TANU songs and slogans into their *ngoma* performances, thus placing them in the forefront of the politicization and overt "nationalization" of the Swahili language through TANU.

Examination of women's life histories illuminates important questions related to agency in Tanganyikan nationalism and constructions of "nationalist consciousness." At the level of individual agency,[13] we can begin to understand the conditions and structures that enabled urban women both to use and to challenge aspects of their shared Swahili identity in their TANU activities. Following Callinicos, the term "collectivity" seems appropriate to describe women's coordinated actions because of their belief in a common identity, and their consciousness of themselves as agents.[14]

---

[11] "Egyptian," "Alwatan," and "Bombakusema" were the names of specific *ngoma* (dance) groups; *lelemama* was a specific style and form of competitive dance, although as Laura Fair has noted, *lelemama* as performed by women in Mombasa was different from *lelemama* in Zanzibar, and therefore probably had a specific Dar es Salaam version as well. See Fair, "Pastimes and Politics," 270–73.

[12] Annual Report of the Arnautoglu Community Centre, 1954. TNA 540 27/6.

[13] See Alex Callinicos, *Making History: Agency, Structure and Change in Social Theory* (Cambridge, 1987), 134.

[14] Ibid., 135.

Although women activists committed their energies to TANU, the organization had no extended organic structure in 1954 beyond the Central Committee in Dar es Salaam and similarly constituted regional branches whose level of activity tended to depend on local politics, issues, and grievances.[15] In Dar es Salaam, TANU as it existed beyond the walls of headquarters on Lumumba (then, New) Street was created by the organizational networks and neighborhood committees tapped into and established by its women members.

A comparative profile of these TANU activists points to the conditions and structures that constituted their affective community and collectivity in the 1950s and facilitated their continuing relationships in the 1980s. First, as indicated previously, all were Muslim and identified with the broader social and cultural milieu of the Swahili community. The vast majority had little or no formal Western education—four years of primary school at the most—though many took advantage of adult education programs in the late 1950s and 1960s. With the exception of Halima Hamisi, who had a teaching job in a Muslim school, none was employed in the "formal" sectors of the economy; rather, those who earned money participated in the "informal" economy, selling pastries or firewood, locally brewed beer, or bread. The income earned from such activities was probably less salient to their political activities than the flexibility self-employment provided over wage or salaried employment.

These women also shared aspects of life experience. At the time of mobilization, the TANU activists we interviewed were betweem twenty-five and forty years old—"middle-aged" by Tanganyikan cultural norms. Having experienced a first marriage by age fifteen, divorce—and in many cases, remarriage and second divorces (and even third marriages)—meant that all were freer than young women in their first marriages, who were closely confined if their husbands could afford it.[16]

As a cohort, the TANU activists we interviewed had very few children. Many had only one. Several had none. The largest number was five.[17] All of the women had participated, prior to their involvement in TANU, in active women's networks in Dar es Salaam—most commonly in an *ngoma* group, but also through economic activities. Taken together, these conditions and structures help to clarify their responsiveness to TANU. As divorced, "middle-aged" women, they were no longer as constrained, socially or economically, as either younger Muslim women or the small urban minority of Christianized "elite" women. By their membership in a pan-ethnic community, they had already rejected tribal exclusivity and had fostered in its place an ever-expanding sense of broad "sisterhood" through their dance associations.[18]

As organizers of a "modern" political party, TANU founders were, in principle, open to women's participation. After years of all-male membership, the TAA

[15] For an overview of these issues, see Iliffe, A Modern History, 523–28.

[16] Geiger, "Women in Nationalist Struggle."

[17] Many scholars have noted (without explaining) the relatively low fertility of women on the East African coast. See, for example, Mirza and Strobel, Three Swahili Women, 10 and note 24.

[18] I am using the term "sisterhood" here to convey the Swahili term ushoga, defined in the Oxford University Standard Swahili/English Dictonary as "friendship—between women." The Swahili term shoga, defined as "a term of endearment or familiarity between women," conveys, in my view, a relational bond and closeness not unlike that intended by the Western feminist use of "sister."

had belatedly called for the equal participation of men and women; and TANU's first constitution had also pledged to promote the equal participation of women through the establishment of a women's section.[19] Julius Nyerere demonstrated his own recognition of Tanganyika's "woman question" when he wrote a prize-winning college essay applying J. S. Mill's analysis to the subjugation of women in African society.[20] Yet there is no evidence in his later writings that Nyerere was troubled by the absence of women elected to office when he became president of TAA in 1953,[21] and it is doubtful that he imagined, much less planned for, women's vigorous involvement in the nationalist cause. Nor would he have targeted Swahili women for this role. First, Nyerere's background and associations—his rural chiefly family, his Catholicism, and his training in secondary (Tabora) and higher (Makerere College) educational institutions—did not include women as intellectual or political peers. Second, in 1955, Nyerere was only familiar with the broadest outlines of coastal urban society, and similarly unacquainted with large segments of the country he was now trying to organize.

Through participation in the Dar es Salaam branch of TAA, Nyerere came to know and respect prominent men in the Swahili community, and to appreciate their political influence.[22] Yet Nyerere did not associate politically with women of this community until 1955. Nevertheless, one of his most important gifts was an ability to grasp a situation quickly and seize the opportunity presented. In this case, the events that took place as a result of John Hatch's June 1955 visit brought into focus the strength of Swahili women's networks and the political opportunity they provided for TANU organizing.

Kinship ties provided the first opportunities that stitched three important women activists, Titi Mohamed, Tatu Mzee, and Halima Hamisi, into the TANU fabric. Two prominent Dar es Salaam businessmen and TAA politicians, Sheneda Plantan and John Rupia, were instrumental in this process.[23] When John Hatch provoked TANU officers to claim the existence of a women's section, as mandated in TANU's constitution, these men had the knowledge and connections to reach potential women leaders within the community who were capable of creating such a section and much more.

title of an elder

Tatu (Mzee[24])

Tatu binti Mzee was initially singled out for a prominent role among women by Bibi Titi Mohamed, when she insisted that Bi Tatu accompany her to the pivotal

---

[19] TANU Constitution, Appendix "A" in R. de S. Stapledon to W. L. Gorell Barnes, Col. Office, ABJ.22 Secret of 26 Nov. 1955.

[20] Hatch, *Two African Statesmen*, 17.

[21] Dome W. Okochi, Hon. Sec. Gen., to Chief Sec., 11 April 1953, TNA 41736.

[22] See Iliffe, *Modern History*, 408–12, 507–13, and 528–30; and Anthony, "Culture and Society," passim, for biographical information on Dar es Salaam community leaders active in TAA and TANU.

[23] For additional biographical information on Sheneda Plantan and John Rupia, see Hatch, *Two African Statesmen*; Iliffe, *Modern History*; Anthony, "Culture and Society."

[24] Except where noted, this section on Tatu Mzee is based on an interview on October 18, 1984, in Kinondoni.

Photo 6: Tatu binti Mzee, no date. Courtesy of *Daily News/Sunday News,* Dar es Salaam, Tanzania.

meeting organized to assuage John Hatch's concerns about the existence of a Women's Section. Related to each other through Titi's half-brother's mother, Bi Tatu was also connected to Bibi Titi through her (Bi Tatu's) father's second wife, who was the sister of Bibi Titi's third husband, Boi Suleiman, and of Sheneda Plantan. Both Bi Tatu and Bibi Titi had purchased TANU cards from Sheneda Plantan prior to the meeting with John Hatch, but neither had been tapped for a leadership role until that meeting. On the contrary, Bibi Titi told E. B. M. Barongo that she had initially been rebuffed when she expressed interest in playing a more active role to Plantan and others, on the grounds that men would not accept the idea.[25]

Tatu Mzee was born toward the end of World War I in the coastal town of Kikale in Rufiji, south of Dar es Salaam. There, her father, Mzee bin Abad, a Yao from Kilwa, married her mother, Hadija binti Fundi, the sister of Bibi Titi's father's first wife. While still a very young man, Bi Tatu's father took a job at the New Africa Hotel in Dar es Salaam. The family moved, and Bi Tatu was entrusted to her grandmother's care. After some time, Mzee bin Abad left the New Africa Hotel and worked as a dry cleaner. When Bi Tatu's parents separated, her mother supported herself by making and selling *vitumbua* (rice flour fritters). Later, after Tatu matured, her mother returned to Rufiji to farm. Bi Tatu never went to school. Confined at puberty for nine months, she was then sent to be married by[26] her first husband, Hamisi bin Suleiman, a water engineer. Prior to joining TANU, Bi Tatu never worked outside the home or participated in any overtly political organization. Like Bibi Titi, she first learned of TANU from Sheneda Plantan. From Sheneda, Bi Tatu learned that TANU was "fighting for our country so that we could live as others live—so that we could decide what to do and what to agree or disagree about." She promptly registered as a member and paid for a TANU card (probably in early 1955) but did not immediately become active.

> I kept [the TANU card] without knowing what to do with it. You know our houses are full of rats but that card was not destroyed; all other papers were destroyed by rats. After staying away for many days [Sheneda] came back and he said, "You know women are wanted in the organization. We are only men. Women are wanted so that they can mobilize others to join." And I agreed. I sent him to Bibi Titi because she was my relative. And Bibi Titi didn't refuse. She came. We used to meet in Hamza's house. That's where they started the job. When Nyerere was teaching, he used to come to Hamza's.[27]

In their initial house-to-house recruitment efforts, Tatu Mzee and other women activists encountered suspicion from other women. Although close social relations

---

[25] Barongo, *Mkiki wa Siasa Tanganyika*, 93–94.

[26] Here, and elsewhere when marrying and marriage are discussed, I follow Swahili usage, which specifies that men marry (*oa*) and women are married by or to men (*olewa*). As Anita McWilliam explains, *-oa* is the base form of the verb "to marry" and *-olewa* is a passive derived form, characteristic of a number of Bantu verbs. See Anita McWilliam, "Is There Sexism in Kiswahili?" Occasional Paper No. 3, Women's Research and Documentation Project, February 1988, 3–4.

[27] Hamza Mwapachu was a fellow student of Nyerere's at Makerere, where they created a political organization called the Tanganyika African Welfare Association (Hatch, *Two African Statesmen*, 17).

were characteristic among Dar es Salaam women, visitors were expected to be known by occupants. Moreover, many Dar es Salaam residents were skeptical about TANU itself. Strangers who introduced themselves at the door were frequently perceived to be "after something." Several TANU activists interviewed indicated that they had to respond to questions such as, "How could TANU do what it said it was going to do?" "Who were TANU people *really* working for and why?" "What would responding lead to and why were these TANU people asking for money?" "How was that money actually going to be used?"

> So we started moving here and there, explaining to people about the organization. But whenever we told our friends, they said "Ah, you liars! You have come for our husbands! Have you lost your husbands? That [TANU] is a government organization. Is it possible for us to become officials?" They were talking behind our backs and sometimes we heard them but we didn't care, we carried on with our work and we moved from place to place and got our leaders, some of whom have died.

For Bi Tatu and other women mobilizers, approaching groups of women proved to be easier and more fruitful than house-to-house canvassing.

> We tried to keep in mind what type of people to look for. We looked for *lelemama* groups and beer brewers because these were the groups which had many people. And through these groups we could spread propaganda about our organization.... then they could encourage their people and those people could go and encourage other people.... There was one woman leader in Gerenzani area, another in Temeke, another in Ilala and in Kinondoni. But we had to start with Dar es Salaam.
> We worked through [musical] organizations such as *taarab*, *ngoma* such as *lelemama* groups, religious groups, "Gombe Sugu" [a Dar es Salaam Zaramo *ngoma* group]. That organization tried to pull us fast! [was very aggressive, politically].... I was in "Roho Mgeni" with Titi. She was a singer and I was also. We cooperated with the group "Al Watan."

If women had to overcome initial suspicion, men who worked for the government were afraid of losing their jobs if they identified openly with TANU. Women were therefore essential not only to the recruitment of other women, but to the recruitment of urban men as well. As individuals, women were most influential with relatives; but as a group, they were effective because of their ability to collectively if gently "shame" men into joining. Those who spoke at rallies and meetings also exerted important pressure on men.

> The government didn't allow them [men] to join and if they joined they lost their jobs. Now what we used to do ... was to buy cards for them and keep them in our suitcases. Some of them took courage after a while and took their cards; others decided to leave their cards with their wives until they were allowed to join.

Following the initial recruiting efforts in the Dar es Salaam area, Tatu Mzee also travelled extensively on behalf of TANU, especially but not exclusively in the coastal region.

> ...sometimes, when we went to a town where there was a *shehe* [Muslim religious leader] it was not easy to find women because they were

kept inside.... But if we found this to be the case, we would talk politics with the men to convince them, and when we went the second day, we might be able to find five women. So we would keep arranging visits and the number of women would increase. At last, we would mobilize the women. That's how the women joined us. The people who were convinced were those in the coastal region. It was big. We travelled to Rufiji, Kisarawe, Bagamoyo, Mafia. Then we travelled to Kilosa, [and] Morogoro, [where] we got Hadija [Swedi].... I travelled a lot throughout the country—to Lushoto, Mwanza, Shinyanga and Mbeya. [And after independence] Mwalimu also sent me to China and Moscow.

Tatu Mzee shared with several of the early TANU mobilizers a view of colonial rule and its termination as evolutionary and inevitable.

I see colonialism as a natural thing. One person leaves and another comes. First there were the Arabs. They left. Then came the Germans. They left. Then came the British. They have left. And now it is us, ourselves. That's how it is.

Her view of traditional gender relations was equally matter-of-fact, and after two marriages and two divorces, she refused to marry again. This decision, while not socially condoned within Swahili culture, was at least possible as an option for women who could support themselves in Dar es Salaam.

...a [married] woman had no voice. If she was asked to do something, she had to do it; and if she was told not to pass, she had to obey. She was afraid of her husband. And whenever you wanted to go out, you had to cover yourself with *ushugi* [a headcloth].

Within the developing organization of TANU, however, women and men were elected on equal terms and women activists clearly seized upon the gender equality experienced in the political arena, which contradicted the gender inequality experienced and expressed as social ideology.

Along with Bibi Titi Mohamed, Bi Tatu Mzee became one of the first women members of the party's most important decision-making body, the Executive Committee.

It was 1956 or 1957 [when I became an Executive Committee member]. We sat together, discussed, and arranged meetings. We went around explaining policy to people and whenever they had problems, they told us and we explained the problems to our organizational leaders. And when there was a meeting for the whole country, we discussed many issues. We adopted the good ideas and left out the bad ones.

Halima Hamisi[28]

Like Bibi Titi and Bi Tatu Mzee, Halima Hamisi was first informed about TANU by Sheneda Plantan; but it was only through Bibi Titi's persuasion that she

---

[28] Halima Hamisi was interviewed in her home on Amani Street in Dar es Salaam on October 23, 1984.

agreed to join and become active. Born in Bagamoyo in 1925, Halima Hamisi identified herself as Swahili, explaining "my parents came from different places and as such we call ourselves Waswahili." Bi Halima's father was a teacher during German colonial rule, a clerk and later a businessman during the British period. Her mother, Shiri binti Gulu, was expert at sewing. Because her father valued education, Bi Halima attended both Koranic school and Mwambao Primary School in Bagamoyo from 1936 to 1940. To continue beyond Primary Standard IV, however, required going to Dar es Salaam, and in this, Halima was thwarted by "the prevailing attitude whereby parents would not allow their daughters to go to Dar es Salaam for further education. To them Dar es Salaam was very far; they used to say that children who went beyond their town were bound to develop rotten behavior."

Instead, a year after finishing school at fifteen, Bi Halima was married. Her husband worked as a driver at Government House and frequently drove the governor. On moving to Dar es Salaam, Bi Halima busied herself with "social organizations and dance groups, ... gatherings for mutual help and welfare, with a view to starting cooperative ventures." Then she taught religious studies for six months at the Muslim School in Lumumba Street (then, New Street) before leaving there to teach at the Habib Punja Muslim School in Ilala when it opened in 1952. That was where Sheneda Plantan went to recruit her in 1954 and told her that TAA had become TANU. Sheneda explained to Bi Halima that TANU needed men and women to come together and demand freedom, but she was skeptical:

> I did not agree with him. You know, in those days women did not easily take men's views at their face value. I did not share his ideas. I left them with him. However, since we have had some comradeship with Bibi Titi since we were young, she followed to explain what Sheneda had told me.... I told her that I had already heard about that organization but I did not believe what I had heard since the news was passed on to me by a man. [But, I told her,] "Since you have called me, I will come." She succeeded [in convincing me]. Unfortunately, I did not appear at the meeting. She called again and told me that they had met at New Street, where TANU was born, on the previous day and asked why I didn't turn up. I assured her that I was going to attend their meeting that day; and I did.

Bi Halima's observation that "women did not easily take men's views at their face value," and her reliance on Bibi Titi in making her decision to become active in TANU, reflected the importance of women's sub-culture in the mostly gender-segregated Swahili adult society. Like many women mobilizers, Bi Halima sought and obtained her husband's written permission to act as a TANU leader. Her father, however, was difficult to convince:

> My late husband put it in writing that I could continue helping as a leader of TANU if its aims were honest. However, before he was well informed, my German-trained father was upset and told me very bluntly that it was very dangerous to agitate against the government. He told me that since I was a grown person, he would not stop me from what I was doing. However, he stressed that what we were doing was dangerous; I could lose my life and they could as a result be jailed or hanged. Later on, since he had

some education during the German era, it was possible to explain to him. He too was persuaded to join TANU and later became the TANU chairman at Bagamoyo.

Although she did not experience seclusion as an adult, Bi Halima was distressed by the situation of many of her Muslim sisters who did, and saw in TANU a force for social as well as political change.

Is it not so that we women used to be locked up inside? We used to be imprisoned in our houses and therefore we could not engage in anything. It was your problem if your husband was not able to provide for you. You had no right to reply to anything that a man said to you. We women were far behind; we were far behind. We couldn't express our thoughts in front of men. They wouldn't be acceptable. Today, however, a man and I have equal rights and each of us has the right to explain herself or himself.

Halima Hamisi brought a higher level of formal education to her work for TANU and for the Women's Section than other women activists in Dar es Salaam, and also differed from them in terms of her work as a teacher. Because she could write, she became the Women's Section's secretary. In working to recruit other women to TANU, however, Bi Halima encountered occasional problems because of her education. Dar es Salaam residents did not automatically assume that educated people had their interests at heart.

Many women who did not understand TANU complained that they had previously been swindled by many organizations which called for subscriptions.... "You who are educated and have progressed want to rob us of our money." It was therefore tough going. We cooperated with groups and organizations of housewives or domestic women such as "Submarine" and "Safina." After we had explained to these groups, they would turn up at Arnautoglu to listen to what we had to tell them regarding the aims and objectives of TANU. They too would contribute to the discussions....

Bi Halima Hamisi, Bi Tatu Mzee, and Bibi Titi Mohamed travelled together, especially in the early days of organizing. There was certainly no precedent for women travelling for political purposes, or in the company of men who were not relatives. But while the presence of women in the TANU entourage caused some initial criticism at various locations, the three women together experienced less hostility than they would have had any one of them been travelling alone with unrelated men. They went to Mwakanga with Nyerere and opened up a branch there. Then they moved on to Kigamboni and held a meeting. When they visited Bagamoyo, her home town, Bi Halima "stressed the point and emphasized that women also had the right to join TANU."

I remember we held our first meeting at Mwanamakupa on the way to Kaole. We were Mwalimu, Bibi Titi, and Mzee John Rupia.... My work was to organize and to issue cards to members.... And I kept minutes of meetings too. After a while, I was transferred to Morogoro.... My job was to open TANU branches. Whenever men addressed meetings, we too stood up to urge fellow women to join the organization.

Like Bibi Titi, Bi Halima remembered well her first public speech and appearance at Arnautoglu:

> It was indeed the first time we were going to stand before a large crowd. I was so worried that when I first held the microphone I wanted to hide behind the table. However I plucked courage and stood up to speak somehow. Bibi Titi also boldly stood up to speak. Her performance removed my fear. I threw fear overboard.

There were difficulties, Bi Halima noted, with some men who looked upon TANU women organizers as "evil people who were trying to persuade their women to roam around outside their homes."

> They said we were already spoilt [prostitutes]. That was the main issue. However, later on they understood that we were not what they thought.

In Bi Halima's view, women were strong supporters of TANU despite their lack of education because "we felt we were backward." When asked what she meant by "backward," she replied, "we were economically backward." Since the vast majority of women who earned money were self-employed, Bi Halima was one of the few in Dar es Salaam to experience female wage discrimination directly.

> For example, as a teacher, I used to get only 35 shillings a month. Men got 60 shillings. The head teacher was getting 80. We women were really backward. Thus when the message for the struggle reached us, we felt like joining. We too would have dignity like other human beings. It is a good thing.

In addition to the problem of economic inequality, Bi Halima was aware of aspects of colonial discrimination such as segregated hospitals.

> Right here in Dar es Salaam, the hospitals meant for Europeans and Asians would not attend to Africans. And the services and facilities available to Europeans and Asians were not available to Africans.

The fact that Halima Hamisi was better educated than most TANU women activists did not preclude her strong identification with Dar es Salaam's Swahili community and Islamic norms for women. In October 1984, she was one of two recently widowed women (the other was Asha Ngoma) who were observing a four-month, ten-day period of seclusion and mourning. It was therefore necessary for her to seek special permission to talk with me and Mr. Chiume. Having received it from the proper religious authorities, she spoke in low tones, with her back to us—a shrouded figure in white, offering her perceptive recollections in a muffled voice. Following the interview, she went to another room in the house and requested that I come to see her. There, in the absence of any non-kin male, she greeted me face to face and said that she was glad that we had come despite the difficult circumstances. Halima Hamisi had not been well for a decade or more and illness had taken its physical toll. Nevertheless, despite her poor state of health and the recent death of her husband, her eagerness to discuss her early work in TANU was a stronger force than either adversity.

Bi Halima Hamisi and Bi Tatu Mzee were Bibi Titi Mohamed's closest associates in the first year of women's participation in mobilization efforts. All had bought

TANU cards prior to becoming engaged in popular mobilization and in the establishment of the TANU Women's Section. Through their efforts, and those of other groups and individuals with connections among various communities, TANU began to achieve mass popular support, first in Dar es Salaam and soon after, throughout the territory.

Mwamvita Mnyamani[29]

Mwamvita Mnyamani's initial interest in TANU was sparked by the proximity of her house to TANU headquarters and the meetings taking place there. Mwamvita was born in Dar es Salaam at the end of World War I; her Zaramo father, Mnyamani bin Mgeni, died when she was still very young. Her mother, Mwachombo binti Hassan, was a farmer and Mwamvita was the last born of her seven children, two of whom, including Mwamvita, were still alive in 1984. Bi Mwamvita was raised in Dar es Salaam by her grandmother, who lived in the Kisutu area. She did not attend public school, though she went to Koranic school for a while. She was married to a Nyasa, Athuman Shamte, and had one child before her first husband died.

> I don't know [how old I was when I got married.] In the past it wasn't easy to know your age.... Twelve men came to get engaged to me but I refused. I only agreed to the Nyasa man. He was lucky! And I agreed, I wasn't forced. I made my own choice, and once we got married I went to my husband. He was a soldier. [After his death] in 1930, I went to Zanzibar. I came back after I learned that my mother's sister had said that I wouldn't come back to bury her. When I heard that I returned to Dar es Salaam. And it was just at that time when TANU was started. I was then living in New Street.

Prior to her participation in TANU, Bi Mwamvita had been a member of the Zaramo Union, but her (first) husband had forbidden her to participate in any dance organization. She was married and divorced twice more.

> I then married a man from Rufiji. He was a driver. But later on, he divorced me before TANU started; and then later I got married [again]. After my marriage, my husband divorced me because of TANU. I said, "If you don't want TANU you can divorce me." That's why we divorced.... I was divorced because of TANU. They [some of our husbands] didn't like TANU but we did, with all our hearts.

She remembers the early days of TANU and her own involvement:

> So when it [TANU] started, they didn't meet in Arnautoglu. They used to meet under a bamboo tree and there were seven of them...Nyerere, Abdul Sykes, Dossa [Aziz] ... then Titi and others. Oscar Kambona, Tatu Mzee, Mgeni Saidi—dead.... He [Nyerere] was still a student. He used to come there wearing shorts. The Union house was a simple house—a small one—number 40. And that's [near] where we were staying. So after meetings then Titi started moving around to mobilize people and Tatu Mzee joined too and Saidi Ndonge....

---

[29] Mwamvita Mnyamani was interviewed in Buguruni on October 26, 1984.

I heard them when they were talking at the tree and even when they were going to Lumumba Street. I saw them. I lived near there. I was among those who went to buy a card. When we had our [women's] meeting we elected our leaders—Tatu Mzee, Titi Mohamed, and me.... We used to meet and discuss and decide where we should go to explain to people about TANU. We were not free in our country and we explained to the women that when their husbands came, they should tell them to join TANU.

I was [also] cooking rice fritters (*vitumbua*) and whenever TANU came we were asked to carry what we had made for TANU. [Selling] *vitumbua* also helped me support my children.

We could sometimes collect 10 or 15,000 shillings....

Bi Mwamvita became a TANU activist because

we were looking for a better future for our children ... and wanted independence—the freedom to decide what we wanted. We saw people being beaten by the colonialists and we experienced this a lot. [For example] I was going to Kinondoni for a meeting. During the meeting, a policeman came. My secretary ran away and I bent to collect the files from the table, and when I put my head up, the policeman hit me. So I ran to our car with my files. I didn't drop any; but I left the table there!

We expected independence to bring peace. That's what we prayed for. Equality...to be together, and to live peacefully. We didn't expect to get money. Even if we are not rich and don't have big houses, we should still unite and respect each other.

Like many other women activists, Bi Mwamvita saw in TANU a mechanism for forging new rights for women.

To speak the truth, during colonial rule it was not easy to see a woman chairing a meeting. We had to follow what our husband told or commanded us to do. And if he said you have to stay inside, you had to do so. You won't go to market. You have to obey ... and if you wanted to attend a funeral, you had to ask your husband.

[But] in TANU, we were all equal—men and women. We were free and working shoulder to shoulder. We discussed things together. You shouldn't laugh at a poor person, because we are all equal, because we respect equality.

Like most of Dar es Salaam's women mobilizers, Bi Mwamvita spent a great deal of time recruiting new members and collecting money for the organization's needs.

We had to travel by foot. You couldn't take a bus into the *pori* [wilderness]. We had to travel the whole day—sometimes from here to Kinondoni. At that time, Kinondoni was just *pori*. As we were going along, we could hear a lion roaring. We had nothing to eat. We had to travel the whole day. You would take tea at home and if you happened to find some groundnuts you bought them.

Sometimes, we were able to get money for food from the TANU office. But the office people had to calculate carefully. Sometimes we were only given two shillings and if Oscar [Kambona] wasn't there, we got nothing. [Steven] Mhando did nothing except buy and drink beer.[30]

---

30   Steven Mhando succeeded Oscar Kambona as TANU organizing secretary when Kambona went abroad to study. He was removed after one year for "profligate expenditure."

At points in her recollections, Mwamvita Mnyamani employed the metaphorical language of pregnancy and childrearing for women's mobilization efforts:

> We would sometimes carry "unknown luggage." You don't know what is inside; but after you have given birth they say, "Oh, she has got a baby." But before, you couldn't tell whether you had a snake or anything else. After birth, the child grows up. He talks and laughs. So it was necessary for us to be in the front of the struggle because we were not afraid. Men were workers and they were thinking about what would happen to their children if they lost their job. It was not easy for women to get jobs in Dar es Salaam. It was just a matter of life and death. Men were afraid to lose their jobs.

Although several of the activists interviewed expressed their political views and consciousness in the language of motherhood, their themes and purposes varied widely. Some did so to contrast women's situation and conditions with that of men, as Bi Mwamvita does above. Others emphasized that the struggle for independence was absolutely necessary to ensure a better life for the next generation. Perhaps the most common usage involved establishing claims to Nyerere's consideration ("Nyerere, our son, should not forget us"). Still others, most notably Bibi Titi Mohamed, emphasized the fact that men who thought of themselves as more significant than women needed to remember where they came from.[31]

Salima Ferouz[32]

Salima Ferouz was born in Kilwa and came to Dar es Salaam "at the time of Hitler." Her father, Ferouzi bin Maftaha, a Yao, sold ivory with the Arabs and her mother, Zalia Msuli, farmed. Bi Salima never attended school, was married at around fifteen and divorced soon thereafter. At some point in the 1940s, she went to Zanzibar, and, like Mwamvita Mnyamani, returned to find TANU already "fighting to get freedom for the benefit of the people."

> I then sold *vitumbua* to get money to buy my own TANU card. [I joined because] I wanted to get our independence and get out of colonial slavery.

Like many activists, Bi Salima conflated the personal and political lack of freedom experienced under colonial rule:

> Colonialism was difficult. We were put inside. Let's say you were married. You stay inside and everything is brought inside—fish, vegetables.

---

31 An essentialist reading of African women's deployment of motherhood and fertility denies them the possibility of symbolic and metaphoric speech. Such readings are not uncommon. See, for example, Caroline Ifeka-Moller, "Female Militancy and Colonial Revolt," in *Perceiving Women*, ed. Shirley Ardener (New York, 1977), 127–57; Julia Wells, *We Now Demand! The History of Women's Resistance to Pass Laws in South Africa* (Johannesburg, 1993); Belinda Bozzoli, "Intellectuals, Audiences and Histories: South African Experiences, 1978–88," *Radical History Review* 46, 7 (1990): 207–63, especially note 7 (262), which distinguishes South African women's "motherist" from "feminist" interests.

32 Salima Ferouz was interviewed in Magomeni on September 26, 1984.

What is going on outside, you don't know. You don't know what is happening in the world. So we thought if we didn't get it [independence] ourselves, our children would get it. But we would work to get out of slavery.

The colonial problems people had were many. It is difficult to remember them now, but one of them was that our children were punished by being jailed, eehee, arrested, chained and forced to pay taxes.... So when we saw them getting such punishment and saw a chance for respect coming...we thought, it is better to fight for independence....

We [women] were very strong. Men didn't want to participate. Women led the way because of our children's pain and how we were put inside. Because of our children, we advised men to join with us together.

As you know, women had to get support from men. But they didn't want us to work and be together. But we worked together anyway. We joined the committee [Women's Section] and worked for TANU, collecting money and encouraging many more to join and work together. Sometimes the committee called us and we went and sat together. When visitors came or whatever, we all celebrated together with our chairman [Nyerere]. We became united. Although he was our superior because of education, we wanted to get our rights.

Salima Ferouz provides one of the more detailed summaries of the processes by which women used their culturally separate spaces and networks to persuade other women to join TANU. She hints that the techniques of persuasion could border on coercion and sometimes included deception.

We [women] organized ourselves. We did it ourselves! We started by choosing the committee from the group that had joined TANU. After we bought cards, we were chosen for the committee. And then, during the committee meetings we discussed the means of getting others to join us to be united. Then we went out and scheduled a meeting. We would say on such a day, Bibi Titi is coming. We said this to motivate more people to come and we said if someone didn't come we would do this and that. When they came, we would give them the news about politics and joining TANU. They got their cards, until we were many.... Seeing things getting hot, we went on like this, attracting many more. And they joined when they saw us.

Those of us who were active were many. But many of them are dead. Those of us who are still living are very few. Many are lost. One of them was our chairman, Khadija Jaffari. Then there was Zubeda Mambo. Then this grandmother who we are now burying. Many of them have left; they are not seen above ground. We are very few who remain and we are half asleep. We don't know what we are doing.

Bi Salima's last remark above, "We don't know what we are doing," was the dejected comment of a very elderly woman who was in poor health and "had difficulties." "In fact we are old now," she observed at the end of our interview. "We have forgotten some things; [we must speak carefully] lest we say what is not needed [i.e., not accurate]."

Mashavu Binti Kibonge[33]

Mashavu binti Kibonge was born in Tabora town (Ng'ambo), during "Kibanga nazi" (between the two wars).[34] Her parents, Baba Kibonge and Asha binti Hasan, were both Manyema farmers. Bi Mashavu's brother and sister were still alive and living in Dar es Salaam in 1984. While Bi Mashavu was still very small her parents moved to Dar es Salaam, chased by hunger, but they found life just as difficult once they got there.

> I remember that they came here at the time when we used to have to "fall in" [queue] for food. We had food scarcity in those days ... after the first war.
> I grew up here in this house. It was a small house before the addition was built. This is where my mother used to live, so I grew up here, I menstruated here and I got married here. Then I moved to Kikwajuni. That *mkwaju* [tamarind] tree was at the center of my yard. It was my husband's house—Kikwajuni court.

For Bi Mashavu, as for many of the women interviewed, early childhood memories tended to be vague, and were overshadowed by a more vivid recollection of the experience of puberty and early marriage.

> My life when I was young was very nice. At that time, we were not allowed to do anything before our first marriage. According to the Manyema, when a girl menstruates there are puberty rites and celebrations for seven days, and then she can go outside. She waits for a husband.
> After menstruation you got married to the first husband. Then you go and sit inside the house without doing anything. Your duty is to cook and serve.... That is your only job.
> I didn't stay in [seclusion] very long because I had been promised to a man from the time I was ten years old. So I was married to a certain man called Selemani bin Hamisi who was also Manyema.... He was a driver and I wasn't doing anything. I just sat inside. And if I wanted to go to visit friends, I had to put on a *buibui*. It was not proper to show your face.

Bi Mashavu could not recall exactly when she first learned about TANU nor how, specifically, she learned about it.

> A woman would register herself for TANU and then she would pass the word to another woman within the house and when the women in that house were all registered, they would pass the word to their nextdoor neighbors. And this is how many women came to be TANU members.
> We were very excited about that party. We wanted our own independence, so that we could become citizens of our own country.... We wanted to be free to do whatever we liked in our own country. We didn't hope to become rich, to build big flats or houses; but we didn't want people to interfere with us.

---

[33] Mashavu binti Kibonge was interviewed in her home on Ngarombe Street, Kariakoo, October 23, 1984.

[34] From the words, "breaking open coconuts"—a time when people ate coconuts because of hunger.

As for my feelings about colonialism, I only saw people being sentenced, being jailed, being hanged. You couldn't say anything— you had no voice. But after independence, we were able to say whatever we wanted. And you, friends. God has blessed you. You come to visit our country, and we can converse together.

Bi Mashavu echoed a concern for education expressed by many other women, and an awareness of how she and other women, most especially Muslims, had been denied schooling under colonialism—something that TANU promised to rectify with independence. In addition, she was acutely aware that women had lacked access to paid employment, even when educated.

[We knew that] *uhuru* [freedom] would bring education and literacy. We would all be able to get an education, because during colonial times, if we were not Christian, we couldn't go to school—especially women. After independence, women were given the opportunity to attend [adult education] classes at Arnautoglu.
[During the colonial period] even if a woman had an education, it was difficult for her to find employment. It was difficult to find even 100–300 employed women.

Bi Mashavu also reiterated women's centrality to TANU mobilization, and the common wisdom about why men in Dar es Salaam were hesitant about participation.

To tell the truth, it was women who brought TANU. It was truly women who did so. Because many men were afraid of being fired from their jobs. The men were told by their employers that whoever joined TANU would be sacked immediately; so they joined secretly. Some joined after independence; that's when they joined the party.... But most women were not discouraged. So they secretly went to join TANU by purchasing the membership card. And they hid it. Women were strong believers in and supporters of TANU.... And some were actually divorced [by husbands who didn't like their political activities].
As for me, I was not only a TANU member but also a TANU chairman three times. I was also a UWT leader [after independence].

Although the issue of employer disapproval figured centrally in women's accounts of why men were less active in TANU politics, other differences in their economic activities affected political participation. Employed men were expected to keep regular hours of work and did not have the flexibility that self-employed women had. A few women managed to become quite wealthy, especially through an active business as beer-brewers or as prostitutes. However, harassment from authorities was a frequent liability of self-employment and husbands often objected to their wives' work.

It is true that we were frying fish, preparing fried fritters (*vitumbua, mandazi*), porridge and beans and *pombe* (millet beer). Up to now we have a *pombe* shop at the DDC [District Development Center]. In the old days, we used to sell beer from our homes....
You can't say that [women's businesses] brought sufficient income. There is a difference between sufficiency and daily survival. Daily survival means you get what you can use immediately for your family. And sufficiency means that you have more, to put in the bank. There wasn't a single woman

who was able to put money in the bank from this kind of business.... [M]en preferred to seclude us. Even the preparation of *vitumbua* was done by women only. And many men didn't like their women to engage in such businesses. They preferred women to sit inside and wait to serve them.

Bi Mashavu regarded extending TANU membership and collecting money for the party among women's most important duties. Many women pawned belongings if they did not have cash to contribute.

At Pugu, [where Nyerere was teaching secondary school] Mwalimu was told to leave teaching and continue with TANU or leave TANU and continue with teaching. But since we, the men and women, had seen Mwalimu as an able leader, we advised him to leave his teaching job. "And we will look after you." And it is true. We collected money. We sent him to UNO. And he came back.

Women collected money to send our delegates on tour to get them fares and some money to use. So women were ready to give whatever money they had to assist. Even if you didn't have money, you took whatever you had—even a gold necklace or bracelet[35]—and you pawned it. The aim was to get money.

And if our delegation was leaving, say, at 10:00 p.m., women were not satisfied to let a delegate go to the airport accompanied by men only. After all, the men were few. The majority were women.[36]

Binti Kipara[37]

Binti Kipara was also Manyema and born in Kigoma before the First World War. Her parents, Kipara bin Kitate and Nia binti Mgimba, were originally from the Congo (present-day Zaire). Manyema people had long been conscripted as forced labor[38] and Binti Kipara's father was no exception.

[My father] had no employment. At that time they were doing forced labor—repairing roads. I went to ask the British if they could release my father because of his old age. So I rescued him and he stayed home farming. I told the British that he was very old and asked permission for him to go home and they agreed.

When I was young, I just stayed at home. My mother refused to allow me to go to school because she thought if we went to school, we would become Christians. And if we read Arabic, she thought we would be beaten. So we did not go to any kind of school. I finally came to learn to read when I was here—already grown up—at the education center. But I didn't continue. And then I started to learn Arabic but before finishing, I became handicapped.[39]

---

[35] Jewelry was often part of a woman's dowry and belonged to her, while gold jewelry was a common gift from a husband to his wife—if he could afford it. A woman's jewelry was her savings, her security.

[36] Kibonge interview, October 23, 1984.

[37] Binti Kipara was interviewed at her home in Temeke on October 17, 1984.

[38] Anthony, "Culture and Society," xvi.

[39] The handicap to which Binti Kipara refers was a problem with her legs that made it difficult for her to get around.

Binti Kipara was first married to an Arab in Kigoma, Hamrain Amed, before she had reached menarche. She doesn't know how old she was, but remembers reaching puberty after she was already married—"perhaps three years" later.

> I did not do any work—not even farming. I became pregnant but had a miscarriage. He divorced me, not because of this but because he went back to Zanzibar. In fact, I wasn't the only one he divorced. There were two of us. He spent his life in Zanzibar until he died.

Binti Kipara was then married by Shaban Marijani, a laborer who brought her to Dar es Salaam. They did not have children, because, according to Binti Kipara, her husband was sterile. In Dar es Salaam, she built the house she was still living in in 1984 and joined two *ngoma* organizations, "Kiua" and "Warumba." She rented rooms in her house and learned about TANU from one of her tenants.

> [He] told me that one day our country would be ruled by an African, "so go and buy your card." I asked him where I could buy it and he said in town, at Lumumba Street, so I went and bought my card. It was during the time of John Rupia. John Rupia was a staunch TANU member. God bless him. Rupia, and John Hatch, the Englishman, told people to buy their cards. Many people bought cards. Although it is a long time ago, I still remember the scene.
> ...We had no car so we had to move around on foot carrying the cards [to sell] in our hands. I was alone in this area for a while; then a man called "Mkubwa" joined me. We were not allowed to hold public meetings and if we were caught we would be jailed. We had to hold meetings in secret.
> Titi used to join us from Ilala where she was staying. I was keeping the money collected and would later send it to Titi, who was our leader. She had our book—registration book. Her office was at Lumumba. Our meetings took place at Lumumba. At that time, the area was still not good—muddy, and bananas everywhere. We organized until we got our independence.

As with several of the women interviewed, Binti Kipara tended to express her recollections in a rush of memories that clearly attached to different periods of struggle. For example, when we asked her what she had expected to achieve from joining TANU she replied:

> What we wanted was to be together, because unity is strength and separation is weakness. Even when Bwana [Nyerere] travelled to Europe we continued united. He went three times without success. Even Chamwenyewe [distinguished elder of coast region] was still alive. Chamwenyewe was always getting caught by the whites. He was even imprisoned. But we kept on struggling until we got TANU.
> ...I was sometimes the chairman and sometimes a committee member for women in Dar es Salaam. I was the chairman in Binti [Asha] Ngoma's area before she took over.... She volunteered her house to be used as a TANU office....
> God helped us in our struggle until we got our independence. When it was announced, many people carried Mwalimu.... Nyerere was completely covered in dust! On one occasion, he called all the people who struggled for independence to meet at the State House. We dressed in *kitenge* [lengths

of patterned cloth] and blouses and went to meet him. We ate together and later took a group picture. And on independence day, I was with Mtemvu and Kambona cheering the raising of our flag. We rejoiced and sang, "We have achieved our independence" with all the other people.

Colonialism caused us a lot of problems; but thank God, we are now ruling ourselves. Do you remember colonial taxes? Being tied with ropes? You were caught and a rope was tied to your neck? [Now] we eat, we dress. So many clothes in shops. The Indians are selling freely [not cheating], don't you think so?

Binti Kipara recalled that Nyerere was supported by both Christian and Muslim leaders—that this was extremely important to his success. "Even during the independence ceremony, the priest was the first to step up for prayers for Mwalimu, followed by a sheikh. They both liked Mwalimu."

After 1977, Binti Kipara began to experience poor health and, in her words, a "bad life." "I was all right during the independence struggle," she recalled. "I used to jump and cheer; I collected money for TANU, and met with Mwalimu...." Offered a job as a street sweeper after independence, she refused "because I suffered a lot during TANU [the struggle]," and wanted to be in an office. "So I was employed at Ardhi House as a sweeper in the offices; and I got my salary."

In October 1984, during the time of our interview, Binti Kipara was troubled by illness and concerned as well that new corrugated iron sheets for her house, promised her two years earlier, had not materialized. She did not link either of these problems to the stark economic situation of the country generally; rather, she believed their cause lay in the fact that there was nobody she knew in a position of authority "to remind Mwalimu" of her needs and of his responsibility to her as there had been in the past.

Mwasaburi Ali[40]

Mwasaburi Ali, a native of Dar es Salaam, was employed as an observer in a Primary Court (a position frequently held by older women) when I interviewed her in 1984. Born in Segera village, Bi Mwasaburi identified herself variously as Shirazi ("I am just from the coast, eehee?") and related to the "Kila Kisoma"—a reference to learning and more particularly in this case, to readers of the Koran, grouped together in a kind of college. The Dar es Salaam Shirazis, who had exercised considerable influence on the East African coast, traced their roots to an area known as Brava in present-day Somalia.[41] As long-time inhabitants of the coast, the Shirazi occupied a higher economic/social class position than did newer immigrants. While Swahili culture in many ways homogenized and disrupted ethnic difference, an individual's kin-based advantages and opportunities reflected and reinforced earlier status hierarchies and inequalities.

---

[40] Mwasaburi Ali was interviewed in Dar es Salaam in a small waiting room at the primary court where she was working on September 10, 1984.

[41] Anthony, "Culture and Society," 14–15. I specify Dar es Salaam Shirazi because this is the group Anthony's study is based on and because, like Swahili ethnicity, Shirazi ethnicity and origins are extensively and fiercely debated. For the Zanzibar situation, see Fair, "Pastimes and Politics," 243–47 and 243, note 132. See also Glassman, *Feasts and Riot*, for further discussion of Shirazi on the Mrima, or coast.

Mwasaburi Ali's father, Ali bin Mussa, worked for the government as a railway technician from the time of German rule, and her mother, Nyembo binti Mwinyi, one of two wives, was "just a housewife." Bi Mwasaburi remembers her childhood as a time of playing, learning Arabic and reading the Koran—all within the confines of her house. She was married at fifteen to a driver-construction worker who had his own trucks. As a wife, she continued to stay inside and eventually had five children. When she spoke of the importance of TANU to women, then, she spoke as one who had directly experienced strict seclusion as a girl and young wife. Indeed her recollection that "[TANU] started gradually, just at the time when the women were expanding their thoughts," seems likely to have been as much as a personal as a general description. In explaining why so many women became TANU activists, she continued:

> The women had no say. We had nothing to say, and whatever we wanted to say we had to follow what [someone else] said. That was why we increased our efforts. We had no freedom at all. We were considered useless people. A woman had no say even if she could do something useful...still, she was regarded as a useless person because she was a woman. That's why we put in more effort after learning the saying "all people are equal." We understood well what that was supposed to mean and we said, "We shall see if all people are equal; we must cooperate if this saying is to become true."

Mwasaburi Ali emphasized the importance of women's *ngoma* and *taarab* groups in organizing women's support and raising money for TANU.

> These societies, like *ngoma* and *taarab*, I was in one of them. There was also "Egyptian".... Everyone participated in her own *taarab* society. Then we would call Mwalimu to visit us—not openly, as a leader, but just as a special visitor—to join us. And after playing our *taarabs* we contributed money which we gave him as a gift. Our aim was to contribute to independence ... so he could travel to Ghana, to UNO, and other places and we wished him the best in his journey so we could all succeed in gaining independence.
>   The dance groups were like "Egyptian" and "Al Watan." And there was "Lelemama" and also "Bombakusema." Our mother [leader of Masuburi's group] was Bi Hawa Mafuta.

Bi Mwasaburi spoke of singular successes for women.

> And it [the hope of equality] has come true, because you have seen that many women are doctors, others are magistrates, others work as clerks and in offices. But in the past a woman was in the kitchen and was regarded as a person without power.

She spoke of her own successes as well.

> My life has been good, as I have told you. In the past we had no opportunity to go anywhere, but after achieving independence, I became a UWT Central Committee member, and up to now I am still a CCM committee member. I have contributed ideas of various kinds to the leadership. I have travelled to different places. I travelled with Mwalimu to India. I know

the whole of India. And now, I must be thankful because if we had not achieved our independence I would not have been able to travel there.

And up to this time, I can speak anywhere in meetings, eehee? I can talk freely and I will be heard. My contribution will be heard and followed. So I am very thankful.

Given her continuing role in UWT, it was perhaps not surprising that Bi Mwasaburi's list of important women's leaders began with Mrs. Sophia Kawawa, who replaced Bibi Titi Mohamed as UWT chairman in 1967. Although Mrs. Kawawa herself was not involved in pre-independence politics, her husband, Rashidi Kawawa, a trade union leader in the mid-1950s, held significant government posts (including that of vice-president) from 1961 on. Calling her "the first woman of the Tanzanian mainland," Bi Mwasaburi Ali asserted, "as Mwalimu is, she [Sophia Kawawa] is the same to the women." She also mentioned Tatu Mzee, Halima Hamisi, and Asha Ngoma as important to the struggle; but whereas all other women credited Bibi Titi Mohamed with the leading role in TANU mobilization and in the Women's Section, Bi Mwasaburi's only reference was oblique. After observing that many leaders had died, she simply added, "and you can't speak about one person due to circumstances."[42]

Fatuma Abdallah[43]

Fatuma Abdallah was one of the most enthusiastic TANU activists in a generally enthusiastic group—and one whose animated descriptions and recollections frequently captured a sense of past events in particularly vivid ways. She was born in Ubungo just outside of Dar es Salaam.

I don't remember the year as there was no counting of years; but at the time of the First War, I was this age [she indicates the height—probably four]. I am Matumbi. My mother Shida binti Mkewaju was Zaramo. My father Abdallah Athumani Mbonde was a launderer, and my mother farmed.

Life was good when I was a child. I used to help my mother in the farm by guarding against birds and cultivating rice. I didn't go to school....

I was married to Abdallah Mwitanga when I reached maturity. I was about fifteen. When we were married, we moved further to Mbezi Kibamba. My husband and I farmed at that time. And, of course, my [other] work was cooking, sweeping and washing pots. [Except for farm work] I was still being confined inside.

Fortunately, it was after I divorced my first husband and got married again that I first heard of TANU. At that time, I was staying in town. We

---

[42]   In two other cases, the women we interviewed seemed constrained in their responses. In one case, we later learned that the person herself feared that she was under CCM surveillance. In the other, the person thought I might be a spy. These concerns were not unique to my particular research. Another American researcher noted that almost every Tanzanian she met "ventured to guess that up to 50% of the population operates at least part-time in an intelligence-gathering capacity for the state." Kerner, "The Social Uses of Knowledge in Tanzania," preface.

[43]   Fatuma Abdallah was interviewed in Magomeni, September 26, 1984.

used to go and sell firewood. Luckily, I found John Rupia who said that women should be active because there is something coming....

It was a secret that TANU was about to be established. It couldn't be talked about openly. Things went on that way and I thought they were good and made every effort to join my colleagues who had joined earlier. We started being very active. Our meetings were being held secretly at different places until we were able to establish branches. When strangers came, we used to hide. We continued that way until the time when the journey [Nyerere's] to UNO was due.

We were very active at that time because we were fighting for something that concerned all of us. Men used to join, but very quietly because they were employed and when they wanted to buy cards they were afraid. With me, I had already joined and I had no problem because I wasn't employed. My work was to sweep but at the same time, I was very active. I used to go tell the men to bring money and I went to the Executive Committee of TANU and talked about politics. I told them that my husband wanted a card but he feared that if his employers heard about it, he would be fired. So I registered his name and took the card to him.

We continued that way until Baba [Nyerere] came back from UNO. We wore grass on our waists [she dances] singing "*Baba kabwela* UNO, *kabwela*" ["Father has come from UNO"]—with his white handkerchief riding in a car. We were very happy and joyous with Mtemvu, Mtemvu—*kukuru kukuru* [showing how they struggled actively.] We didn't care about our children or cars. What we cared about was politics so we could get our country and be proud like other people.

Women had no voice. Who would recognize you even if you had something to say? Who would have listened to you? But today there is politics. We have our father of the nation. We have our independence. We go to meetings up to the Jangwani Grounds even during the night and even when it rains. We just hid our cards from the rain. But we continued until the end. We continued, thanks to our father of the nation who was leading.

He said "Ha! Women, our work is still the same. Do you agree? Like what? I want people who are strong and healthy to begin to work. We should change the whole of Magomeni. Change its face so that when visitors come they see things are O.K." "But how do we change, sir?" [we said]. "We should change it by removing all the huts and building new houses, and when visitors come they will say that the town is well built."

"What do the men say? Do the women agree?" "Yes, we agree." "O.K. Will you hold spades and make bricks?" "Yes, we will. Let's go!" And we went to Mwembe Chai and built ten houses without being paid anything! It was a contribution. "You should plan your things properly, what do you say?" "It's true, sir, we totally agree," and truly, we built those houses..... Now we are happy. The rain doesn't pour on us and the rats don't fall on us. Now we are glad Nyerere did his work well, and we pray to God that he continues well with his work. This is the joy of getting our country. This is why now women have a voice....

When we were going around then, there was Mama Zembwela. Khadija Jaffari was in. The others were old and have died, like the daughter of Fundi... ahaa. Salima Ferouzi, daughter of Mambo ... Zubeda Mambo.... The others have died. That team would decide to meet at a certain place and then we had to make contributions because visitors were coming...!

We had to meet them—people like Mzee Mkale, Hamisi Sululu ... Mzee Sululu, you see. And others.... That was the group of men we had during TANU politics—this was the TANU committee. Women and men were elected to welcome visitors and we did it well. I would make rice cakes until I got enough money to entertain guests. This was the unity we had and this way it was our pleasure up to this day. We are very proud, very proud. Mmmmm.

Our problems today are only the normal ones. But colonialism! We were sick at heart! The clothes of my husband and my colleague used to be tied together like this [demonstrates, with a laugh]. You see? And when they had to go to the toilet, one would start and the other followed. This used to really hurt. People used to be beaten like drums here [whooooop! the sound of beating] and taken away in cars. We parents would cry, "My poor son! My poor son!" When I got the money, I paid for his release and when he came back I mopped his head with hot water. With conditions like this we felt it was better to fight for our independence, whether it killed us or not.

Of course, we have forgotten a lot of things. There are things which happened a long time ago, and we have grown old and our brains have too [memories fail us]. During those days this *bibi* [gesturing to an older woman in the room] used to talk a lot, but now her tongue is stuck. But I thank god that this *bibi* used to blow the trumpet, paaaah, and even the chairman himself [Nyerere]—we used to talk to him—tele la te. He used to sit opposite us and be entertained by Zaramo songs; and we weren't shy. We spoke what we needed to say. Ahaa! [she laughs] History! You can stay for the whole night if it gets too late to leave!

When the president was about to be detained, we used to stay for the whole day, from six in the morning until six at night. All we ate for our meals were groundnuts. Eventually, we were told to contribute ten shillings. So we left the European area and ran all the way home, since we travelled without money. I ran home and went to my suitcase. My husband was away in Kigoma at that time. I opened the suitcase and the only money there was ten shillings which had been left for me and the children. I said, "To hell with it." And I took the money and went to Lumumba [TANU headquarters]. I went to register my name so that we could save our father from being detained.[44]

We ran from Jangwani Grounds to Magomeni to come and collect money to save our son from being detained. We used to go around with tins for donations even to the colonial residential areas. Even those quarter houses where we found a Jaluo [Luo from Kenya or Musoma] who was very stern. But I begged for five cents ... five cents ... and he asked what it was for. And we ran, but we passed through all those areas. And we collected money for that purpose, eh? We say, "You, daughter of so and so. Take this tin until we have many tins full of collections." And we went all over town looking for money, eehee. You go to a house, you knock.... And you speak to the madame. You start, "Good morning, madame, how are you

---

[44] In May 1958, Nyerere called the administrators of Lake Province "lunatics" and was sued for libel. When Sir Richard Turnbull replaced Governor Twining in June of that year, Nyerere, around whose libel trial thousands of TANU supporters mobilized, decided to pay the fine rather than become a prison martyr. According to Iliffe, his decision was in part based on his impression that Turnbull was ready to cooperate with TANU regarding independence. See Iliffe, *Modern History*, 564.

doing," and pretend to laugh. Then, "My daughter ... there is a meeting, eehee. The Big Man is coming to give his speech. I don't know what he'll talk about, but if you have 20, 30, 40 shillings ... my child, as a contribution...."

So those who thought TANU was, what ... would speak to their husbands and you would give him the tin and he put some coins in. You'd thank him and leave. And actually, his excellency wasn't coming. Your intention was only to mobilize people to contribute....

[Three other TANU activists, sitting in the room with Fatuma during the interview add:] And we are thankful, thankful that we are still remembered. We thought we were already dead and forgotten; but our father, Nyerere, still remembers the people he started with, and we are very thankful.

Careful readers will appreciate the hidden coherence in Fatuma Abdallah's apparently rambling, shifting, and punctuated account, and will grasp the enthusiasm, the intense engagement, and the singular commitment that characterized women's TANU participation in the period of mobilization. Like many others, Bi Fatuma reiterated the importance women attached to the thought that Nyerere, still president in 1984, and powerful as head of CCM even after that, continued to "remember" those to whom he owed so much in the 1950s. Historical continuity resides in this conviction, and the concrete ways Nyerere has "remembered" them are frequently incorporated in women's recollections. In referring to Nyerere, Bi Fatuma sometimes calls him "son," and sometimes "father" or "father of the nation." In doing so, she collapses pre- and postindependence terms—the former, "son" being most common among women nationalists in the 1950s. With independence in 1961 and the creation of a Tanganyikan nationalist metanarrative, Nyerere became "father of the nation." TANU women who had treated him like a son—giving him advice, supporting him financially, morally, physically—now regarded him, simultaneously, as father (respected, admired, praised) *and* son (respectful, caring and attentive to their welfare and needs as required).

Women's Nationalist Consciousness: Continuity, Collective Memory, and Affective Community

TANU women's narratives from Dar es Salaam suggest that a sense of the continuity of relationships must be added to Halbwachs' conditions for collective memory and affective community. For the women of TANU's early years, this means a sense of being "remembered" in Nyerere's ongoing gestures of gratitude to early activists, including his statements of public recognition on important party and state holidays as well as material assistance. Binti Kipara, for example, needed false teeth and Nyerere saw to it that she received them free of charge.[45]

Earlier in this chapter, I suggested that certain conditions and structures promoted a political consciousness and sense of collectivity among a particular group of women in Dar es Salaam. But "conditions" and "structures" do not explain why these women, and thousands of women like them in many respects, became TANU

---

45   Binti Kipara, Temeke, October 17, 1984.

activists. It is one thing to say that it was easier for divorced middle-aged Muslim women with little education and no small children to become TANU activists than it was for either young Muslim women or educated Christian mothers to do so; but this does not explain the attraction of TANU politics as such.

What was it about TANU politics that appealed to urban Swahili women? Several themes emerged in these interviews. Women were drawn by notions of "dignity," "the right to rule ourselves," "the right to decide what we want to do," equality among all persons, regardless of race, gender, or educational background, and "lack of discrimination in any form." They juxtaposed these positive goals of independence and self-government against conditions of colonial exploitation, both generalized and specific, which women readily identified as arbitrary controls, racial discrimination, inequalities and hardships, lack of access to education and jobs, and a failure to accord Tanganyikans the respect all human beings deserved. Women's relative lack of direct and daily contact with the colonial regime through wage labor relations, as well as their lack of experience with direct social control, contributed to their ability to perceive and analyze colonial conditions. Subjugation, they observed, could lead to a "colonial mentality," but women did not see this as evidence of African inferiority vis-a-vis Europeans; rather, they saw it as proof that colonialism was harmful and distorting.[46] Gender clearly shaped women's experience of colonial oppression, and TANU's commitment to end discrimination based on sex or religion struck a responsive chord in women who sought for their children, and especially their daughters, the education and jobs they themselves had been denied under German and British colonial rule.

The women also used TANU ideology to challenge aspects of gender inequality and oppression within their own society. Throughout the interviews, women referred to their experiences of restriction and lack of freedom in marriage; their feelings that women were not regarded as competent or fully human by men; and their sense that this situation was unjust. Women quickly realized the possibility of using TANU as a movement that stressed not only equality for all people, but the need for men and women to work "side by side" as an aspect of "respect and dignity" necessary to challenge their social situation. In this sense, gender and political struggles were mutually supportive—the former legitimated by the ideals inscribed in the latter. Women might still explain that they needed and received written permission from their husbands to participate in politics, but they were fully aware that the party supported their right to engage in public activity. As more women became TANU activists, it became increasingly difficult for husbands to withhold their permission without attracting community censure. As women experienced the power of their collectivity as a political force and the effectiveness of their efforts, their self-respect increased.

Had women's political consciousness been limited to Dar es Salaam, it would be difficult to argue for its significance in the making of nationalism beyond coastal and essentially urban society and culture. But women's nationalist mobilization elsewhere in the country indicates that this was not the case.

---

[46] Interview with Hadija Swedi, Morogoro, September 7, 1984.

5

Bibi Titi Mohamed: Travel for TANU

By the end of 1955, Bibi Titi Mohamed had become an integral member of the TANU leadership and had demonstrated her abilities to mobilize large numbers of Dar es Salaam's African population to support for the nationalist movement. In Dar es Salaam, however, Bibi Titi was in home territory, and once aware of her political talents, comfortable on the urban political stage. To move beyond the familiar city and the coastal region, where she "sort[ed] out the different groups" of TANU supporters in Rufiji district in July 1955,[1] was a large step. Yet it was one that she took with enthusiasm, convinced of TANU's centrality to the goal of independence, and fully aware of her own important role in the party's success.

In this section of her life history, Bibi Titi recounts her TANU work and experiences "on the road" during the period of expansion beyond Dar es Salaam. Meetings had to be arranged in areas where native authorities were hostile, or competing local political organizations held or sought power. New members had to be recruited; and money collected in the face of suspicions (fueled whenever possible by the colonial administration) that the funds padded individual pockets. TANU branches needed to be established or in some cases—where men who were not considered reliable had set up party shop—closed. And seemingly endless permits and forms had to be filled out to satisfy government officers ever watchful for reasons to halt the spread of TANU. Bibi Titi also had to make a choice between politics and marriage.

> On our first trip together we went to Tanga, on January 1, 1956. Those of us who went were Bwana Mkubwa, myself, the late [Rajabu] Diwani, Zem Semshanga[2] of Soni, the late [Elias Amos] Kisenge,[3] and Mbbuta

---

[1] Iliffe, *Modern History*, 519.

[2] Zem Semshanga was a seasoned political activist from Lushoto District who was trying to amalgamate the Usambara Council, of which he was the secretary, to TANU. Feierman, *Peasant Intellectuals*, 177–79.

[3] At the time Bibi Titi met him, Kisenge was TANU organizing secretary for the Same branch in Tanga Province. In 1957, Nyerere chose Kisenge to be the TANU general secretary, and it was under his leadership that TANU branches and women's, youths' and elders' sections multiplied. See Iliffe, *Modern History*, 558; R de S. Stapledon to W.L. Gorell Barnes, Col. Office, No. ABJ.22 Secret, 26 Nov. 1955, EAF 46/7/01, PRO.

Milando.[4] Mbbuta was still young—quite young. He had just left school. We went to Tanga and to Korogwe—the whole region [by road]. We completed the journey in twenty-one days, and on the twenty-second day we returned to Dar es Salaam. Eventually, the Central Committee decided I could do well on my own.

You see, Tanganyika is big. If we all went to the same place together, other parts would be forgotten. So after traveling together for six months, we divided. Bwana Mkubwa went one way and I went the other way. We were the only two who were capable of doing so. In those days, it was me and him.

*I travelled a lot and it was not just on behalf of the mainland women. All my meetings and speeches were for both men and women, and I was accompanied by men leaders on these *safaris*.[5] I used to travel for one to three months at a stretch. Let's say I would be in Mwanza, and then Musoma, and then I would get a telegram instructing me to go to Dodoma. While in Dodoma, I got another telegram to go to Mbeya and I found Mohamed Kissoky and Mwakitwange there. At one time I was coming from Mbeya and I was instructed to go to Tabora; another time I was in Musoma and I got a message instructing me to start collecting contributions to pay D. N. Pritt[6] during the trial [for libel] of Mwalimu [Nyerere] in 1957 [actually 1958]. Also, when I was in Musoma I got a message to go to Dodoma and Mbeya. In Musoma, I met Kitundu [the TANU regional leader] with whom I worked. In Mwanza, it was Paul Bomani[7] and in Dodoma there was Haruna Taratibu.

Fortunately, God gave me a talent [for making powerful speeches]. Outside of Dar es Salaam I used to be very impressive. These were very strong speeches and men were very much moved to see a woman traveling for the struggle in their country. It really motivated them—impressed them, my courage to travel up country for the struggle. *Especially when the DCs and CID [government intelligence] were there. I got really wild!*

[As for the people who called TANU women prostitutes],[8] we thought they were just ignorant. People were doing things without knowing what they were doing. We felt that the time would come when they would realize the gain to be obtained when we won the battle. Then they would regret what they did in the past.* [As for me, when I joined TANU] I didn't expect anything [personal gain]. Even my friends were asking me, "Are

---

4   Mbbuta Milando was attending secondary school in Mwanza in 1954, and remembers becoming aware of Mau Mau in Kenya and the role of Kwame Nkrumah in Ghana at that time. After a brief period of employment as a clerk, he became a trade unionist, leading a group of domestic employees and hotel workers in Mwanza. He left that work when he feared imprisonment by the government, and became a bus conductor on his father's bus until leaving for Dar es Salaam. On the train, between Manyoni and Dodoma, Milando was recruited into TANU by Joseph Nyerere, Julius Nyerere's younger brother. Later in Dar, Milando began working as a political secretary at TANU headquarters. Personal interview with Mbbuta Milando, Dar es Salaam, September 2, 1984.

5   A *safari*, in Swahili, is a journey, often involving several people travelling together, not simply a game-watching trip.

6   A well-known British lawyer who defended many African leaders.

7   Active in the Lake Province Branch of TAA and in the organization of a cotton cooperative in Mwanza in the early 1950s, Paul Bomani, along with Bhoke Munanka, was instrumental in keeping TANU alive in Sukumaland after party activities were banned and the registration of TANU branches prohibited in the province in October 1954.

8   In response to a question Kanyama Chiume asked about this.

you going to be the queen of the country?" I didn't want to be queen, I wanted to be free. I didn't expect anything else. That's why I didn't hesitate for a long time—because I didn't expect anything.

I was interested in building my country—to make our lives better. Education for our children; to have land. Some European capitalists had many farms, earning a lot of profit. And we were simply used as workers in our own country. Why? Why should we do that in our own country? That's what I didn't like. I didn't expect to become a minister one day. I didn't even understand the meaning of being a minister or member of parliament. I came to know it only when I was in parliament. I wanted progress for the people.

Most of our children could only be educated to Standard IV. If the child failed there, that was it. Out of 10,000 perhaps only one could go further. But now, our children go from Standard I to VII free. We didn't have this before independence. Now, if you don't send your child to school you'll go to prison. Children now go to school at five or six, according to Nyerere's government. If parents just let their children play around, they will be imprisoned. The colonialists didn't do that.

*At that time, women's problems didn't vary much from province to province; the differences were between rural women and women from the town. Women in the rural areas had one main problem: they were subjected to both agricultural labor and housework—a lot of work.

Men and women had different problems. Men were regarded as superior to women before independence. Women were always disregarded, even if they had knowledge. A woman was treated as if she knew nothing. That was the first problem. Few men would agree with what their women suggested. Some men also just used women as tools for the house. But independence has given freedom to the woman to exchange ideas in the house with her husband. And the man realized there was someone to share with in the house. But before, the woman had no say and was kept in the house like a package and the man had control of everything. Whether good or bad, you had to follow.

Women had no opportunity before independence. This was the habit of African men. TANU changed this because women themselves volunteered to struggle for independence and were ahead of the men. They were not afraid.*

What about the time I gave my first TANU speech in Bagamoyo? It is true that at that meeting, I said that the cloth barrier [shiraa, in Swahili] shielding women from men should be pulled down.[9] It was usual to put a barrier between men and women in meetings. This was outside, not inside. Stretching such a barrier was common practice along the coast, even in Mafia, Mbwera [it was] the same. I asked [the people of Bagamoyo] why:

Now if you put a barrier, if she [a woman] is bad, do you think the barrier will change this? The behavior of a person is an internal thing. [Regardless of] how bad a woman is, even if you put her under cover, if she wants to do something she will. Because she has brains. Even if you

---

9   This cloth barrier was described by Bi Kaje as "a cloth like a tarpaulin to cover a steamship. It was a large cloth; it came from here to here, and slaves surrounded the cloth around the outside.... All of us women were inside in the middle. Even our legs should not be seen by men." (Quoted in Mirza and Strobel, *Three Swahili Women*, 46). See also Glassman, *Feasts and Riot*, 156. Kanyama Chiume says that a sail from a dhow was used as the *shiraa* at the Bagamoyo meeting.

(margin handwritten notes: "Bwana Mkubwa of Mwalimu - Nyerere"; "Barrier")

see a woman as useless, she can be of some help. You might not know, and she won't tell you. She is keeping it a secret.

Women weren't able to get education as they do now. [To Mr. Chiume:] Did your mother get such an education? No, never!

The purpose and work of the Women's Section was to support TANU. It worked for TANU. [As for women's affairs] there was the Tanganyika Council of Women, there was the UMCA [Universities Mission to Central Africa], the YWCA. They were concerned with women's development. Those were the organizations or associations for the development of women in matters such as child care, literacy, homemaking, handicrafts, gardening, hairdressing, knitting—things like that. There were no TANU politics involved. They were involved in development matters that concerned the administration of the country at that time.

*Those very people of the Tanganyika Council of Women used to go looking for members—to teach handicrafts as a way of attracting [women] away from TANU. They used to follow them right up to the rural areas, using the same methods of teaching handicrafts and so forth. And they went into the areas teaching the women while at the same time quietly using community development to dissuade them from joining TANU. Our responsibilities were different. Our work was political and we were called stupid women who had no shame as we were not educated. We used to be called "ordinary women in the district" while the educated women were in the Tanganyika Council of Women, the YWCA.

TANU was very separate from these organizations. The wives of big people were the leaders of those organizations—for example, YWCA, etc. The chairman of the Tanganyika Council of Women was the wife of the governor, Lady Twining. *These were your relatives! [in a joking tone, to Mr. Chiume:] Mrs. Martha Bulengo, Leah Lupembe, and Mary Chips [Ibrahim].[10] But with us, our responsibility was to struggle for the country. Those [women] who were in the rural areas used to prepare *vitumbua* [rice flour pastries], *mikeka* [mats], *vipepeo* [fans], and *makawa* [food covers] and sell them. Those are the ones who struggled for independence. Even the rallies—the educated women never attended. They used to drink tea with straws and they used to be invited by Lady Twining; but with us, we used to have our recreation in the poor areas of Ilala, Magomeni, and Temeke.*

*The Women's Section used to give strong advice to the TANU Central Committee because I was a member of the Central Committee. At first, I was alone; but later Tatu binti Mzee was a member for a short time. Then Tatu Mzee left after one year. So we were strong because I was there, and later on Lucy Lameck joined. She was the [one] educated woman who joined TANU from her home, Moshi. And when we visited Moshi, she met us and I actually slept in her room where she was staying with her mother, Coleta, in Majengo.

Women's education, especially, was minimal before independence. We used to discuss these problems in the Women's Section, and we explained in meetings and this was taken to the TANU Central Committee. Up to the Annual Conferences these things were discussed. TANU helped a lot, and went on doing so. Women's lack of education was the main problem we were fighting. Women should have education equal to men. It should

---

[10] Martha Bulengo, Leah Lupembe, and Mary Ibrahim were important UWT leaders from the time of its formation in the early 1960s.

depend on a person's ability. A woman should be equal to a man. She could be a doctor, head teacher, professor of any type, eeehh? And get the education she is capable of.

In education, one shouldn't say this is only for men and this is for women. Even in religious education, a woman was educated only to know how to pray. She should know what's good and what's bad. God is forbidding this and the *Shehe* [Muslim religious leader] has forbidden that. What for? Does this help the women? We are now fighting to say that God has created man and woman the same. Sometimes a woman can be brighter than a man; and sometimes the reverse.

Women of all ages participated in TANU. Especially at that time for younger women there was the [TANU] Youth League throughout the country, and the role played by women in the Youth League couldn't be played by older women. Christians or pagans, we were all one. Religious factions didn't exist [within TANU]. We were all one; we built the unity of this country. Some priests were against TANU—even *shehes* because there were societies formed such as AMNUT.[11] The *shehes* were perhaps afraid, thinking that we would all have to become Christian because the leader was a Christian. And there was the Muslim brotherhood. It was led by the uncle of Abas, Mzee Mashado Plantan. Then there was the father of Muhidin Hussein. He was in UTP [United Tanganyika Party].[12] He thought people would get lost. He was afraid.

I was followed by [Catholic] priests many times. They abused [TANU] in the newspapers. The priests even came to our homes. Like one big bearded priest who came from Pugu. He used to come to my house and ask me, "What are you going to gain from TANU? Will it help you in the future?" He even tried to tell me that I was being used. But the next thing they would say was, "She doesn't have any education. Let's give power to those with education." So I argued with the priest and told him that my spirit would be high; whether they were using me or not, I would continue with my work. Other priests [who were against TANU] came from Kipalapala [mission, near Tabora].

What happened in Usambara [region]? Well, we went to Vugiri mission coming from Korogwe with Mr. Nyerere in 1956 [January]. I can't remember the dates, but we were in Tanga Province. We started with Tanga Urban. From there we went to Mombo where we met a Greek settler, Steven Emmanuel, and slept at his home at Kwalikonge. I don't know if he is still alive. He used to stay in Kwalikonge about twelve miles from Mombo.[13] Mbbuta Milando, Kisenge and Rajabu Diwani and Zem Shemsanga[14] were known there because that is where they come from. We went and held a meeting at Mombo and later on Emmanuel took me and Mr. Nyerere to his house to sleep.

At that time, Emmanuel was trying to establish good relations with TANU. This was before ... the UTP started.... We went to sleep at this house and he gave us a very warm welcome. They discussed with Mwalimu the

[11]   AMNUT was an organization limited to Dar es Salaam whose leaders were drawn from older TAA activists. In 1959, the organization favored delaying independence to allow Muslims to gain educational parity with Christians. Iliffe, *Modern History*, 551–52.

[12]   Party sponsored by the British administration as a counter to TANU.

[13]   For a comparative account of this tour, see Feierman, *Peasant Intellectuals*, 179–80, 220–22.

[14]   According to Feierman, Zem Shemsanga was Chief Kimweri's chief minister in 1954, but joined the "opposition" to become a leading TANU activist in the Korogwe area. See Feierman, *Peasant Intellectuals*, 177–78.

whole night and then we went to sleep. In the morning, we found that our colleagues had already left for Bungu [Vugha?][15] so Emmanuel gave us his car and a driver called Hassan. He told us that he would take us to Bungu [Vugha?]. There were very steep mountains. You've never been there? So he took us to Vugha. Mbbuta and the others had reached there the day before. While there, we used the market place. [Here, Bibi Titi is talking about Vugha.] It was Sunday. People were bringing their produce to sell in the market and that way we got people. If you just summoned people to come for a TANU meeting, nobody turned up because they didn't know about TANU.

So Mbbuta put a table at the market place, although Chief Kimweri had told him not to. At that time, before we had reached Vugha, Mbbuta had obtained a permit from the provincial commissioner, Tanga. When we travelled, Mr. Nyerere and I had to first meet the people [leaders] of the area before we did anything. So on reaching Vugha, we found about two or three people who had come to meet us, including Zem Shemsanga. So we went to meet the chief and we introduced ourselves there and left. In Bungu we held a meeting of about seventeen people. Bungu has a big population but we got only seventeen people because their chief had prohibited them from coming. From there we went to Bumbuli. I refused to go further because I am not used to mountains. So when we reached Lushoto, I refused to continue and we held our meetings in Lushoto and I went back to Korogwe and met Hamisi Kalaghe who was the leader there. Others went on to other areas like Vugiri.

In Vugiri the chief refused to allow Mwalimu Nyerere and his people to spend the night, saying that people might cause a disturbance which he couldn't control. So they were asked to leave for Korogwe. He didn't even offer them a cup of tea. Nyerere, who is normally very calm, arrived in Korogwe quite upset at around 11 p.m. and they found me there.

The next day, I went to plait my hair for our next journey to Upare. Before I had even finished my hair, Rajabu Diwani came and told me, "Bibi Titi, you are being called." I wondered what was wrong. "The big man is calling you." So I finished doing my hair and rushed to the car and went to Mr. Rajabu to find that the elders had come there bringing chicken and eggs for us. There were about twelve of them. They didn't tell us why they had come until two days later. They told us they were very disappointed about what had happened at Vugiri. They were looking forward to a meeting with Nyerere. They expected him to sleep there and hold a rally the next day but Chief Kimweri refused and sent them off saying that they might cause chaos there.

Then the elders explained that when the women learned later that Nyerere had been sent away by Kimweri, they were furious and they refused to go to fetch water or to cultivate. Then they learned that Mr. Nyerere and his group had gone to Korogwe and were staying at Kalaghe's place. The women argued that they wanted to hear Nyerere. After all, Chief Kimweri didn't rule the whole country. Nyerere had held meetings all over the country and also at Vugha which was under Kimweri, so why shouldn't it be so here at Vugiri? Therefore, the women urged their leaders to bring Mr. Nyerere, and told them they also wanted to meet the strong woman. They said they wanted to see Bibi Titi in Vugiri. "We have heard and read

---

[15] It is not clear to me whether Bibi Titi was confusing Bungu with Vugha. In addition to Korogwe, Mombo, Lushoto, Bumbuli, Soni, and Mlalo, the TANU leaders were supposed to visit Vugha, Bungu and Vugiri. Feierman, *Peasant Intellectuals*, 179.

about her but we have never seen her. If you don't want to listen to the strong words of Mr. Nyerere, that is up to you. We want to see our companion, Bibi Titi."

So the women refused to work on the farms. The elders told me that they had come to see me to ask me to go to Vugiri where the women wanted me there. "If you refuse, we are bound to fight with our wives." They convinced me to go and said that due to the heavy rains at that time, we would go in a Land Rover which was strong. So we agreed, reluctantly, not because we did not want the meeting, but I was afraid. So we agreed to come with Mzee [Nyerere], for how could I refuse when Mzee had already agreed to come and we had planned to go elsewhere from Korogwe to Upare? I couldn't be left as the only one saying no, so I agreed.

The next day we started off by car but there was a heavy rain the whole day. We went over mountains and when we were about to reach Vugiri mission where we would hold the rally—say, about one mile from the destination—the car slipped and turned in the direction we had come from. I refused to go further although they tried to convince me that we could walk to that mission because it was only a short distance further. But I refused. Mr. Kisenge tried hard to get me to go but I was firm because I was afraid. Mr. Nyerere left for Vugiri where he held a meeting, and then the people left Vugiri mission and followed me [to my car].

First I thought that maybe I had angered Nyerere, so seeing many people going to the meeting, I tried also to go. I was wearing boots and tried to walk, but it was slippery and I fell down so I decided I couldn't go further, and it was in the forest so I went back to the car and slept. In the Land Rover, there was also a relative of Sheikh Aboud Jumbe, called Mzee Mwinyi [Mgeni Mwinyi], who was the driver. He asked me why I didn't go there. I told him that I had fallen down. All my clothes were muddy. So people from the meeting followed me and I delivered my speech there outside the car. * Both men and women came. They were many.* I climbed on top of the Land Rover. There were many people. From there, we left and went to Upare. In Pare we went to the home of Mr. Kisenge.

Vugiri wasn't the only difficult area. Many areas were difficult. But [usually] the chiefs did not oppose us publicly like the one who told Nyerere that he should not put a table there where we used to hold meetings at the market place. If we couldn't use the market, it was not easy to get people. So that is how we got people. When they heard about TANU and especially if Nyerere himself was coming with Bibi Titi, then there used to be a big response although they never knew what was going to be said.

The chiefs used to fear the colonial government because during those times Governor [Edward] Twining [1949–1958] went all out to oppose TANU. So when he heard that we had visited a place he would go there also to inquire about what had been said. Or sometimes he visited these areas before we got there so the chiefs were afraid because he had been around. They did not cooperate. Although not all chiefs were against TANU, they were afraid of losing their chieftainships—like the threats in Mahenge, where Lila Mwinyi Kondo, who was then a chairman of Eastern Province [Morogoro] was thrown into the water in the river. Politics was dangerous at that time.

Another area that was difficult was Mwalimu's home town, Musoma. There was a subchief who was the husband of Nyerere's sister, Nyangeta. He was totally against his brother-in-law and he wanted to arrest Nyerere's brother, Chief Wanzagi. I remember going there to get them to contribute money for Nyerere's [libel] case. Every member of the regional committee had to contribute 100 shillings and I used to stay collecting money up to three in the morning. Members of the committee were supposed to contribute immediately; and immediately a receipt was issued and the amount collected was announced to members. In order to get them to give money to keep Nyerere out of jail, I would tell them how bad it was to be imprisoned and I'd cite examples like Nkrumah, Kenyatta and Gandhi of India.

The next day we held a rally and I told them that we had to save Nyerere from prison and by doing so we were saving our leader and our country and ourselves and the Party too. So the people—party members—were asked to contribute one, two, or three shillings each—they contributed and the receipts were issued and the money kept. So when I left Musoma, Selemani Kitundu posted 10,000 shillings to Dar es Salaam.

I arrived in Mwanza to find that Paul Bomani had organized well. In Mwanza TANU was banned so there was no TANU [branch] and rallies could not be held there; but there were secret members. When I passed there from Dar es Salaam, I stayed at Bomani's house. And we agreed that I should proceed to Musoma and when I came back, he would have everything organized. So when I came from Musoma, he met me and he had done a lot of work. He had informed Geita, Uzinza, Maswa, Magu [small towns in the area], and elsewhere [of a meeting].

I arrived at around 4:00 p.m., and by 6:00 p.m. people started coming. At 8:00, people were still arriving! Some came in boats and they had brought money with them; so we collected about 28,000 shillings and Paul posted the money to Dar es Salaam. I got a telegram to go to Dodoma and there I found Haruna Taratibu. We collected money and I posted it to Dar es Salaam. Again, I got a message from Dar es Salaam that I should go to Mbeya. Abas Max came to pick me up and take me to Mbeya. There I met Mohamed Kissoky. I was there with Hadija Swedi from Morogoro. She followed me there. She came to Iringa which was in the same province as Mbeya. We collected about 6,000 to 8,000 shillings.

Again, I got a telegram to go to Tabora. Nyerere was there and Tom Mboya [then general secretary of the Kenya Federation of Labor]. I first met Tom Mboya in Tabora. I reached Tabora and found Nyerere, who said to Tom, "Do you know how many months this lady has been away from her home?" "How many months has it been since you've been home?" he asked me. I told him three months. Tom told Nyerere, "At home [in Kenya] we do not have such a woman."

The meeting in Tabora [in January 1958]—that meeting was the one that brought us to independence, the meeting that produced the "Declaration of Tabora." The British had told Mr. Nyerere that TANU had to agree to a tripartite vote; that is, we had to vote for a slate which had Europeans, Africans and Indians. This was brought to the Central Committee and we were obliged to summon a meeting for the whole country to discuss the matter. That meeting was held in Tabora at the market place. When we got there, there was strong opposition. People did not agree with the British proposition, but due to Nyerere's wisdom, he could explain that the colonists had many tactics to delay independence and now they wanted to delay us. If we refused their proposal we might not get [our own] government soon and we might have to struggle for such a long time that people would ignore us and get tired, thinking that the struggle was not succeeding for they wouldn't see any achievement and that would greatly reduce our strength. "So [Nyerere reasoned], let us accept the tripartite voting": "Because once we have independence we can do things our own way and no one can instruct us as to who to elect or not. We will make our own constitution and the elections will not be by force but by the free will of the country. Those whom we will choose should not be our opponents but our friends. At this time of struggle there are Indians and Europeans who sympathize with us. Some of the Indians are our friends even if they don't contribute to us materially but give us advice and show us sympathy. So if they know we are leading the country to independence they will be more sympathetic and they will support us more. Although we might get opposition from our own side, when we attain our independence we should not be selfish."

At that time, Mr. Nyerere had a real problem, and I am sure he stayed for three days without eating anything and just drinking milk. Because people were saying we should fight, and Joseph Nyerere [his brother, a TANU representative from Musoma] said he would go and beat him up. Everybody was against him! Mr. Munanka came saying he wanted to fight. Wambura also. It was very chaotic. They were completely against this [tripartite voting].

One person, Mr. Abdallah Sembe, asked for order, and Mr. Selemani Takadiri went and told one man, Jumanne Biasi in Tabora, that they should pray the prayer of "Kunuti." This prayer is like your church service. So people prayed in the mosques for the meeting so that things wouldn't get worse and lead to divisions and break TANU. And on the third day Abdallah Sembe said, "He is our leader. He has been leading us for quite some time and we have faith in him. And if that is the case why don't we support what he has said in his wisdom." At that time, Mwalimu had left the chair [of the meeting] for he had defended his stand. Otherwise, as chairman, he couldn't have been able to defend it.

Mwalimu Kiheri of Tanga chaired the meeting and he defended Nyerere's position. Another man stood up and said, "This man should be cursed. This man who is defending Mwalimu Nyerere does not love this country. He wants to betray us to the colonists." Mwalimu Kiheri talked wisely saying, "It is our leader you are cursing—if we listen to you we will fail to get what we intend to get. India fought for years for their independence—more than 100 years. We will also take a long time and the Europeans and Indians are using this tactic to delay our independence so they can stay here longer. So let us agree. Why shouldn't we agree," eeh?

He talked a lot of wise words and on the fourth day, people agreed; but we decided to rest and give ourselves time to think it over in prayers in the mosque. And the next day it was agreed to have three slates so long as we agreed that we would not be forced regarding who we would elect or not elect. In other words, we would choose the Indians and Europeans we want [not just Indians and Europeans respectively]. And people started reasoning that after all, Mr. Mponda who went to oppose us in UNO, was he a European? Was Rattansey, who supported us at the UN, an African?

So we reached a consensus and from there we summoned the biggest meeting in our history. At that meeting I had to wear a hat because it was

so hot. And meanwhile, [Zuberi] Mtemvu[16] had started the African National Congress, an opposition party. We got this information from newspapers while in Tabora at the end of 1957 and beginning of 1958.

I didn't deliver any speech at this meeting. It was only the president
who talked a lot of inspiring words, and on leaving there, we elected TANU
candidates [to run for the Legislative Council, or LegCo]. We were about
fifteen representatives. First we elected five, the second time five, and the
third time five. It was in this last selection that Nyerere got in. But Nyerere
didn't stay long in the LegCo because he resigned to devote full time to
the party.

[When asked about the personal consequences of all this travel, Bibi Titi
explained:] Boi himself allowed me to join TANU and he even bought me
the membership card. [She repeats the story of how she became head of
the Women's Section.] Also, TANU wrote a letter to him [Boi] asking his
permission for me to assist in TANU and he consented. But eventually—
and it was not only him—no man could tolerate this [all the travel].

As I told you, I was away from home for three months and even when
I was at home I could not stay for ten days before other arrangements
were made to travel. So eventually Boi told me he was tired of that type
of married life and wanted to marry [another wife]. I said that was fine,
but asked him to leave me with my work as I was already used to it. I
could not leave it at this stage.

So Boi married a girl called Khadija, daughter of Leila. After he got
married, I used to leave him with his wife; but Boi couldn't cope with this
woman so they divorced. Before they divorced, I came back home and he
told me, "Titi, I am divorcing this woman tomorrow." I asked him what
had happened and he said she told him she was pregnant, but she was
not, so he divorced her.

So one day, when I was about to leave for my activities he told me that
he didn't think he could be left to marry. [He didn't think marrying again
solved the problem of her leaving all the time.] "So you better leave your
work if you love me." And I told him, "As I've already told you, I can't. If
you want to marry again, you can do so." He refused, saying he couldn't
marry again. So he forbade me to travel.

And so I thought this was a problem—to be forbidden to travel. Boi
drove a taxi and was usually out until after midnight, so I packed my
things during the night and asked my young sister, who was staying at
Ilala Quarters, to make bread for me—I was going to Musoma. She did so,
and she bought a chicken and cooked it. And the next day the train was
leaving at half past noon. I hid my packed bag at her place, and that night
we slept and I didn't announce my departure the next day. Boi had arrived back about 11:00 p.m. and he had already been to see John Rupia to
complain that they [TANU] shouldn't take his wife. He totally refused.
And Rupia told me that I shouldn't go if my husband didn't want me to.
I told him that he had been the one to consent to my working for TANU.

---

16 Formerly TANU provincial secretary, Eastern Province (Dar es Salaam).

"You have a letter, so why are you afraid? I will go tomorrow." He told me that I shouldn't leave if there were problems, but the next day I left. John Rupia heard that I had passed there in a taxi and that I had gone to say goodbye to Bakampenja [?]. John followed me to the station and said, "Titi, you are really leaving!" The child brought me my luggage and food and at 12:00 a group of people came to escort me and we were still talking when Boi came and found the people. By then, I had already boarded my coach, so I left for Mwanza and was met by Bomani who made my travel arrangements.

Two young men came. One was Selemani and the other Hussein. They were twins. They were together with Mr. Bomani and were well off in Mwanza. So they volunteered a car and gave it to the late Yusuf Masha to take me to Musoma. So I left for Musoma, and Wambura was there. He was secretary of that area and we went to Ukerewe and Mriti and went back to Mwanza where I received a letter from my child saying that her father had moved from home and that he had left me a letter which she didn't want to open. So when I got home, I found that the letter was a divorce and he had taken away everything. So that is how I was divorced— in November 1959.

From the account Bibi Titi provides of her experiences working for TANU outside Dar es Salaam, we can get a sense of her place in the party leadership, the significance of her presence "on tour," the personal cost of her political work, and her views of the differences between what TANU meant for women versus the women's organizations of the 1950s. Bibi Titi's speeches were calls to action—persuasive, often fiery, but necessarily cautious when it came to the public encouragement of married women. Many TANU branches had women's sections, which, according to Iliffe, had "'Lady Chairmen' and officers, much like beni societies."[17] (A more appropriate analogy would no doubt have been lelemama groups rather than their male equivalent). Whereas Gogo men reportedly supported women's membership in TANU insisting that unity was "not for men alone," the men in one Haya village "closed down the women's section."[18] At a party conference held in Tabora, Bibi Titi advocated employment opportunities for women, but said married women should have their husband's consent in order to work for TANU. Mzee Takadiri, an elder, echoed Bibi Titi's statement about the consent of husbands and was applauded by the gathering.[19] Whether Bibi Titi voiced her opinion before or after learning that her own husband intended to divorce her is not clear.

As other activists indicate, Bibi Titi was not the only woman to be divorced while working for TANU. Hadija Swedi, another prominent TANU activist who also travelled for the party, was divorced by her husband (in 1957 or '58). As she put it,

---

17   Iliffe, *Modern History*, 531.

18   Ibid., 531–32.

19   Ibid., 532.

People convinced him and told him that if I, as his wife, continued to be a TANU member and involve myself with TANU activities I could lead him into trouble. People advised him to either stop my participation ... or leave me.

He therefore wanted me to decide either to leave TANU or he would leave. I didn't leave TANU because somehow I saw it must progress.... I cautioned him ... that a lot of other people had understood the meaning of TANU, and among those others were colonial govenment workers who remained TANU members. I told him that if we refused membership now, we might later fail to get it [independence] when we wanted it.... So I decided to remain a TANU member.[20]

Bi Swedi attributes her divorce to her husband's fear that he might lose his employment because of her public TANU role. TANU's official position that equality was for everyone had to mean that "politics" was for both men and women. But this position was modified to accommodate the fact that husbands who were angry at TANU for "attracting" their wives were unlikely to support the party—thus, the "consent of husbands" policy that even Bibi Titi adopted. Lucy Lameck, remarkable for being among the few educated women to support TANU actively during the anticolonial struggle and to continue as a significant politician into the 1980s, astutely observed that TANU women whose husbands divorced them were as likely to be divorced because of what they were *not* doing for their husbands as for what they *were* doing in TANU.

[A TANU activist] who was divorced by her husband—what was the reason? The reason was because the woman attended too many party meetings. And the husband didn't want that. This wasn't a question of seclusion. The women wanted to work for freedom and the husband didn't see that. Just as some women didn't see it.... They saw it in the narrow sense. If my wife goes out ... she's going to mess about somewhere. Which is ridiculous.... Whether she was messing around or not, she wasn't doing the things that she would do if she stayed home.[21]

Although she was involved in many debates and meetings concerning the appropriate course for TANU to take in the face of various attempts, local as well as colonial, to undermine the movement's growing popularity and subvert its goals, Bibi Titi was not a major party strategist or ideologist. She was an activist and a publicist, a highly intelligent and popular "voice," whose presence demonstrated, among other things, that women had a place in the TANU leadership, and that the actions and understandings of "ordinary" women and men lay at the heart of the kind of nationalism TANU was now mobilizing.

As Bibi Titi indicates, the meeting at Tabora marked a crisis point in the party's development. The idea that TANU should agree to a "tripartite" future in which 20,598 Europeans and 76,538 Asians[22] claimed the same number of seats in the Legislative Council as the African majority of 8 million was anathema to many Afri-

---

[20] Interview with Hadija Swedi, Morogoro, September 7, 1984.

[21] Interview with Lucy Lameck, Upanga (Dar es Salaam), November 12, 1984.

[22] Population figures from Tanganyika, *Report on the Census of the Non-African Population, 1957* (Dar es Salaam, 1958), 6.

cans. The rift caused a number of former TANU supporters to leave the party, and led to the creation of the only African-based nationalist opposition group to emerge prior to independence. Nyerere won the day by preaching moderation and a strategy that proved TANU could outwit the colonial administration, even playing with racially skewed colonial rules.

Although the TANU leadership could not have known it at the time, Governor Twining's fanatical belief that "multiracialism" had a future in Tanganyika had little support, economic or ideological, in the Colonial Office in Britain. As early as 1956, W. L. Gorell Barnes, secretary of state for the colonies, was expressing serious doubts about Twining's plans (to encourage multiracialism) and timetable (ten years of gradually increased local, unofficial representation in government). It was not realistic to "plan politics in detail beyond 1961," wrote Barnes, given scarce resources, the actual "size and importance of non-African groups in the territory" (i.e., small and relatively insignificant), and nationalist activities in neighboring Uganda and Kenya.

> Does the Governor really believe that even with the most gratifying social circuses it is realistic to plan on the assumption that a majestic progress with three horses of equal docility is to be counted on beyond that time (1961). The dark horse will surely be restive in such strict harness.[23]

The interplay between Twining's policies, TANU's progress, and the making of Tanganyikan nationalism will be addressed in more detail in the next chapters, which describe women's activism in Kilimanjaro and Mwanza.

---

[23]   W. L. Gorell Barnes to Twining, 6 July 1956, EAF. 297/7/01. Secret and Personal. co82/1143 PRO.

6

Nationalisms in the Hinterland: Kilimanjaro and Moshi

I should perhaps reiterate here that the division of Tanganyika into a large number of separate and geographically separated tribes, relatively small in size, while it makes the abstract ideal of African nationalism no less emotionally attractive, does not make it easy for stranger busybodies to persuade a tribesman to part with his money. So that what the Union has already achieved is by no means an insignificant effort, but also one that is not going to be easy to keep up and to improve on.[1]

TANU spread rapidly throughout much of Tanganyika between 1956 and 1958, despite the colonial government's efforts to discredit its leaders and counter its popular appeal with propaganda and red tape, alternative local initiatives, and a rival "national" party—the United Tanganyika Party (UTP). Governor Twining's defensive strategies toward TANU included applying restrictive measures wherever possible, prohibiting certain publications, tightening laws such as the Incentive to Violence Bill, refusing branch registration, and of course, barring government employees from party membership. His offensive was designed to "canalize nationalism into local or tribal patriotism" by "such means as producing popular tribal histories and by the further development of African councils and multi-racial local government bodies." "We are stepping up our public relations organization," Twining enthused, "and we have an excellent broadcasting system."[2]

Twining envisioned an alternative political party with "strong financial support from the sisal industry, the mining industry, commerce, European farmers, the coffee industry and "various other powerful bodies," and a "really first-class po-

---

[1] Extract of Governor's letter to Secretary of State for the Colonies, 2 May 1956. EMF 46/7/01 SECRET, PRO.

[2] Twining to Alan Lennox-Boyd, M.P., Colonial Office, GH. 1033/2 Secret, 31 October 1955. EAF 46/7/01, PRO; also, R. De S. Stapledon, to W.L. Gorell, Barnes, Col. Office, No. ABJ. 22, secret, 26 November 1955.

litical organizing secretary" (understood to be a European) who would be "given an Asian and African colleague at the party's headquarters in Dar es Salaam." The party platform would include the acceptance of a multiracial society under the existing constitution, equal opportunity for "men of all races," "more rapid development of the African, particularly in relation to economic matters," "the protection of the position of minorities and so on." It would be, Twining summarized, "a Conservative Party with a liberal programme." The extent to which the Governor was seriously out of touch with the realities of the territory was apparent in his belief that such a party would "receive support from a good solid conservative and 50 percent Muslim population which runs from north to south through the Centre of the territory."[3]

Local Politics and TANU in Northern Province

Mount Kilimanjaro and the town of Moshi, which grew up to serve the economic, political and transportation needs of the diverse populations resident on and near the mountain,[4] were among the most difficult targets facing TANU mobilizers. Long considered an "advanced but fractious tribe" by colonial functionaries, the successful Chagga farmers grew coffee as a cash crop and sent their children—90 percent in 1956[5]—to the Lutheran, Catholic, or Native Authority primary schools dotting the mountainside.

Sharing Moshi District with the over 300,000 Chagga were Masai pastoralists and, increasingly, African migrants from less well-endowed parts of the territory, who came to labor on plantations owned by a mixed European population of British, Greek, Italian, and Swiss settlers, and often stayed to establish scattered settlements on the mountain, in Moshi town, or along the road linking Moshi to the neighboring town of Arusha. Although members of several East Asian communities also lived and worked primarily in the town, there were 3,000 Chagga traders in Moshi district in 1951, and Africans "owned 80 percent of shops [in Moshi District] and were apparently in the process of forcing Asians to quit Kilimanjaro."[6] Competing Lutheran and Catholic missions had long since divided the mountain, and British, American, French and German missionaries, along with British colonial officers, completed the demographic picture as it existed in the mid-1950s.

The particular political history of the Chagga in the late colonial period posed special difficulties for the spread of TANU. One of the greatest of these was the "Chagga nationalism" effectively promoted by Thomas Marealle, the highly educated grandson of the famous chief, Marealle I.[7] Urbane and sophisticated—the very model of a modernizer—Marealle had been a prominent spokesman for TAA while working for the Social Welfare Department in Dar es Salaam. In 1951 the Kilimanjaro Chagga Citizens Union (KCCU), a political organization opposed to

---

3   Ibid.

4   Joel Samoff, *Tanzania: Local Politics and the Structure of Power* (Madison, 1974), 17–19.

5   Iliffe, *Modern History*, 445.

6   Ibid., 449.

7   Marealle had attended both Cambridge University and the London School of Economics.

the system of divisional chiefs established by the British administration in the late 1940s, persuaded Marealle to run for the position of *mangi mkuu* (paramount chief). With KCCU backing and the strong support of Chagga Muslims, who provided the Union with a unifying base that "cut right across the barriers of individual chiefdoms,"[8] Marealle won handily. As paramount chief he promoted the continued educational and economic advancement of "his people," and the solidification of his own power by cloaking his authority in cultural nationalism.[9] The date of Marealle's inauguration was celebrated annually as "Chagga Day," and a Chagga flag and anthem were created.[10] Here, then, was a local leader who fit perfectly into Twining's plans for thwarting TANU through the development of tribal "nationalisms."

But the *mangi mkuu*, while paramount, was not the only politician to be reckoned with. Although Marealle abandoned territorial (TAA) for local nationalism in 1952, veteran Kilimanjaro politician Joseph Kimalando, "the most experienced"[11] of those present at the July 1954 meeting at which TAA became TANU, returned to Kilimanjaro and applied for registration of a TANU branch, which was granted at the end of the year.[12] Soon, however, quarrels over the disposition of the TAA branch bank account dating from 1948 signaled a division among local politicians: even the account's original authorized signatories couldn't agree to its disbursement. As the exasperated Moshi DC wrote to the registrar general, some original TAA members were now TANU, others were KCCU, and others, part of a "recent splinter group" of TAA.[13]

With these kinds of internal divisions on Kilimanjaro, Twining had some reason to hope that a combination of "tribal patriotism," relative wealth, and education would work against TANU, provided that the administration could support Marealle effectively but discreetly, and that Marealle himself could maintain popular backing. For a while, Twining's hopes seemed well-founded. When TANU was making serious inroads in many parts of the country, only a minimal presence was established on the mountain. In December 1956, for example, TANU provincial secretary M. K. Simon was forbidden to speak by a number of local chiefs and recruited only a few members at the meetings he was able to hold. In early 1957, the Moshi District branch almost closed for lack of funds; as late as February 1958, the branch had only 7,710 members out of a district population of 365,000. Five thousand of these were registered in the town of Moshi itself,[14] and of the 2,630 TANU members living on the mountain, 2,000 were from Hai division, whose chief, Abdiel Shangali, shared his peoples' op-

---

[8] Kathleen M. Stahl, *History of the Chagga People of Kilimanjaro* (The Hague, 1964), 359. Chagga Muslims living on the coast also supported Marealle and the KCCU.

[9] Among the traditions Marealle sought to reinstate was the "now famous Chagga ngoma," ROSI, which required 230 colubus monkey and 50 eland skins, 60 ostrich and 400 eagle feathers, to enable 60 men to perform (TNA 5/23/57 Tribal Ngomas, Moshi).

[10] Samoff, *Tanzania*, 21.

[11] Iliffe, *Modern History*, 513.

[12] M.K. Simon, Prov. Sec. of TANU, to Assistant Registrar of Societies, Ref. No. N.PROV/HQ/12/28 of 18 February 1957. TNA 25/9.

[13] TNA 25/9 Moshi, TANU.

[14] Iliffe, *Modern History*, 525.

position to Marealle II's overrule.[15] In Stahl's view, at least one reason for TANU's "belated conquest" of the mountain was "that Islam had already been harnessed by the party machine of the other side."[16]

If Moshi District proved difficult for TANU organizers, it was equally clear that the Chagga were unlikely to support the administration-sponsored UTP, formed in February 1956 to counter TANU. Marealle thus advised Twining to establish a Chiefs' Convention as another alternative to TANU's appeal; the governor did so in May 1957.[17] This move probably hurt both Twining and the *mangi mkuu*, whose star was falling in any case along with coffee prices.[18]

Before the 1950s, individual Chagga women had been able to influence formal political structures and relations in their communities—sometimes as powerful chiefs, more often as influential wives or mothers of chiefs or lovers of other powerful men.[19] In 1937, however, "ordinary" women initiated, led, and dominated the "Chagga coffee riots"—the most significant "disturbance" to erupt on the mountain during the period of British rule. In response to the reduced prices growers received after the administration moved to control and centralize coffee marketing, women attacked coffee-weighing facilities and equipment, verbally abused complicit native authorities, and confronted police reinforcements sent to quell the protest.[20] Thus, women on Kilimanjaro, as elsewhere, expressed their politicization during the years of colonial rule through direct action rather than political association.[21]

At the same time, daughters of successful coffee growers, of Christian catechists, and of chiefly families interested in modernization and therefore education, were benefiting from gradually expanding educational facilities. By the 1950s, however, it was clear that school expansion beyond Standard IV was not keeping pace with population growth and local interest; nor was school access for girls keeping pace with parents' increasing interest in educating their daughters.

Meanwhile, district officials and native authorities continued to exchange a stream of memos detailing men's complaints about runaway or abducted wives, and women's pleas for assistance in the face of nonsupport, abandonment and neglect by husbands and sons, beatings and other forms of physical abuse from husbands.[22] The paramount chief warned local colonial administrators not to take seriously the claims of "loose women," "teases," and prostitutes.[23] Thus, Marealle could support girls' education on the one hand, and hold a low opinion of women—especially young, unmarried women—on the other.

---

[15]   Ibid., 525.

[16]   Stahl, *History of the Chagga*, 359.

[17]   Iliffe, *Modern History*, 535.

[18]   Ibid., 568.

[19]   Stahl devotes a considerable amount of attention to influential women. See Stahl, *History of the Chagga*, passim.

[20]   Rogers, "The Search for Political Focus on Kilimanjaro," Ch.5.

[21]   For the Pare women's Mbiru protest of 1945, see Jean O'Barr, "Pare Women: A Case of Political Involvement," *Rural Africana* 29 (1975–76): 121–34.

[22]   See various letters in Native Affairs General Moshi 25/14 Vol. VI, VII, and VIII.

[23]   TNA 5/39/17 Mangi Mkuu to D.C. Moshi, Ref. 3/I/Vol. II/67 of 5th September 1955.

The Club Movement and Kilimanjaro's Women and Girls

By the time TANU began to make inroads on the mountain, women and girls on Kilimanjaro were receiving considerable attention from social welfare officers. Attention came to Chagga girls early in 1955 as an indirect result of administrative concern for the ever-increasing population of adolescent male Standard IV leavers, who, having "failed" and "let their parents down," were "drifting off" to the towns of Moshi, Arusha, Mombasa, and Tanga, where they often fell prey to the "spivs" and "bad hats."[24] Unlike male Standard VII leavers, viewed by the administration as dangerously responsive to TANU, Standard IV leavers were considered potential juvenile delinquents.[25]

In January 1955, education and social welfare officers in Moshi (none of whom were African) proposed neighborhood-specific Boys and Girls Clubs to cater to twelve- to eighteen-year-olds who had completed Standard IV. Several months later, representatives from Lutheran and Catholic missions, Native Authorities, and the Education and Social Development Departments met in the Chagga Council to initiate training courses for youth leaders who had achieved Standard VIII.[26] In their most ambitious formulation, the clubs were to offer groups of no more than thirty-five participants four years of instruction two or three times weekly in English, arithmetic, current affairs, civics, physical education, singing, carpentry, smithing and simple building. Lessons in boxing, swimming, and rope climbing were expected to provide a "healthy outlet for youthful exuberance and the desire for adventure."[27] Apprenticeships would fill the days when there were no classes.

Girls were to learn mat- and basket-making, simple domestic science, and child care, with netball for physical activity. Attachment to local women's clubs would take the place of apprenticeships and it was hoped that the Red Cross would provide proper health and home nursing lectures. *Vihamba* (plots for cultivation) projects were emphasized, while suitable home projects were to include care of poultry, vegetables, cattle, and goats and cultivation of "Russian Comfrey" as cattle-feed.[28]

These clubs were intended to promote interlocking communities of citizens focused on domestic improvement.[29] Marguerite Jellicoe, the Woman Social Devel-

---

[24] Report of John H. Worthington, SDO, District Office Moshi, 29 October 1956, "The Boys' and Girls' Club Pilot Scheme in Moshi District," 5/S.D.4723. By this time, there were reported to be over 4,500 Kilimanjaro children leaving Standard IV annually. Some were encouraged to leave home by their parents.

[25] Ibid.; Iliffe, *Modern History*, 532.

[26] Proposal of 22 January 1955 for Boys and Girls Clubs on Kilimanjaro; Minutes of meeting held at Moshi Boma 19 January 1955. Mimeo on boys and girls clubs; Circular from Director of Education to all Provincial Education Officers, Ref. No. 141/8/46 of 28 July 1955, re: Post-Standard IV Informal Education; Worthington Report, 29th October 1959, TNA 5/S.D.4723.

[27] Report of John H. Worthington, SDO, District Office Moshi, 29 October 1955.

[28] Circular from John H. Worthington, SDO, Arusha, 25 October 1955; J.P. Moffett, CSD, to SDO, Arusha, Ref. 22/116/19, of 6 October 1955. 5/S.D.4723.

[29] Report of John H. Worthington, SDO, District Office, Moshi, 29th October 1956. "The Boys' and Girls' Club Pilot Scheme in Moshi District." TNA 5/25/14, Vol. VII, Native Affairs General Moshi, Boys and Girls Clubs 5/S.D. 4723.

opment Officer in Moshi, suggested that Chagga girls should learn about changes in the lives of women in England and India. She noted that in Sierra Leone, "filmstrips on [the] 'Life of Florence Nightingale' and 'Changes in the Position of Women in the Last 100 Years' [were] very popular among semi-educated tribal people (women) as well as the elite."[30]

On a more practical level, girls club members were to learn about proper child nutrition and psychology, first aid, home nursing, and handwork, with "a talk on choice of colour and style in dress" deemed "useful and popular." They would learn to cook using a "debi-oven" for "scones, biscuits, bread, and baking meat." Jellicoe realized that for classes to become genuine clubs, they had to have African leadership, but she worried about Muslim fathers and husbands, who were "liable to object ... unless it can be proved that the girls and women are not getting "uppish."[31]

Like the Girls' Clubs, the Women's Clubs on Kilimanjaro were supposed to raise homecraft, child care, and home hygiene standards, and to produce handicrafts. But they were also intended to encourage African women "to play a fuller part in the life of the community," and to give African housewives "wider interests and more enjoyment in life" through "communal amusement such as singing, acting, [and] competitions." In short, the clubs were to be an "African edition of the English rural village institute" with "activites ... learnt at the Club ... practiced at home."[32] Despite their predetermined goals and content, clubs were supposed to reflect the initiative and desire of women themselves, with small initial grants from the Social Development Department and help from voluntary organizations such as the Tanganyika Council of Women and the wives of administrative officers. Eventually, however, the clubs were expected to become self-supporting.[33]

Just as Girls'and Boys' Clubs were limited to Standard IV leavers and not intended for youth who had never attended school, Women's Clubs were limited to "respectable [i.e., married] women," admitted by the consent of the Club Committee on the vote of members. To start a new club, organizers and prospective members needed approval from local native authorities, and from their husbands. Club presidents were drawn from the wives of chiefs and headmen, or "leading" men in the area, and local teachers were expected to serve as club secretaries and treasurers.[34] Clubs were encouraged to arrange performances and competitions for such things as "[b]est latrine, kitchen, well arranged house; needlework; children's clothing, fancy needlework, embroidery, baby shows." Husbands were to be invited to at least one performance per year.[35]

---

30   Ibid.

31   Ibid. Unsigned, typewritten memo, 5/S.D.4723.

32   TNA 5/47/26 Women's Clubs – Policy and Organisation. "The Organization of Women's Clubs – Brief Notes" [unsigned].

33   Ibid.

34   TNA 5/47/26 Women's Clubs – Policy and Organization. "The Organization of Women's Clubs" – "Brief Notes."

35   A "best latrine" contest had a particular irony—since according to custom, Chagga men did not need to defecate. See Sally Falk Moore, "The Secret of the Men: A Fiction of Chagga Initiation and Its Relation to the Logic of Chagga Symbolism," *Africa* 46, 4 (1976): 357–70.

Badges, Rank, and Federation: Club Politics

The politicization of Girls' and Women's Clubs on Kilimanjaro in the mid-1950s was perhaps inevitable. Three issues in particular pointed to the ways in which Tanganyika's Trust Territory status influenced social development schemes and trapped clubs between the Chagga nationalism of the chiefs and the territory-wide nationalism of TANU: the question of "proficiency badges," the importance of rank within the clubs, and the dilemma of federation.

Women's Clubs in Northern Rhodesia awarded badges to individual African women for best needlework, embroidery, cakes, and so on. When Lady Twining urged that Tanganyikan women's clubs adopt a similar "badge scheme,"[36] Miss Jellicoe opposed the idea. Whereas women's clubs in Northern Rhodesia (and in Kenya) were organized and funded by the government, and run by Europeans, Tanganyikan clubs, she insisted, were grassroots efforts, and lacked the "trained local staff" necessary to run a badge scheme. In any case, she stated, women on the mountain had no time to work for badges.[37] Jellicoe's complaint about lack of funding and trained personnel suggests that the virtue of grassroots self-reliance was as much a product of necessity as philosophy.

Meanwhile, however, the Chagga Council liked the badge idea, and the "selection of Kilimanjaro area for a pilot scheme." Rather than a badge with a Tanganyikan design, however, they proposed a local badge with the Chagga flag and "an inscription such as Chama Cha Wanawake wa Kilimanjaro [Women's Club of Kilimanjaro]." Defending the Council's position and stressing that it favored "territorial federation ... built from the bottom upwards," Jellicoe suggested that a national federation bar badge could be added to the Chagga badge at a suitable time.[38]

If the Chagga Council's desire to maintain control of the nationalist movement seemed obvious in their intervention regarding a badge design, tensions among women at whom clubs were directed were equally apparent. Jellicoe quickly learned that club leaders wanted "an extra mark of rank" and clear distinctions between senior and junior sections so as not to "drive the older married women from the Clubs...."[39] The need to reconcile older women's demand for *heshima* (respect) with younger women's greater educational and other skills was the most troublesome problem, but there were others, with broader implications, as well. Club leadership was too closely tied to the chiefly system; moreover, local notions of competition meant that past winners would not compete again for fear of losing prestige, and past losers would not participate for fear of losing again.[40]

Jellicoe resisted the pressure for a federation of women's clubs coming from Commissioner Moffett. Agreeing that "some sort of federation should be achieved ... while we still have full powers of guidance," she insisted that imposing it would result in further fragmention. Moreover, Jellicoe feared that

---

[36] J. P. Moffett, CSD, to Miss Jellicoe, Woman SDO, Moshi, Ref. No. 22/128/11/13 of 6 April 1956, TNA 5/S.D.47/28.

[37] Jellicoe to C5D, Ref. No. 3/77 of 30 May 1956, TNA 5/47/26.

[38] Ibid.

[39] Ibid.

[40] Ibid.

Photo 7: Three "races" of women together: the club ideal in the 1950s. Courtesy of the Government Information Office of Tanzania, Dar es Salaam, Tanzania.

any encouragement of "national sentiment" could "land up the women's clubs in the laps of some political party." In Jellicoe's view, both TANU and the Chagga Citizens' Union were mainly interested in the women's clubs for "vote-catching and fund-raising." [41]

The desire of Tanganyika's Social Development Department to channel women's interests into clubs was not as intense as the Kenyan program to entice women away from Mau Mau through Maendelo ya Wanawake.[42] Nevertheless, it is clear that contending political and social forces were vying for women's attention and seeking to influence their attitudes in the 1950s. In his first detailed memorandum to Lennox-Boyd, cited above, Governor Twining recognized that TANU was "making a bid to gain the support of women," a fact "which has its dangers."[43] The attachment of Kilimanjaro's Women's Clubs to the local chiefdoms fit into Twining's emphasis on "tribal patriotism," even as the concept of a gradual federation proposed by Jellicoe paralleled the council of chiefs. The club emphasis on "respectable" women exposed the conservative and controlling strain running through the movement. Single women were a problem

---

[41]   Woman SDO, Moshi, to CSD, 27 May 1957, Ref. 47/30/20.

[42]   Audrey Wipper, "The Maendeleo ya Wanawake Organization: The Co-optation of Leadership," *African Studies Review* 18, no. 3 (1975): 99–119.

[43]   Twining to Alan Lennox-Boyd, M.P. Colonial Office, GH. 1033/2 Secret, 31 October 1955. EAF 46/7/01, PRO.

for married women; young, for old; and educated girls, for "uneducated." It was all a dilemma for Jellicoe.[44]

TANU Townswomen

Women joined and supported TANU for a range of reasons that invariably included the desire for freedom from colonial rule. But with few exceptions, they joined TANU without prior formal political experience. Relative inexperience was a repeated theme in interviews, along with women's sense that their subordination and men's refusal to take them seriously posed particular problems prior to the coming of TANU.

The political and cooperative associations that proliferated in many parts of Tanganyika after World War II were no more likely to invite women's participation than had their earlier counterparts. Of course, women had *acted* politically in organized protest to express grievances and opposition to debilitating administrative regulations, economic hardship, and the injustices and excesses of native authority rule.[45] However, women were notably absent from the ranks of leadership or membership in TAA, or in the citizens' or cooperative unions—all regarded as precursors to TANU. TAA was primarily an organization of educated and salaried civil servants or wealthy businessmen, and women's lack of land and cash crop ownership explained their absence from the emerging cooperative unions. Local political organizations—the citizens' unions—often depended upon women's capacity and willingness to organize against colonial practices; but these were male, like the colonial administrations and the native authorities they confronted. And while agricultural work constituted women's most significant involvement in wage labor, that segment in turn was the least organized in the mid-1950s.

Of Kilimanjaro's local political associations, only the Chagga Congress, whose eleven listed leaders were "old members of the now defunct [Tanganyika] African Association, Kilimanjaro Branch"[46] seems to have considered admitting women members. Shortly after the formation of the Congress in 1954, "it was agreed that women should be allowed to join the Society and that methods of choosing women members should be studied."[47]

---

[44] By September 1957, with a total of 183 women's clubs in the territory, there were 48 in Northern Province, including 17 in Moshi District and 31 in Arusha District. Central Province had the fewest, with 2 (Kondoa District). There were 13 in Eastern Province (6 in Dar es Salaam Municipality); 7 in Morogoro District; 34 in Lake Province, including 21 in Bukoba, 5 in Ukerewe, 2 in Mwanza, 2 in Musoma and 4 in Ngudu; 27 in Southern Province, 15 in Masasi and 12 in Newela; Southern Highlands Province had 9, with 3 in Mbeya and 6 in Rungwe Districts. Tanga Province had the most clubs—3 in Tanga and 47 in Pare. (List attached to a memo from Moffett to various SDOs and Women's SDOs.)

[45] Further research may reveal that more women in colonial Tanganyika expressed their political protest as members of associations, as was the case in Ujiji. See McCurdy, "The 1932 'War.'" For other examples of women's protest see O'Barr, "Pare Women"; Feierman, *Peasant Intellectuals*, 218–20; Susan [Geiger] Rogers, "Anti-Colonial Protest in Africa: A Female Strategy Reconsidered," *Heresies* 9, 3 (1980): 22–25; and Mbilinyi, "This Is an Unforgettable Business," 116–22, on the 1934 struggle of Dar es Salaam's women beer brewers against government controls.

[46] Mangi Mkuu to D.C. Moshi, Ref. 10/5/42 of 8 January, TNA 5/25/23.

[47] TNA 5/25/23.

Yet changes were occurring for and among women that would affect their politicization and willingness to direct their energies toward TANU. This was sometimes in spite of, but in other respects because of, the pull of missions, increased access to education, administration-sponsored women's clubs, and the continuing controls exercised by husbands, fathers, native authorities, and district commissioners.

The local politics of TANU support and opposition appears to have had very little to do with the actions of women in the district. Moreover, Kilimanjaro politics, though seemingly mountain-bound at one level, had long been infused with the cross-currents of trade and travel that had the mountain as a place of departure or destination. During the twentieth century, the movement of Chagga away from the mountain in search of employment opportunities, and the reverse movement of laborers from less well-endowed areas to Kilimanjaro in search of wage labor on coffee and sisal estates; the movement of people from the mountain down to Moshi for work, for trade, for escape from the confines of life in the homestead and villages of the mountain—these realities were not contained within the bounds of notions of community, citizenship, and progress posed by the colonial administration, the Chagga Council and *mangi mkuu*, or the Social Welfare Department's "Club Movement."

The women of Kilimanjaro and Moshi who joined TANU and became activists during the second half of the 1950s shared some of the characteristics of women activists in Dar es Salaam, but their profiles also reflected the particularities and colonial experience of that region. To understand these similarities and differences, I turn to the life histories of TANU women collected in Moshi in 1988.[48]

Halima Selengia Kinabo[49]

When we met in 1988 at Basilla Urasa's office in the Moshi Regional Development Block, Halima Selengia Kinabo was the leader of a women's group which for twenty-five years had owned the Shangazi Hotel in Moshi, an operation whose success could be measured in the fact that shares had divided "more than six times."

Bi Halima was born in the Marangu chiefdom in the village of Sembeti (Sendichi, in the transcription by Anita Urasa) in about 1929. Her father, Selengia, was a chief who divorced her mother, Hija, a farmer who cultivated bananas, coffee, eleusine and beans. Brought up by her mother with her three siblings, Bi Halima was not sent to school but pestered her brother and others to teach her how to read

---

48   Mrs. Basilla Urasa, then regional community development officer, whom I first met through a mutual friend, Eva Pendaeli Sarakikya, was instrumental in helping me contact and arrange interviews with TANU women activists in Moshi. On several occasions, she participated in the interviews—invariably in a positive and perceptive way. Well-known and highly respected in the area, Mrs. Urasa also helped me secure a seat on a flight to Mwanza, when after several disappearances of my name from the reservation list she accompanied me to the ATC office (Air Tanzania Corporation, commonly referred to as "anytime cancelled"). To my additional good fortune, I was able to employ Mrs. Urasa's daughter, Anita, as a research assistant. Anita, who had completed national service and was soon to go to Dar es Salaam to study architecture, transcribed and translated most of the Moshi tapes and several from my research trip to Mwanza as well. She also assisted in many of the Moshi interviews.

49   Interview with Halima Selengia Kinabo, Moshi, October 7, 1988.

and write. She also watched her mother go to town to "do small business" and worked with her until she began to do business on her own.

When she was about nineteen, Bi Halima married Athumani Abdallahrahmani, a policeman and later police inspector, with whom she had one of her two children. Eventually, they separated "for unavoidable ... inexplicable reasons, by religious law," and she did not remarry.

Bi Halima explained her introduction to TANU as follows:

At the time I joined TANU I was doing business. Often, as I went home from work, I used to meet the local TANU chairman, Yosufu Olotu. He used to tell me, "Bi Halima! Join TANU." And I asked him, because I didn't know at that time, "What is TANU?" He said, "TANU is independence. Independence means that we will rule ourselves." I told him, "But I hear TANU is bad!" And he said, no, that wasn't true. I really said that to him.... I met him four times and each time he urged me to join. I asked myself "why does he keep asking me to join?"... [apologizes for failing to bring her membership cards] Anyway, when I joined, finally, I started to try to persuade others to join. "Join TANU. TANU is a good thing. TANU is the country, we will be independent," and so on. Some said, "Oh no, we don't want to join that party. We are afraid of it." And I said no, it is a very good party. I used to sit with people for hours discussing this issue. So slowly, they started to join until we got internal self government....

"I must tell the truth," continued Bi Halima; and she went on to explain how the local TANU leaders met to discuss their difficulties in countering UTP and other anti-TANU propaganda, and their decision to ask Nyerere to come, assess the situation, and help out. When five elders (TANU leaders) asked her if Nyerere could stay at her house when he came, Bi Halima agreed, and both he and Bhoke Munanka[50] stayed with her. It must have been at the time of the tripartite elections because Bi Halima remembers that along with members of the TANU Youth League, "the Indian lady, Bibi Sophia Mustafa[51] from Arusha," TANU candidate from the Asian community, was there as was TANU's choice among the Europeans, Derek Bryceson.

Many people came, but these stood out because they had drive. They stayed there and held discussions. I cooked and they ate and went off to meetings.... When I asked Nyerere what he wanted to eat, he asked for bananas. He said he was tired of rice. So I cooked bananas and he came and ate.

After Nyerere left the house to address meetings—Bi Halima mentioned Majengo, Kilema, Mamba, Useri and Arusha—she locked the doors and followed. Women used to guard Nyerere when he came, she explained; and they also spread

---

[50] Trained as a clerk at Tabora school, Isaac Bhoke Munanka was secretary of TAA's Mwanza branch in 1950, and sought to revitalize the flagging organization in 1952 with Paul Bomani and Saadani Kandoro. Adamantly opposed to the tripartite voting established for the elections of 1958, Munanka nevertheless continued as a loyal TANU leader. From 1958 he administered the Pan-African Freedom Movement of East and Central Africa (PAFMECA) designed to foster liberation and unity in these regions. See Iliffe, *Modern History*, 480, 490, 504–507, 511, 514, 555–57, 561, 568 and 574.

[51] Sophia Mustafa has written an account of her life and political career, *The Tanganyika Way*. I interviewed Mrs. Mustafa in Dar es Salaam in 1984.

the word about upcoming events. Bi Halima wanted to help TANU, she said, because she was committed to independence.

> Colonialism was something the people had somehow come to accept out of ignorance of anything better. To tell the truth, the colonists were not bad people. They just didn't show everything clearly. They didn't think we had a right to what belonged to us ... and didn't like people to express their own views.

As for women's situation, Bi Halima felt, as did virtually all other women I spoke with, that before TANU, women had no say.

> If she spoke out, she was told, "Ah! Woman. What are you saying?" But now, women have a voice; they can speak out, and so long as what they say is sound people believe it and their words are accepted.

Like many women activists in Dar es Salaam, Bi Halima also understood that beyond freedom and dignity, what independence would bring depended upon good plans and hard work. "We couldn't expect independence and then sit back and wait for aid from the colonists," she pointed out. Women sought the same privileges and opportunities as men from independence, she stressed. "Like now," she observed, gesturing to Mrs. Urasa, the community development officer. "In those days it wasn't at all easy or possible for you to sit here at this desk. Nowadays, if you are well-educated and lucky, you have the chance to travel here and there."

Bi Halima's success as a businesswoman in Moshi provided her with a degree of wealth and mobility that few women farmers on the mountain enjoyed. Familiar with both village and town life, she had earned her status of respectability in the context of the latter. As a Muslim, and divorced, it is unlikely that she would have been attracted to or accepted into the women's club movement. Had she been Christian and married, it is equally unlikely that she would have been a TANU activist in the 1950s.

Mwamvita Salim and Zainabu Hatibu[52]

Mwamvita Salim and Zainabu Hatibu discussed their participation in TANU with us in a very old Swahili house near Moshi's major market. Although it was bright daylight outside, the room in which we sat on beds for the interview was windowless and dark with the flickering of small kerosene lamps offering the only light. A neighbor's funeral had kept the women up all night.

Mwamvita Salim remembers that she was already born "when the British hoisted up their flag" [following the defeat of the Germans in World War I]. By that time, her father, a Zigua from Tanga, was dead. Her Maasai mother, Asha, died when she was five years old. "My mother had twelve children, but ten died leaving only two," she explained. "Now I am the only one still alive. The girl who just came in is my niece."

Poor and orphaned, Bi Mwamvita grew up with foster parents and remembers her early life as very difficult. She was married to Omari Mzira, a railway station

---

[52] All information and quotations from Mwamvita Salim and Zainabu Hatibu are from interviews with them conducted on October 13, 1988. Anita Urasa assisted with these interviews.

master, who divorced her when she was about twenty-five years old. Although she did not specifically link the divorce with her difficulty bringing pregnancies to term, Bi Mwamvita went on to tell us about two miscarriages. With no children of her own, she raised her younger sister's five offspring when her sister died. To support them, she baked buns and cakes and had the children sell them on the street. Turning to her involvement in TANU she explained:

> I didn't belong to any kind of group before TANU, although the DC started a sewing group for us [women]. I heard of TANU when my late younger sister was in Dar es Salaam and was one of the first TANU members. She sent me a message saying "TANU is coming. Don't refuse to join." I can't remember what year that was; Nyerere came here in 1954, didn't he? So from the time Nyerere came here, we have been with him. We supported him until we gained independence. We even dressed him in a *buibui* so he wouldn't be recognized. I was his guard. I cooked his food [as did] Zainabu Hatibu and Fatuma Makwia. But I was the one who was chosen expressly by TANU to look after his welfare so that he wouldn't be harmed....
>
> I volunteered to cook, to do the laundry, to put up guests—people like Munanka, Shemsanga, and even Kambona who left us. They were all under our care.... If TANU needed something [we] women would provide it immediately....
>
> I was in an *ngoma* group that used to dance for money which went to the government [TANU]. I also ran a dance hall at the KNCU [Kilimanjaro Native Cooperative Union] together with Dadi. The money went to TANU. I organized many TANU events: football matches, dances, a bar where we sold soda. I worked hard so that TANU would rule.
>
> Women were braver than men, in fact; we weren't afraid even of dying. The men were the ones who got scared; never the women. I used to sell membership cards. Sometimes I went up to someone and told them, "Buy a card," and they would say, "No, I'll be jailed." And I'd say, "Buy it and hide it in your suitcase and go on with your government job. After independence you'll produce it and show you are a TANU member."

Because Bi Mwamvita grew up speaking Maasai, she became invaluable in TANU's efforts to gain members and establish branches in Maasailand.

> I thought I'd die in Maasailand. All those party branches that you see were established by us. Since I spoke Maasai, I used to go there to teach the Maasai about TANU. I explained; they understood and bought membership cards....
>
> One day, at our meeting grounds, several white men came up to me and asked, "Mama, do you like TANU?" I answered, "Very much." "How much do you like it?" I said, "Like my soul." "And if you couldn't have TANU" "It would be like my soul had been taken away." I told them the truth. They patted me, laughed, and then they left.

A Muslim, Bi Mwamvita was adamant that religion had helped both TANU and women, and that TANU, in turn, had helped women a great deal.

> Why shouldn't [religion] help TANU and women? That's what religion is for—to help the oppressed!
>
> Women's problems were different from men's because women were treated like donkeys. Up on the mountain, women cleaned the cowsheds, cut grass for the animals, split firewood and tended the farm while the

husband lived in town.... After independence, we refused such treatment. Those of us who had the guts said "It is not right for human beings to be treated like beasts of burden...." Before independence, women didn't dare say anything in front of men or expect to be taken seriously. They would beat you up and laugh at you. Women weren't allowed to do anything; but these days women are beginning to become more aware of themselves and their capabilities. They speak out and make their own decisions; but in the past even if they were whipped they didn't dare object.

I was interested in TANU because we wanted to rule ourselves. So why shouldn't we be interested? Colonialism didn't particularly harm me, but I knew that Nyerere was the teacher and that independence would remove trash from the town. By trash, I mean people who don't know how to wash themselves and their clothing and to look after their welfare. As for women, we would be able to speak out. TANU brought democracy. Everyone had a right to speak out. Women could gain a voice, an education. I was completely illiterate....

Born December 29, 1939, and perhaps twenty years younger than her friend, Mwamvita Salim, Zainabu Hatibu was also of mixed parentage. Her mother, Mwamvita Athumani, was the daughter of Maasai and Chagga parents; her father, Hatibu, was Pare and Maasai. Bi Zainabu remembers that her life as a child was good. Her father was a doctor (probably medical assistant) at Mawenzi Hospital, and she attended school up to Standard VI. She then attended Koranic school, but stopped at the age of fifteen when she was married by an Arab hotel-keeper in Moshi.

Bi Zainabu was still quite young—perhaps sixteen or seventeen—when she joined the TANU Youth League, having heard about TANU from activists such as Abdul Rahmani, Bakari Abdi, and Akida Hamisi, who were all deceased by 1988.

There were three women's groups in the Youth League. The first was the women singers; the second was the young women's group—Mwamvita and others—they were the guards here in Moshi; and the third group dealt with guests. They catered for the TANU Youth League guests when they came to Moshi. We were the ones who looked after them. Halima Rajabu was also one of us.... I [also] belonged to a TANU *ngoma* group. We performed to earn money for [the party]....

Personally, I was very active in TANU up until we gained independence. I volunteered to look after guests; I gave them food. When Youth League members from the rural areas were sick in Mawenzi Hospital, we looked after them. I personally took them tea, food, everything. I even used to beg my father for money; then I cooked food and took it to the hospital.

We joined the TANU Youth League to strengthen [TANU]. We were real youths, not like the ones today! [A reference to the many elderly women and men in Tanzania who still express their political personas as members of the TANU Youth League]. We didn't discriminate against each other; we were a mixture of many tribes. There were Somalis and an Indian who now lives in Zanzibar. He was even disowned by his parents for the sake of TANU.

We were like the CID [Special Intelligence Division of the colonial administration]—informers for TANU. We spied on other people and provided information. We used to hold meetings in Arusha, but in the morning we would be seen in Moshi, and so people never knew where we had been....

I was the first messenger sent [from Moshi to Dar es Salaam] to take Nyerere money; the Youth League collected it. I saw him and gave it to him personally. We also went to the hearing of Nyerere's court case. Me, Mwajabu Selemani, Fatuma Makuria, and some men, Jumanne Abdallah, Ali Badri ... he's still alive. This was when the colonial administration prosecuted Nyerere in 1958. Nyerere won.[53]

Bi Zainabu shared the view that women's problems differed from men's prior to independence, and that men gave their wives little freedom. But TANU changed this. Stated Bi Zainabu, "Almost all Tanzanian women, especially *buibui* women [Muslim women, in this case] came forward to join and campaign for independence."

Mario Kinabo[54]

Amina Mario Kinabo, as she introduced herself, welcomed us into the sitting room of her home in the suburb of Pasua, Moshi, on October 8, 1988. The daughter of Chief Kinabo Namfua of Mkuu Rombo, Bi Mario was one of four children born to her mother, Ndekusara. Because her father was a chief, Bi Mario explained, her childhood was good; but "we saw that other people had difficult lives." All women and girls had to cut and fetch grass for the cows, which were kept in sheds. "If you refused to cut grass, then, mama, you were not considered a woman. Women cleaned the cowsheds and cooked, and we used cow dung for fertilizer. People look down on it now, but it was very good."

Bi Mario attended mission school for two years but decided it was worthless. Her marriage had already been arranged, and since girls were not allowed to do anything, she didn't see the point. "If you went out, your reputation was spoilt. And then who would want to marry you? No man would love you if you were promiscuous...so I decided it was no use going to school when I was going to be married."

Bi Mario was married to Lot, from Mashati, Rombo, when she was eighteen or nineteen. Lot worked as a casual laborer, and they lived in Mombasa for seven years. However, Bi Mario became bored, and when she heard that the coffee-curing factory in Moshi was hiring women to sort coffee beans, she returned to Moshi and was hired along with six or seven hundred people. Eventually, she was chosen by her fellow workers to be the women's supervisor. "I showed the women how to sort coffee beans and grade them. 'This is grade C, and this is how to sort.' I knew all the different grades of coffee beans."

---

[53] Many women throughout the country organized to raise money for Nyerere's defense in the case of criminal libel brought against him in May 1958. As Nyerere was leaving the courtroom, he had to be "protected by the ushers against his over-excited followers," which included hundreds of women who had travelled from all over the country to be there: "some ... women who had not understood a word of the proceedings thought that he was being taken to prison" and would have attacked the ushers had Nyerere not reassured them. Listowel, *The Making of Tanganyika*, 327, 331–32.

[54] Basilla Urasa participated in the interview with Mario Kinabo, held in Mrs. Kinabo's home in Pasua (Moshi) on October 8, 1988.

At the coffee-curing factory, my salary as supervisor was Sh. 60/ per month. That was a lot of money. A kilo of meat cost 50 cents. The sorters got Sh. 40/ per month. I campaigned until they got a raise to Sh. 60/. Then my salary increased to Sh. 120/. So I worked for 18 years....

Bi Mario's experience as a worker in the coffee-curing factory fueled her interest in TANU, and her role as a supervisor there gave her confidence and authority among the workers. She first heard about TANU in 1954 in Moshi "from a reliable man called Metseri Simon, Mama Coletta's in-law. Because we believed in him, we elected him our leader."

I joined TANU because I thought it would be a good thing to get independence. As the supervisor of six hundred women and between two and three hundred men, I had seen discrimination at the factory.

For example, workers weren't allowed outside to drink water; we had to drink from taps in the toilets. I felt bitter about this and asked myself why [it should be]. One day, I confronted the white man [curing works manager] and told him I didn't want to work any more. He asked why, and I asked him whether it was right for us to drink water in the toilets. He asked if this was bad and I told him it was, that the drinking tap should be put outside. That they were degrading us by making us drink in the toilet. He told me he was going to fire me, and I said I didn't care. "Whether you fire me or not, we are only looking for equality between the black and white people. That we should eat what you eat. If you eat eggs then so should we; if you eat meat then we should eat meat...."

When TANU started we began to sell membership cards secretly because other people weren't allowed to enter the coffee-curing premises. Then the leaders selected me to speak at meetings all over the district. I said I was willing, but that they had better not regret later.

So I spoke in Arusha and everywhere. I told the men that although the women worked to produce coffee, they didn't get any of the money after the coffee had been sold. The people who did all the work were the women. "But you men go to town and get drunk on all the money. The women don't even get five cents." I was the district chairperson of the TANU women's section, so I said that out of five bags of coffee, the women should get at least two. "And the husband, you can go get drunk on the other three. But if you get drunk, tomorrow, when you are old or you have problems, that will be your own business. It's your own drunken foolishness." The men and women cheered. So I went on making speeches at meetings in Arusha and other places.

Bi Mario's parents followed traditional religious practices' and she became a Muslim after leaving home. She brought to her political interests and perspective an awareness of the lives of women and less fortunate people on Kilimanjaro (Rombo was well known as the poorest region of the mountain), the experience of living in Mombasa, and her years as a wage laborer in the coffee-curing factory. Despite or perhaps because of her father's position as a chief, she believed that it was important to support TANU not only to bring independence to the country, but because she felt that people were oppressed in the chiefdoms of Kilimanjaro. Having felt restricted herself as a young girl, she also had a heightened sense of the importance of personal freedom —that it was important to be able "to go freely where you please, without being harassed for no reason."

Bi Mario believes that she was harassed for her political activities and that her life threatened by persons who favored the United Tanganyika Party. On one occasion, she was near the police station when she was almost struck by the car of Mamdani Shariff, a UTP member. "God told me to look back and when I did I saw the car and jumped out of the way just as it reached me. A big crowd gathered around me. Yes, by God, he intended to kill me!" She went on to recount an even more dramatic attempt on her life.

And then, they shot me at home. They came to my house at one o'clock in the morning and I got shot at four times. Something told me that the people who were outside shooting were not thieves, they were TANU opponents. So I called a child—my grandchild. When the first bullet came—tap! I was on the floor, and the second and the third and the fourth. They ran out of bullets. They said, "Let's go now, she's dead." By the grace of God, I was about to take up a spear and I told them, "Enter then! You have no more bullets. Enter!"

I fought them alone. My children were across the road, and when they tried to come there [to her aid] they were prevented by tear gas. Yes, my children had tear gas thrown at them so they couldn't come. So I fought, and I told the child to get under the bed. I knew that if I let go of the spear, they would catch me and kill me. So I fought until they were tired.

The tenant of the second room had a pregnant wife who told him to help me since those people were UTP members, not thieves. But the man didn't help me, and I was so tired. I opened the door...and left that room quietly and went in to the sitting room. The door is very strong and it would take four or five blows with a big rock before you could break it. I decided to stay there. They entered the other room and took my case and other possessions. I owned a small shop. At three o'clock, I took a sword [*panga*?] I didn't even go see the children and left the house.

However, the police had heard the gunshots and were now coming. "What's going on in Pasua?" they asked.

I could not verify Bi Mario's impassioned account of the attack on her house and person. At the very least, it can be read as evidence of the conflict between TANU and UTP that was felt in the area—a conflict also discussed by several other women interviewed in Moshi. The potential for violence was, of course, among the reasons why political and public activity were thought to be wrong for women. The following TANU activists further illustrate the situation.

Violet Njiro[55]

Violet Njiro was born in 1930, in Marangu, to Semalik Samu, a butcher, and Ndeambilisia Mtui, a farmer. Although her mother had only two children, her father had four wives, and Violet had many half-sisters and brothers. As a young girl, Violet stayed with her mother and farmed, took care of the cattle, and went to fetch fodder. Her father was neither educated nor a Christian, but he wanted his children to go to school and sent Violet through Standard VI. At that point, she

---

[55] Anita Urasa participated in the interview with Violet Njiro, which took place at UWT headquarters in Moshi, October 20, 1988.

decided she wanted to become a nurse; having read about a nursing school in Kenya, she applied and was accepted. With her father's permission, she attended the school and then returned to Kilimanjaro, hoping to practice nursing in villages on the mountain.

At the age of twenty-one, Violet married Gideon Njiro and moved to Moshi where her husband worked as a mechanic while she worked at Mawenzi Hospital.

> The first time [I heard about TANU] we were at work. We got into trouble. I was almost sent to jail. Our doctor was a *Banyani* [Indian]. I remember the year was 1954 and some clerks were sent to prison at that time. I was asked, "Did you buy that [TANU] card?" I didn't dare admit it; one just kept quiet, so I said, "No, I don't know anything about it."
>
> Now the doctor told me I would be jailed because we used to associate with the clerks."We will send you to jail; we've noticed that you're starting a bad political party here."
>
> But we just kept quiet. Luckily, by the grace of God, they [the clerks] were released because by then TANU's influence was widespread; they were released because the government said they had to be and the doctor stopped bothering us.
>
> [Very soon] TANU was everywhere. When we heard that there was a meeting in town after work, we would go....

Mrs. Njiro was one of several women to speak of an accident that occurred during one of Nyerere's visits—a terrible accident that could have had very negative consequences for TANU and Nyerere.

> When Nyerere came, they [the visiting TANU leaders] used to hide in the back streets. Once while he was talking to people who had been with him at a meeting, a small child crawled underneath his car. Now when the car moved off, no one knew that there was a child under there. The bulk of the car hid the child, and it was knocked down and killed. The child's father had spirit. He said, "You are not to blame." He said that even he had not seen the child. And fortunately, we were able to strengthen the party. We said that the child was TANU's since it had been killed there. And when we got independence, Nyerere looked after that child's father very well. He built him a house.

Like Mario Kinabo, Violet Njiro was attracted to TANU in part because of the terms and conditions of her working life. In addition to poor pay, she explained that once she got married, she was no longer considered a full-time nurse and could have easily been dismissed. If you had a baby, you were immediately fired. Like many other women, Mrs. Njiro also spoke of the importance of TANU's support of women's organization. Women were able to start projects, she noted, and to hold meetings. "In the past, women didn't even know what a meeting was. That's the truth!" Mrs. Njiro herself had never seen her father go to a meeting; nor had she attended any meeting prior to TANU.

TANU's insistence on the equality of all people helped women who had previously been unable to leave the house without permission and could expect a beating if their husbands returned and they were out. Somewhat younger and usually better educated than the women interviewed in Dar es Salaam,

Moshi women frequently blurred the pre- and post-independence organizational picture.

Elizabeth Gupta[56]

Elizabeth Gupta was born in Same District in 1922. Her father, Stenga, was a Nyamwezi from Tabora who travelled to the northeast to work on the Tanga railroad. His main camp was in Same, and that was where he met and married Elizabeth's mother, Shuhute Mgoloka, a Pare. Not long after the births of Elizabeth and her two brothers and three sisters, the family moved to Tabora where Elizabeth grew up and attended six years of primary school. She did casual labor for a while and when her father moved the family to Moshi, became a storekeeper on a sisal estate belonging to Germans in the area. When she was twenty-one she married Alijansi Gupta, a doctor (medical assistant) and moved with him to Ifakara in present-day Morogoro region.

Mrs. Gupta heard about TANU in 1955 and purchased her first membership card in 1956 after she and her husband had returned to Moshi and settled in the village of Mabogini. In Moshi, she remembers Yusufu Ngozi, the late Mgeni wa Simba, Shabani Mkwawa and Joseph Kimalando as the first TANU leaders.

To Mrs. Gupta, it would have been foolish not to be for TANU and for ending the repression of colonialism, where no one had a voice with the government, neither men nor women, and women suffered the added burden of not even having a voice with their own men. "Because women weren't valued," she insisted. "You had no value at all as a human. Women were like—I don't know—you probably value your dog more because it guards the door. We had no voice."

Mrs. Gupta was most active in the TANU choir and Youth League, which were led by Julius Nyerere's brother, Joseph. "Our job was to sing." She particularly remembers the period after the tripartite elections when Zuberi Mtemvu, former TANU assistant secretary, and his racialist African National Congress[57] sought to wrest popular support from TANU.

> Straight after we left [a meeting place] Zuberi Mtemvu would arrive, or Zuberi Mtemvu would leave and we would arrive. I remember Joseph Nyerere brought us *kanga* to wear. Both men and women wore them. I remember the meeting we held in Majengo. We put up our TANU flags and were immediately ordered to take them down. You know at that time, when we held public meetings the fence around the grounds was guarded by colonial police with guns; but we weren't scared.
>
> Now, when we won the [1958, tripartite] elections I joined the safety and defense section. It was a difficult job. I remember the time when Nyerere used to come, we took him to Lucy Lameck's to sleep but we

---

[56] Interview with Elizabeth Gupta conducted by Anita Urasa and myself at the UWT office, Moshi, on October 20, 1988.

[57] Zuberi Mtemvu left TANU to form the African National Congress (ANC) following TANU's 1958 decision to participate in the tripartite elections. Advocating "Africa for Africans only," the ANC had limited success in national elections but attracted local support from those threatened by TANU's "growing hegemony." See Iliffe, *Modern History*, 572.

guarded Mama Binti Mwalimu's house because the colonialists thought
that he slept at the house which we guarded. But Nyerere was somewhere
else. If we changed his residence we would guard another house. We used
to hide in sacks because we were afraid of the colonials. When the colonial guards passed by they thought we were coal sacks whereas there were
people in the sacks!

We went on like that. I was in the safety and defense corps and our
O.C. [officer in charge] was Mzunda. I remember our last meeting before
independence, we held it at the Memorial Ground and it was during the
hot season, like now. There was no water; the colonials had cut off the
water supply; it was their ground. The sun was hot. There were many
people and we were forced to cut away the brush because the whites refused us the use of their good ground, so we were near the road where
the Memorial Ground is now built. People volunteered to cut away the
undergrowth, so in twenty minutes it was all clear.

Mrs. Gupta also helped to build TANU offices.

I volunteered to build the Mabogini Party office; the house is Abdi Nuru's—
the one whom you see here—he offered his house for an office, but it was
in a terrible state and so I volunteered and took off the thatch. I mended it
and painted the house and put in a cement floor and corrugated iron roof.

Then another house belonged to Mrs. Muhogo. I think you remember
her, she's dead now. It was here, she offered one room but it was unsuit-
able. Then the people volunteered and we mended it; but personally, I
contributed more than my colleagues. Mwalimu came to open it for us.

All the leaders who used to come to Mabogini used to stay at my house.
Ask Yusufu Ngozi. Their base was my house. If we were going to Kahe or
anywhere else, we used the late Kiraia's ... car. We've worked for TANU,
but since that's now past, one can't give a very long history.

But I contributed my wealth and resources to TANU. Even my child,
who's now deceased, found me already in TANU. I used to have nursing
children, but I spent very little time with them; I was sometimes away for
a week at meetings campaigning for TANU in Rundugai and other places.
Even my husband understood. What husband would let you stay away
from home for a week?

Elizabeth Gupta was among several women who wanted to let us know that
not all women who claimed to have been active in TANU during the struggle for
independence actually participated. Many, she told us, really only become supporters afterwards. But those like herself who had been staunch activists in the
Moshi area were instrumental in making arrangements for meetings, providing food
and lodging to visiting TANU leaders, and collecting money for the petrol needed
for the cars donated to TANU for local trips up the mountain. Some local car owner
might offer his vehicle for transportation, she pointed out, but who, if not the
women, would pay for the petrol?

A Christian, Mrs. Gupta felt that the church had helped TANU. As a successful businesswoman and farmer with vehicles and tractors, she believes in the effi-
cacy of hard work, and says her life has been good since independence. Two of
Elizabeth's sons died, leaving her with four children and seven grandchildren. Not
surprisingly, her major concern in 1988 was the attitudes and activities of children
and youth.

Kanasia Tade Mtenga[58]

Among the more difficult people to arrange an interview with in Moshi, and among the women who continued to be politically involved (suggesting at least one possible reason for her reluctance or inability to find time for an interview) was Kanasia Tade Mtenga. During my stay in Moshi, I was living only two blocks from Mrs. Mtenga's house in Majengo, and in fact walked past it almost every day on my way to and from the town center. Moreover, Henry and Audrey Marealle, with whom I was staying in Majengo, knew Mrs. Mtenga, and Henry Marealle stopped by her place on several occasions to help me arrange for an interview.

When I finally met her, Mrs. Mtenga was taking care of her grandchildren and working as the CCM party secretary for Moshi Rural. Although she had been an M.P. in the 1960s, there was little evidence from her living circumstances that she had managed to join the "bureaucratic bourgeoisie"—those nationalists reputed to have taken over in Tanganyika following independence. In the small, sparsely-furnished sitting room of her house, the noise of traffic in front of the house competed with the noise of cows behind. On the walls were many pictures of young men in church vestments. A crucifix hung over the one table in the room.

Kanasia Tade Mtenga was born in the village of More (?) Mwika in Moshi area in 1934 to Jonathan Ngowo and Nathenjwa Jonathan Ngowo, farmers. She was her mother's fifth child and had four sisters and one brother. Her parents were "good farmers" and cultivated coffee. As a child, Kanasia helped her mother pick coffee and fetch firewood. She started primary school at Mwika mission school and then went to Machame Girls' School, finishing in 1955. Following a two-year teacher training course at Machame, she taught for a short time at Msaranga primary school.

In 1956, she married Tade Mtenga, an independent trader, and they moved to Moshi township. Mrs. Mtenga learned accounting, bookkeeping, English proficiency, and typing at the College of Commerce, which later became the Cooperative Education Center. After passing the Royal Society of Arts examinations and obtaining her bookkeeping certificate, she worked as a cashier at the KNCU Hotel.

In the meantime, her husband had joined the Kilimanjaro District Council and was working in administration.

> I also doubled as a storekeeper for five years. At that time, in 1958, I was working on a part-time basis, as a volunteer teaching adult education classes for TANU. I was working part-time, sometimes in the morning and sometimes in the evening. I was teaching *Kufuta Ujinga* [eradicating ignorance?] literacy classes and also teaching English and so on. I joined TANU in 1959.

In 1958, Mrs. Mtenga was nominated by Governor Turnbull to be a councillor in the Moshi Township Authority. She was also an "ordinary member" of the Tanganyika Council of Women, which was active in the Moshi area and involved "the wives of the D.C., P.C., wives of civil servants—and a few women who could cooperate—Asian, European and a few African women...." The Chagga Citizens Union, she observed, was for men; and she had not been involved in the politics

---

[58] All information and quotations from Mrs. Mtenga are drawn from our discussion on October 19, 1988, and our interview, which took place at her house on December 16, 1988.

surrounding the *Mangi Mkuu* movement. In 1958, people in the Moshi area were mostly joining TANU in secret, especially civil servants who were not permitted to join. It was in that year that Mrs. Mtenga also became a member of the Police Special Constabulary.

Mrs. Mtenga first heard and read about TANU in the newspapers while she was in school in 1955; and in 1956, when she became a civil servant (school teacher), she heard it spoken about "discreetly."

> Anyone would have been excited at the prospect of being independent when you understood the way colonialism was. Independence was a dream. That's why I volunteered to teach ... a big group of men and women who didn't know how to read or write to do so ... to drive out ignorance....
>
> We wanted independence in order to have our own leadership; government would be in the hands of the citizens of Tanganyika, and then we would set our own goals, decide things for our own benefit...at that time all the economic benefits were going out of the country. We grew cotton, coffee and other crops and all ended up going out of the country and not benefiting the people of Tanganyika. We remained with nothing.
>
> Now, after independence, we decide what we want to do with our country, our resources. This is to say that the people have the power to elect their own leaders. We removed the governor and elected a person of our choice.

Mrs. Mtenga officially joined TANU on May 20, 1959, when she obtained her first membership card and became a local committee member. From the beginning, she worked to convince women to join the party and work for independence.

> Women were not to be left behind in the independence struggle. Because we believed that the way the TANU Constitution was drafted women had the power to speak out and address any issue that concerned them in particular and the country at large, just as any other member. Besides, women were the majority. Even now, women are the majority in this country.... And you couldn't ignore the majority. Most of the men were in the civil service and could not be openly associated with the party. So the women united and made a lot of noise and that brought a lot of excitement....
>
> The women persuaded their husbands. Some men were afraid, but their wives said, "If you are afraid, take off your trousers, give them to us so that we can go ahead and fight."

Mrs. Mtenga's view of which women needed to "learn confidence" before independence reflected what she had no doubt learned from her mission education on Kilimanjaro, her association with the Tanganyika Council of Women, and her somewhat late arrival to TANU politics.

> You see, in those days [before independence] it was unusual for women to go to public meetings—especially for Muslims. Women are not allowed to go outside, here and there. Because of this, TANU had a difficult job at first to make them understand and have confidence. They had to learn, because they were not used to political forums. But Bibi Titi, who was the leader of the TANU women's section, oh, she did a lot of travelling with Mwalimu Nyerere and other nationalist leaders to go and to talk, to stay on the platform and ... she was good.

*[handwritten margin note: very important quote *]*

She did a lot of good work at that time. So women also got confidence, you know, saying, "Aahha, so it is possible!" That's why we thought of giving them a chance to talk about their problems, to try to improve the economy, how to bring up their children, take care of their houses, their husbands and so forth. And to improve in their education, because most of them did not even have any education.

Mrs. Mtenga pleaded the ignorance of youth to questions concerning the attitude of Kilimanjaro's churches (she herself was Lutheran) and chiefs, including the *mangi mkuu*, towards TANU's activities and message in the late 1950s. "I was still in school, you see, in 1952." She wished to emphasize her work for the UWT and government after independence. And so she did. Mrs. Mtenga was one of the few TANU women who successfully made the transition from pre- to post-independence politics; she managed to maintain a career in and out of office until her tragic death in a car accident in 1990. Her age and her educational level and qualifications at the time of independence were in her favor, as was her cautious approach to sensitive questions and issues.

Natujwa Daniel Mashamba[59]

Like Kanasia Mtenga, Natujwa Daniel Mshamba was a TANU activist from the 1950s who continued to be directly involved in government and politics in 1988. We met at the CCM offices, Kiboroloni (just east of Moshi town) where she was CCM representative for Moshi Rural. Mother of four and grandmother of six, Mrs. Mshamba was the only woman I interviewed who spoke of a history of direct links to earlier anticolonial action, in her case, the Mbiru (tax) protest of the mid-1940s in Same District, where she was born.[60]

Born January 13, 1934, to Yohana Mcharo, a primary school teacher, and Nimwindie, a farmer, Mrs. Mshamba's vivid memories begin with the family's expulsion from Same District. She was thirteen years old when her father and six other protestors were deported from the region because of their opposition to the Mbiru tax. At first, her mother stayed on in the village. "After my father was deported, the women in our village helped my mother a lot. They came to visit and to help with the chores; others came to spend the night so my mother wouldn't feel lonely, until we had to leave." Because her husband was a teacher, Mrs. Mshamba's mother eventually had to move with him: "All our possessions were auctioned—the farm, coffee, everything. My mother vowed never to return."

Natujwa attended Ilembula Primary School; later, a girls' boarding school called Kyimbila; and then, when it was built, Loleza Girls' School. After finishing Standard IX, she went to Tabora Girl's School and graduated from Standard X in 1952.

---

[59] Interview with Mrs. N.D. Mshamba, CCM Office, Kiboroloni, October 19, 1988. Mrs. Mshamba availed herself of the opportunity I offered to all women interviewed to review the typed transcript of her interview in order to make corrections or additions and to review what she had said. I left her a copy and on January 1, 1989, I received a letter from her in which she offered several corrections, all of which I incorporated into a revised version. Most were corrections of spelling.

[60] See I. N. Kimambo, *Mbiru: Popular Protest in Colonial Tanzania* (Nairobi, 1969). For women's participation, see O'Barr, "Pare Women."

After graduating, she wanted to become a doctor, but at that time there was no medical college in the country that accepted women: "The government said that it couldn't help me, and that if I wanted to be a doctor my father should send me to Mulago in Uganda. He couldn't do so, so I learned typing instead."

When Natujwa's father was released from detention, and despite her mother's vow never to return, the family went back to Pare shortly after Natujwa finished at Tabora.

> When we returned, we were given a hearty welcome. Our house had been sold, so we were given a house by a neighbor.... [And] we were given land because our original farms had been sold. People helped us to farm, and since we were still very young, some old men gave us sugar cane farms so we could have sugar, and potato fields so we would have potatoes. Others gave us their maize farms until we were able to provide our own food. When we harvested the crops which they helped us to cultivate they took back their farms. And they let us have that house until my father was able to build another one, with the aid of our neighbors.
>
> So we stayed until TANU was founded. When my father was asked to give permission for me to work for TANU he was pleased. But as I was still very young, he asked the party chairman and the secretary to help me to keep clear of trouble so that I wouldn't be jailed because the colonial government didn't want TANU.

Mrs. Mshamba's first job was with the Pare Council in Same District. While working there, the TANU chairman for Same District, the late Elias Amos Kisenge, gave her TANU papers to type. After a while, she was found out and given a first warning to stop; but she did not heed the warning and kept typing in secret. When her superiors found out, her boss, the most senior of the Pare Council chiefs, summoned her and said, as Mrs. Mshamba quoted, "We have warned you, but to no avail. The government can find out which machine typed the papers and if they prove that it is yours you will be either sacked or jailed. So you'd better resign." Mrs. Mshamba continued:

> I was fined 30 shillings three times. Thirty shillings was deducted from my salary. I used to earn 75 shillings per month. The first time, they took 30 shillings; the second time too. So I was told to resign since I could, through my involvement with TANU, implicate my boss and maybe even the Pare Council—we could all be sent to jail. They didn't even give me written notice, since they would have had to record it.
>
> So I left and told Elias Amos Kisenge that I'd been asked to resign because I'd refused to stop typing TANU papers.
>
> When I was twenty-seven years old, I got married to Daniel Mshamba and we went to live in Kisiwani. He was the regional business and industry officer there, and I did TANU party work. First I was the TANU branch collector. I was initially interested in TANU because I could see that it was a good party and because my father was treated so badly by the British. The colonial period had been full of problems such as the tax which caused my father's deportation, and the low regard in which we Africans were held. In addition, I didn't want to be governed by foreigners.
>
> As for independence, I thought that we would be able to make our own decisions instead of having them made by other people. Through self-government—after independence—we would get the education which we

wanted, people would be able to know and understand their rights and thus be able to solve their problems.

As for what women would gain, since TANU had set down its goals, after independence women would be able to acquire an education so then they would know their rights.

Women's problems were different from men's. Most fathers didn't send girls to school because they believed that educated girls wouldn't fetch bride prices when they got married. Another important fact was that tribal customs suffocated women. They had no right to air their views; the men were the ones who went to meetings and made decisions and then the women were informed of the decisions. Women were belittled and regarded as though they weren't intelligent beings with the capacity to think.

These problems were discussed in TANU because there were women leaders like Titi Mohamed who educated women on their rights. She spoke at mass meetings in the presence of both men and women.

Women were elected to leadership positions in TANU. Also, many women joined TANU because the colonial administration prevented civil servants from joining. Even some religious groups prevented their followers from being involved. But many women joined TANU and increased the membership so that UNO had to agree to independence....

Because I was young, I initially joined the TANU Volunteer Corps [Youth League]. I'm a Lutheran. The church didn't like to associate with TANU activities because the government didn't approve; but some church leaders helped secretly.

During the struggle for independence, life was very hard because we spent almost all of our time with TANU. We had to find other means of surviving—farming beans, or maize or onions—and selling them. But there were some old men who were strong TANU supporters and who helped TANU workers.

Neither Mrs. Mtenga nor Mrs. Mshamba advanced a political agenda for Tanzanian women of the 1980s; and both were uniformly positive about attempts by UWT, government, and CCM to "help women." Their respective positions as party functionaries did not make critical appraisal likely; on the other hand, there was nothing in their responses to my questions to suggest that they were "hiding" criticisms they actually felt.[61]

Lucy Lameck[62]

Lucy Selina Lameck Somi, whose education and youth made her unique among TANU women activists, was to become a nationally recognized politician follow-

---

[61] Lucy Lameck and Teresa Ntare, whose political careers also spanned the periods before and after independence, were less sanguine in their assessments of recent developments for women (Lameck) and politics in general (Ntare). Sadly, and very unexpectedly in the case of Mwame Teresa Ntare, both are now deceased.

[62] I interviewed Lucy Lameck at her home in Upanga (Dar es Salaam), November 12, 1984. I had met her several weeks earlier at the home of a mutual friend, Eva Pendaeli Sarakikya. Ms. Lameck chose to be interviewed in English.

ing independence, and an ardent voice for legislation intended to address inequalities in women's lives. She was born in the mid-1930s in Kilimanjaro. Her father, Lameck Kimaru Somi, was a farmer and sometimes a transporter. Her mother, Petronilla Lameck Somi had also been deeply involved in politics when Lucy and her three sisters were young.

> "On the whole, my mother brought us up, looking after the family and my three sisters. My life growing up was just like any other Chagga girl's life at that time. You go to primary school and from primary school, to middle school and then, if you are lucky, you go to secondary school."

Lucy went to primary school in her village, Moshi-Njoro, to middle school in Kilema, and to secondary school in Tanga, where she also undertook three years of nursing and midwifery. As she put it regarding her education, "I was one of the lucky people at that particular time."

> My life was just like any normal African child, with a poor background, eager for education, full of question marks; and it was during this time when there was all the hullabaloo about colonialism and the party, which had started in 1954, and about getting independence.

After completing her nursing course, Lucy returned to Moshi in 1955, preferring to go home rather than to a nursing position in Tabora. In Moshi, she took evening classes in typing and shorthand and began working for the Kilimanjaro Native Cooperative Union.

> In l955 I joined the party as an ordinary member, but an active member in the sense of attending meetings and recruiting other people. That was true up to 1957....
>
> I was lucky because every time he came to Moshi, Nyerere used to visit my mother, our home...and he knew me, and recognized my efforts within the party. He mostly saw my mother because she was more frequently there than my father; and in fact, we used to have meals together, almost every evening, whenever he was in Moshi. So he became a friend of the family.
>
> Nyerere got to know my mother because she was... politically active in her own right and had been involved in politics for many years—even when we children were younger. When TANU was established, she got involved in recruiting members and so was I, when I came back. I was also very, very active indeed.
>
> My mother was a very intelligent woman and she knew what was right. So, she welcomed Nyerere and called him "my child." .... The majority of government servants were afraid to entertain Nyerere at that time—or even to take him to their home. But my mother had nothing to lose. We were a poor family, we couldn't be poorer, [so] why not? So he [Nyerere] was accepted as a member of the family....
>
> There was a lot of Chagga politics, but Nyerere was not part of it. He had something much bigger, much more honorable, namely TANU.... My mother wasn't involved [in Chagga politics, either]. None of us were.... There are always some intelligent people in the community who can see far ahead....
>
> I was elected a member of the Moshi District committee of TANU in 1956, and remained there during 1956–1957, until I went away [on a scholarship to Ruskin College]. There were many women who were TANU

activists in Moshi, and other women committee members as well. And many strong women who always welcomed Mwalimu Nyerere whenever he came, oh yes. Mgeni Simba, she is dead now. I remember her.... And when I left, my mother was elected; but then my mother became the district chairperson for the TANU Women's section, which I had never been.

You see, after being a member of the branch of the party, she became a member and then chairperson at the district level of the TANU Women Section until [the establishment of] UWT.... Actually, in all the regions we went to there were women; maybe few on the committees, but many in membership and particularly, in mobilization and total support for independence.

I remember, during the president's case, which was [July 1958], hundreds, a thousand or so women were [sitting] outside the high court, cooking and literally sleeping there until the case—if you have read about the famous case—was over.... And none of them budged until it was over. I was back at school then, I wasn't here.

In 1957 I was offered a scholarship to Ruskin College in Oxford where I did a two-year diploma course in public administration, sociology, psychology, and some economics. TANU and TANU's friends—meaning the labor unions and the TUC, the British Trade Union Congress—gave me the scholarship to Ruskin. TANU had many strong supporters. Joan Wicken[63] was especially supportive, even in finding the college, she was very supportive. Plus others, you know, Billy Humes[?], John Hatch, and a few other people.

There were very few Tanzanian students at Oxford when I was there.... We would meet in London [at] East Africa House. So those few who were TANU members would hold our meetings there.... But, the rallying point was always when Mwalimu was there. Whenever he was there, students from all other parts of England would come, and we would sit and listen to him and shoot questions at him, [and] he would reply.

You know, when you are away from home you tend to think that everything is going wrong; and particularly when you get the bookworm inside you, so you feel either Marx, Engels or somebody, you know, "John Smart," whatever, is much much better. So you feel that everything is going wrong.[64] So whenever Nyerere came...he reassured us that things were going [well] at home. He always had time for students.

In 1960, I met an interesting American group [at Ruskin] who wanted to sponsor Tanzanian students for short courses. So I was offered a scholarship to go to United States, and did one semester, I think it was, at Western Michigan University, Kalamazoo. I studied international relations, and the American group helped me to tour a few states in the United States where I spoke about our country, about our aims and aspirations for in-

---

63 Wicken became Nyerere's personal assistant during the years of his presidency.

64 E. B. M. Barongo quotes extensively from a letter written by an Englishwoman who had hosted Lucy Lameck during an Easter holiday. She praised Lucy for her ability to explain political events in Tanganyika, her willingness to criticize the British government for its failings, and her efforts to educate members of the Labour Party about the need to end colonialism. In addition, wrote this enthusiastic woman, "she explained to us the lives of the everday person and their customs. She taught my children to play and sing in Swahili, she cooked us African food, in short she become one of us whom we liked a lot...." E. B. M. Barongo, *Mkiki wa Siasa Tanganyika* (Dar es Salaam, 1966), 193–95.

dependence. I explained the then constitutional set-up and what TANU was all about, and what we were seeking, and I received a lot of support and encouragement.

In 1960 I returned home and worked with the party for a few months. At that time it was very difficult... because we didn't have any funds.... By the end of that year, I was nominated to Parliament by the president—in accordance with the existing constitution.

It is difficult to explain how and why I became politically active in TANU at such an early age. But I do remember clearly that I resented working under a colonial system because there was very clear discrimination based on color.

For example, African nurses were treated differently from the white nurses. As black nurses, we were given different food, different accommodations, different treatment altogether. We were more or less treated ... like a bunch of bananas, as if we don't exist, as if we were not human. Our working hours were different, our meal times were different, our food was different, the whole attitude towards us was so different. In fact, I would say that it started there because I remember early in 1954, in the hospital in Tanga, we went on strike. We went on strike because the meals were not fit for human consumption.... And we all had money deducted from our stipends and some of us were summoned for immediate dismissal. Some of the girls were sent home. Some of us stuck our necks out and spoke the truth. So I would say ... it is an accumulation of many factors that makes you resent a system. When TANU came, it found a ready market among some of us....

Then you arrive at a point where you feel that you are a second-class citizen in your own country.... We used to have European schools for the [small minority of] European children; we used to have Asian schools for Asians who held the economy of the country in their hands; and we used to have poor, dilapidated African schools. So it is the accumulation of all these factors.... And once you see these things and begin rejecting the system, you begin to wonder whether there is a better world or a better life....

Lucy Selina Lameck was not "typical" of the TANU activists who spearheaded the Women's Section of the 1950s. She completed secondary school, trained as a nurse and acquired further education in Britain and the United States. She was more highly educated than the vast majority of women of her generation, and she was not Muslim. As we will see when we return to her post-independence life history in the final chapter, both of these aspects of her identity faciliated her political career into the late 1980s. She died on March 21, 1992, of complications related to liver disease.

The stories and backgrounds of these and other Moshi-based activists contribute to an understanding of women's relationships to TANU and nationalist consciousness outside the capital. As a group, Moshi activists were slightly younger and had more years of schooling than was the norm for Dar es Salaam activists. For those who had grown up on Kilimanjaro, the availability of primary schools, parental (and especially father's) interest in the education of their children, and an older average age of marriage no doubt contributed to higher levels of education. For example, Nsiana Nathan Njau (b. 1932),[65] whose father was a primary school teacher and later Lutheran evangelist, attended school in Machame until 1948, when she went to Dar es Salaam for four years' nursing and midwifery training at Muhimbili Hospital. It was while she was in Dar es Salaam that she first learned of TANU; but she didn't join until 1958, when she and her husband (a medical officer who later became an administrative officer in the government) were living and working in Kibonde village in Kigoma. Although she worked for the party and attended meetings, Mrs. Njau confirmed that in Dar es Salaam the uneducated women were the most active, "and especially the unmarried ones who were able to travel without any problems; because if you have a husband you can't leave the house; your husband can say 'stay.' Women without husbands could go anywhere, even on long journeys." Nor did Mrs. Njau belong to any *ngoma* group, "because [her] job as a nurse made it impossible." In her view, the Lutheran church supported TANU and independence. Mrs. Njau, who retired from nursing in 1985, has six children and eight grandchildren.

As for the women who were raised outside the Kilimanjaro region, their fathers' educational level and employment seem to have been key factors in their own educational opportunities. Six Moshi activists held jobs in the formal sector as adults, and brought to their political commitments direct experience of racial and sex discrimination at their places of work. There were also fewer divorces and more children among the Moshi TANU activists, as well as greater religious diversity. Muslims, Catholics and Lutherans were all represented, and most saw their religion as compatible with and reinforcing their political convictions, even as some noted that particular religious leaders and, in some cases, church policy called for neutrality if not hostility toward Nyerere and TANU.

While some Moshi activists talked about their participation in dance groups (which raised money for TANU and expressed party solidarity), and in the TANU Youth League and choir, others extended the list of responsibilities women undertook for TANU. Some of these, such as housing and feeding Nyerere and other leaders, were obviously related to the needs of TANU organizers on tour. Others, such as "hiding" and "guarding" Nyerere, reflect the particular circumstances in a region where political forces bent on undermining or discrediting TANU were active. Still others tapped into the skills of individuals: translating from Swahili into Maasai and typing and undertaking other office work for the party.

Yet if there were clear differences in activist life course profiles, there were also commonalities in background and experience that, I argue, predisposed these women to "nationalist" thinking and behavior. Two of these commonalities, "mixed" ethnic identity and relative mobility, stand out. The reality of mixed ethnic identity (whether through their parents' or their own marriages) flew in the face of colonial intentions to freeze tribal identities and control people accordingly. Several women activists experienced considerable mobility within the region and the country relative to their age cohort. For several women, these experiences contributed to a sense of themselves—a sense of identity—that included being able to "see"

---

[65] Anita Urasa and I interviewed Mrs. Njau at the UWT office in Moshi on October 18, 1988.

from marginal standpoints of several kinds.[66] While these aspects of a "national" consciousness were critical to TANU's success in building a nationalist movement, they became far less relevant to Nyerere's post-independence conception of "nation building."

Higher levels of formal education meant that several of the Moshi women activists successfully made the transition from preindependence mobilizing activities to the organizational and bureaucratic work of TANU as a ruling party and UWT as the post-independence incarnation of the TANU Women's Section. They enjoyed the experiences of travel abroad for conferences and "study tours." They were concerned about the social and economic problems of girls and women, and children generally, and worried about changes they saw, often attributing difficulties to moral drift of various kinds, including the breakdown of familial and religious authority over children. Indeed, at various points, their concerns seemed reminiscent of those of colonial social welfare officers thirty years before. We shall return to this shift in the postscript.

---

[66]   To be the daughter of a poor and "lesser" chief or to be the daughter of a chief who divorces your mother is, for example, as likely to produce a "marginal" standpoint as is "mixed" parentage and extensive mobility.

7

Nationalism in the Hinterland: Mwanza

Tie two kangas at the waist, very tight![1]

It has been noticed recently that members of the TANU have been wearing distinctive dress signifying association with TANU. I particularly refer to the green dresses worn by lady members at the Kigoma Railway Station on the 15th November.[2]

Colonial administrators of the early 1950s regarded Moshi District as advanced and reasonably manageable in spite of the uneasy relationship between locally and nationally focused Chagga politics. In contrast, officials were sufficiently alarmed by political activities in Lake Province (including the town of Mwanza) to prohibit TANU branches there. Shinyanga DO Birkett's wife Ursula had written home in March 1958 that whites might soon be "sleeping with loaded guns."[3]

In his study of local politics in Sukumaland, Andrew Maguire details the widespread Sukuma hostility to the imposition of local government "reforms," including the unpopular multiracial councils and the more general economic "development" programs, especially compulsory destocking and cattle dipping. Maguire maintains that this hostility "fostered the most active and politically oriented African voluntary associations in Tanganyika" during the decade before TANU's for-

---

[1] In Swahili, "Walijifungwa kibwebe haswa" means to do what you need to do and be strong in difficult times. This, said Pili Juma, characterized women's actions with respect to TANU and the anticolonial struggle. Nyerere used the phrase frequently as well. Interview with Pili Juma, CCM headquarters, Mwanza, November 21, 1988.

[2] Assistant Superintendent of Police, Kigoma, to District Chair, TANU, Ujiji, 21 November 1958. Ref. No. s/14, TNA. The Tanganyika African Association, Kigoma A6/5.

[3] Ursula Birkett's letter, 15 March 1958, RH.

mation in 1954.[4] Just as nationalist organizing in Kilimanjaro subverted Chagga political organization, it was dance and work societies in Mwanza that cut across colonial divisions and united people from different chiefdoms, giving the Sukuma what Maguire called "built-in receptivity" to associations promoting economic cooperation and nationalist politics.[5]

An additional factor contributed greatly to the foundations of nationalism in the area: "Swahili traders"—meaning Africans speaking Swahili as their first language—had arrived in Sukumaland to establish outposts in the late nineteenth century. Along with mission-educated men, "Swahili-speaking townsmen with a sophistication born of travel, trade and perhaps a smattering of Koranic education" constituted, in Maguire's view, "the transitionals"—the nonrural, nontraditional "middle level local elite so critically important to the early stages of the development of nationalist organizations."[6]

But Maguire apparently overlooked women's presence in those transtribal dance and work societies (or in parallel organizations), ignoring the women among the "Swahili-speaking townsmen" living in Mwanza. Maguire's reasons for downplaying the role of TANU women included their lack of traditional authority and their lower levels of education compared to men. His description of women's presence at TANU events is classic: "Self-effacing and reticent, they sit together at the back of TANU rallies and meetings, nursing their children, talking among themselves, but never participating (except for traditional ululations of approval) in the public discussion."[7] Citing the "thirty active members" of the TANU women's section in Mwanza as exceptions, Maguire goes on to explain that political women were anomalies:

> The only really active women have been the handful of leaders who, through educational or vocational experience, or *peculiarities of personal and family life* [my emphasis], have forged for themselves a new and entirely untraditional type of role. Such leaders live, usually, in the major towns and trading centers where they have had some success with activities which include (in addition to political education) domestic science, health, childcare and literacy.[8]

Maguire's male Sukuma with their "built-in receptivity" to transtribal political organizing, and the "transitionals" of Mwanza town so important to the emergence of nationalism in the area, become anomalies in their female form. These women were not anomalies, of course, as this chapter seeks to demonstrate.

Politics, Prostitution, and Women in Mwanza

Formed in Feburary 1945, the Mwanza branch of the TAA quickly became the town's most important African association and was diverse from its beginnings. Members

4   G. Andrew Maguire, *Toward "Uhuru" in Tanzania: The Politics of Participation* (Cambridge, 1969), xxv.

5   Ibid., xxviii.

6   Ibid., 4 n.2, and 59.

7   Ibid., 319.

8   Ibid., and note 2.

included Muslim and non-Muslim, Sukuma and non-Sukuma, and people with varying degrees of education; they were concerned with issues of welfare, rights, and advancement for both urban and rural Africans.[9] In addition, however, the Mwanza TAA branch was unusually diverse in having women members.[10]

By the early 1950s, TAA was, from the perspective of Sukumaland and Mwanza, "perhaps the single most powerful, anticolonial political force in Tanganyika," while the chiefs and other native authorities fell into further disrepute for their close identification with the colonial administration.[11] The strongest evidence of TAA's importance in Lake Province was the administration's decision to ban the opening of TANU branches there. According to Governor Twining, this decision was necessary because "the leaders were definitely subversive and misapplied the Union's funds."[12] With the striking combination of hostility toward TANU and hopeful naivete that characterized his leadership, the governor continued:

> We are taking steps to discredit the Union whenever there is cause to do so, such as the offence which Julius [Nyerere] gave to a large number of people in the Lake Province in one area by appearing on the platform with a well known prostitute.[13]

Whether Maguire's phrase, "peculiarities of personal and family life," was intended as a euphemistic suggestion that women involved in politics were likely to be prostitutes, the association of Lake Province women, particularly Haya women, with prostitution swept through the British colonial period like a psychological epidemic. As a result, it has also dominated scholarly discussions of women in the area to the exclusion of virtually all other topics. While a detailed discussion of the debate between European and African men over Haya women and prostitution is beyond the scope of this study, the furor raised in Mwanza had consequences for women engaged in nationalist politics.

In a region where women and girls exercised few rights over their own person,[14] the fact that a considerable number had left their home areas to sell sex and other domestic services elsewhere had become a source of great concern to many Africans by the late 1940s. The Bahaya Control Union of Prostitution was established in villages, and a Haya man authored and published a self-help advice book for Haya men and women on stopping prostitution, entitled "To Put Buhaya on the Right Path."[15]

In 1949, the Mwanza Branch of the Bahaya Union sought permission from the DC, Mwanza, to return Haya prostitutes in the town to Bukoba, and to prevent the

---

9   Ibid., 65.

10   All of the TANU activists I interviewed in November 1988, who had lived in Mwanza in the early 1950s, made a point of their involvement in TAA prior to joining TANU. Mwanza's Sukuma Union, founded in 1945, also had women members, setting an entrance fee at Shs. 1/ per month for men and half that for women (ibid., 79).

11   Maguire emphasizes that TAA Mwanza grew and developed its militant leadership, extensive membership and regular meeting schedule with no help from TAA territorial headquarters in Dar es Salaam. Indeed the Dar es Salaam TAA was practically moribund by late 1952 (ibid., 113, 131).

12   Twining to Alan Lennox-Boyd, M.P., Colonial Office, GH. 1033/2, Secret, 31 October 1955, PRO.

13   Ibid.

14   Swantz, *Women in Development*, 50–52.

15   Larsson, *Conversion to Greater Freedom*, 132–33.

arrival of others.[16] Multiple attempts on the part of Bahaya Union branches to coordinate efforts to prevent "prostitutes or rather the *Bahaya Women*"[17] from leaving Bukoba, "unless certified as not a 'PROSTITUTE'" [word in capitals and red type][18] and to return Haya women deemed prostitutes to Buhaya, point to the magnitude of concern and anxiety focused on the issue. In June 1950, Governor Twining added the fuel of humiliation and insult to the Bahaya antiprostitution campaign when he told a large crowd in Bukoba that "the Haya had a bad reputation in the rest of East Africa because of the travelling prostitutes."[19]

In light of the governor's inflammatory remark, members of the Bahaya Union were angered by the administration's refusal either to outlaw "commercial prostitution," or, failing that, to permit the Bukoba Native Authorities to act against prostitutes as they saw fit. In the Union's view, commercial prostitution was causing depopulation, famine, the destruction of marriage contracts, and the spread of venereal disease.[20] Arguing that commercial prostitution was a criminal offense and its practioners hardened criminals, they reasoned that since no criminal exercised freedom of movement, neither should a prostitute "BE GIVEN ANY FREEDOM" [to travel outside her own district].[21]

In Mwanza, D.W.A. Stones warned Bahaya Union members that they could be charged with assault if they forcibly removed alleged prostitutes from the town, and reminded them that a Haya woman in Dar es Salaam had successfully sued a Bahaya Union member there for defamation of character. Haya women, he cautioned, could not be

> "sent away from Mwanza"... merely because your Union desires it, and complains about them. I would remind you that responsibility for their trade lies with the men who create the demand.[22]

Undeterred, the Union wrote a lengthy plea to "the Hon. Member for Local Government," warning of rapidly deteriorating conditions and urging the government to require the repatriation to Bukoba of "all the Bahaya women prostitutes all over the Territory."[23] In the Union's view, the government's position amounted to complicity in the destruction of Haya society. There was even a rumor that the government needed prostitute traffic, a traffic set at 5,000 women, to make the East African Railway and Harbors profitable. Warning of "riots and revolutions" if the government did not act, of the increasing enmity be-

---

[16]   Sec. of Bahaya Union, Mwanza, to DC, Mwanza, 19 October 1949, Ref. No. BU/1/149. In his reply, the DC expressed sympathy with the Union's aims, but said that the police could only enforce existing laws (against soliciting and annoyance). DC, Mwanza, to Bahaya Union, Mwanza, 11 November 1949, Ref. 103/8/149, TNA A/6/6.

[17]   Sec. of Bahaya Union to DC, Mwanza, 30 May 1950 Ref. No. Bu/1/159, TNA A/6/6.

[18]   Ibid.

[19]   Larsson, *Conversion to Greater Freedom*, 133, citing DC to PC, Bukoba, 19/6 1950.

[20]   Letter from the Bahaya Union, Mwanza branch, to Chief Secretary, Dar es Salaam, 21/10 1950, cited in Larsson, *Conversion to Greater Freedom*, 136–37.

[21]   Letter signed Y. I. S. Bairu, Pres.; Z. G. Kashumba, Treas., and J. P. Kamuhabwa, Member, TNA A6/6.

[22]   DC to Bahaya Union, 8 March 1951, 103/8/191, TNA A6/6.

[23]   Bahaya Union, Mwanza, to Hon. MLG, Ref. No. BUM/3/61, 20 March 1951, TNA A6/6.

tween Haya men and women, and of the "epidemic" nature of the problem, the Union insisted that if the government didn't outlaw prostitution, children would no longer get married and women would "just go off to get rich."[24] Similar complaints about Luo girls coming to Mwanza as prostitutes were registered by the Ramogi African Welfare Association,[25] but the colonial authorities refused to accede to the demands for either territorial laws or tribal orders banning "commercial prostitution."

The intense if inconclusive debate over prostitution is relevant to the lives of TANU women activists in Mwanza because the port city was one of its major nodes; and in the early 1950s, the conflict between local and native authorities and the colonial administration over prostitution was as serious as any occuring at the time. At the heart of this struggle was whether or not Haya men had the right to control the movements of Haya women, and by extension, the relative freedom African women could exercise under British-inspired legal codes. While it was commonplace among Africans and non-Africans to assume that unmarried women and girls living in towns without a husband or other family members were prostitutes, the intensity of the issue in Mwanza had particular consequences for women residing there. Many TANU activists spoke of being called "prostitutes." Whether any of the women I interviewed had ever engaged in prostitution,[26] all women ran the risk of being called prostitutes if they lived in towns, attended public meetings, sold and kept TANU cards, solicited for the party door to door (especially at night), cooked for and housed TANU leaders, or sang and danced to celebrate and to raise money for the party.

TANU Women in Mwanza

I sought to interview women TANU activists in Mwanza to broaden my understanding of women's nationalist politicization in Tanganyika. But the logistics of conducting life history research there proved difficult from the outset. First, both road and air travel at this time (November 1988) had their complications. Even after a friend with "know-who" intervened to enable me to reserve and use a seat on an ATC flight, Mwanza was not a place I knew; nor did I know people there. My only contacts were the sister-in-law of a University of Dar es Salaam colleague, and the UWT district secretary to whom I had written about my work. Although both provided invaluable assistance, my limited contacts and limited time produced interviews of less depth than those conducted elsewhere. Moreover, my introduction to TANU women through the UWT district secretary, an established authority figure, and her presence at many of the interviews, affected the interview atmosphere and women's responses. For example, in addition to providing introductions, the UWT secretary sometimes offered answers to or comments on questions before the person being interviewed was able to respond. On other occasions, I

---

[24] Ibid.

[25] Minutes from meeting, 9 Dec. 1951, TNA A6/6.

[26] I did not ask this question.

sensed that interviewees were reluctant to offer any but the blandest answers to questions that called for assessment, opinion, or comparison.

Nevertheless, several important points of interest emerge. Unlike women in Moshi or Dar es Salaam, many activists in Mwanza were members of the town's strong and vocal TAA branch in the early 1950s. Although they became firm supporters of Nyerere, their politicization preceded his visits to the area, and their experiences frequently reflected the need for secret organizing during the period when TANU was banned from the province. In addition, Mwanza activists were often still involved in *ngoma* groups of the kind that made performance central to TANU mobilizing in the 1950s. They were therefore able to provide examples of songs that I was unable to record elsewhere, and plays that popularized Nyerere's visits to Mwanza.

At the same time, the life histories of Mwanza activists reinforce a sense of the importance of transtribal identities, experiences, and women's communities that already linked narrators in Moshi and Dar es Salaam. The abbreviated life histories presented here capture the core and the range of women's sense of nationalism and nationalist activity in Mwanza.

Agnes Sahani[27]

Widely acknowledged as Mwanza's most distinguished nationalist activist, Agnes Sahani was also the most reluctant to discuss her past or women's political actions in any but the most general terms. In the days that followed our interview, Mrs. Sahani was present at several other interviews I conducted in Mwanza.

Agnes Geikwa Sahani was born in Kwimba District, Mwanza Province, in 1918, the only child of Sahani Ugolo Chenya, a farmer, and a soldier in the "war of 1914," and Kagura Kwiede, also a farmer. While she was growing up, they lived near the Protestant mission at Kijima. Agnes attended mission school there for about four years. When she was twenty years old, she was married to Jeromini Basunji, a veterinary officer, and gave birth to one child, who died. "I never stayed for a long time with the husband," she added. Although the timing is not clear, Mrs. Sahani eventually moved to Mwanza where she worked at the hospital as an assistant and child minder for nine years. As she explained at a much later point in the interview, she was forced to leave this job because of her politics:

> One time I took part in a meeting and was late for work. Then I disagreed with the woman who was our boss. After we disagreed, many things followed. She told me, "If you want the party, you can leave your work and follow the party." Then she kept on asking me whether I preferred the party or my job. When I responded, she said "I see you are angry; go take

27   Interview with Agnes Sahani, CCM Building, Liberty Street, Pamba, Mwanza, November 19, 1988. Mwanza's CCM chairman, who was among the many people to name Mrs. Sahani as the most important person to interview, also informed me that Mrs. Sahani had gone with Paul Bomani to Butiama to see Nyerere just after Nyerere's return from Edinburgh. They had gone, he said, to ask Nyerere to work politically with the cotton cooperative society. He also said that Mrs. Sahani had visited New York, Washington, DC, Alabama, New Mexico and California in 1978, as a guest of Paul Bomani.

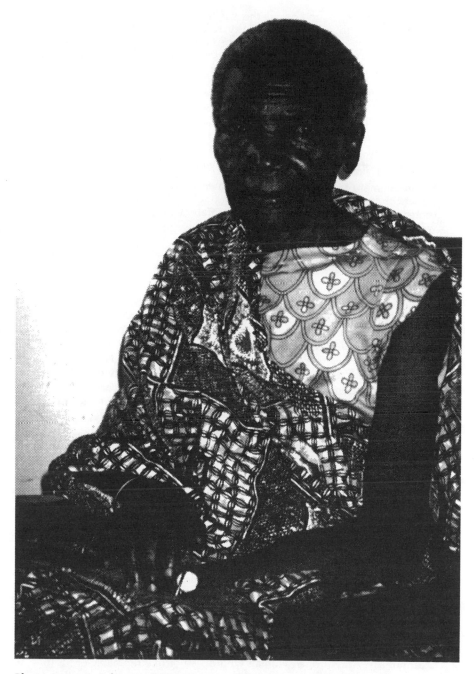

Photo 8: Agnes Sahani in 1988. Courtesy of Susan Geiger, photographer.

a walk by the road, then come back to work." So I decided it was better to go home.

Later, I went back and asked them if there was a letter saying I was fired and if so, to give it to me. They refused, and refused to pay me, saying that they couldn't pay me because I had left work on my own accord. Stopped work? Well, I didn't stop work. Weren't they the ones that told me to go and take a walk by the road?

Agnes Sahani was on the TAA advisory committee and, later, a strong TANU activist. "I was not a visitor to politics," she said. "I thought it was good to participate in the politics of my country, and wanted to cooperate with my compatriots to achieve independence and build our nation." Her response to my question about what she thought women might gain from joining TANU was characteristic of her sense of the importance of unity and party loyalty:

We are women, and because we are women we must be ready to join our leaders, the men and the women of Tanganyika. That is to say, we must be united.... Women's problems were no different from men's, because we were all citizens. All of us were together....

TANU really helped us women, because many of us didn't understand many things; the party helped us.... Many women also assisted in administrative matters. [Men and women] never left each other; we were together; until now, we are united.

When I asked Mrs. Sahani to explain the kind of work she did with TANU, she replied, "I am following our affairs—how it was and our politics. I cannot coin anything to give as an example on my own. I saw how we were progressing. I can only say what I saw. I don't want to guess." I mentioned that I had been told that she had gone to see Nyerere at Butiama and asked if she could tell me about that. Mrs. Sahani replied, "That was about farming, about cooperatives.... The Asians used to buy our cotton. But we wanted to grow, harvest, and market it ourselves, not sell through middlemen. I participated in the Lake Province African Growers Association led by Mr. Bomani."

Mrs. Sahani said that her life since independence has been good. "I have no problems. I cooperate well with fellow party members and all the leaders of Tanzania." In those years, she has been chair of a UWT branch, later provincial chair of UWT and a TANU board member. "In the TANU board we all cooperate and work together. I still participate; I have not stopped."

I don't see that women have any particular problems, because we participate in anything we want to—in the cooperatives, in adult education—we participate in everything equally. Maybe some women have problems. Personally, I don't see any. There aren't any political problems because women are given equal opportunity with men in education. In the colonial period, many women could not get education; but with independence, the door opened for women's education equally with men.

Mrs. Sahani was circumspect in her comparison of the TANU activism of educated and less educated women.

I cannot say. An educated woman who does not like the party or an uneducated one who likes party matters—I think everybody is entitled to their own opinion. But there are some women with whom we work who are educated and in leadership positions who teach us about party matters, and some who are not; you cannot say that educated women don't like the party, because it is the party that defends them. How can they dislike the party? The party is the defender of all women.

Aziza Lucas[28]

Aziza Lucas was born in Ilemara, Mwanza District, in 1928. Her father, Lucas Maneno, was from Ukerewe; her mother was from Sukumaland. They were farmers, and Bi Aziza was one of eleven children—six brothers and five sisters, one of whom died. Bi Aziza remembered her childhood as a time when the wisdom and authority of elders was respected, and you obeyed your parents. Life was good because her parents provided. Bi Aziza did not go to school and was married to Shaban Magi when she was about twenty-five. At that time, she moved to Number 054 A. Kimumba (Mwanza town) where her husband sold timber. She could not cultivate any more because she had no land in the city.

Bi Aziza joined TANU with her husband in 1954. "In the evening," she stated, "I used to go secretly to sell [party] cards without being seen. The leaders here were Paul Bomani and [Isaac Bhoke] Munanka." Along with Saadani Abdu Kandoro, Paul Bomani and Isaac Bhoke Munanka were instrumental in bringing TAA to the political forefront in the early 1950s.[29] Both Bi Aziza and her husband were very enthusiastic about TANU.

> Just to hear that we too could rule ourselves. You know, when you are a free person, you can do your work with one heart, without problems. Our hope was that the people of Tanganyika would be one and remain united without discrimination. As for women, we hoped that when we got self-rule, we would not be oppressed by men, like in the past. We would be free to go anywhere.
>
> For example, my husband didn't allow me to go to the market. I was just sitting while this man brings food, I go to the kitchen and cook, we eat. After independence our men were made to understand that women are the same as men.... But in the past, even going to a neighbor's house, you had to ask for permission from your husband. It was just like slavery....

When Bi Aziza began to talk about her leadership role in the Mwanza Women's Section of TANU, and about welcoming Bibi Titi when she came, the UWT secretary, who was present at this interview, turned the discussion to "helping women." Bi Aziza obliged by explaining that the UWT members cultivated farms together and had opened a tailoring shop. "And adult education?" urged the UWT district secretary:

---

[28] Interview with Aziza Lucas, Mwanza, November 21, 1988.

[29] Paul Bomani was a major figure in the principal African associations of the area. He led the cooperative movement, became president of the Sukuma Union in 1951, and president of TAA in 1952. At the same time, he was a member of the Mwanza Township Authority and the Lake Province Council. For further information on all three men, see Maguire, *Toward "Uhuru"*, 136–37.

And adult education, even me, I managed to get some education, some basic reading skills. And before, I never knew [how to read]. But after independence and the excitement with UWT, we too joined development.... We were given the UWT organization to teach us and to get us out of ignorance.

"And given a representative?" coached the secretary. "And given representation and others even became members of parliament and some women became secretaries. All of this was because of— But before, women could not stand in front of men, even remotely, to speak up."

Asked about other TANU activists in Mwanza, Bi Aziza mentioned Binti Mwajuma Msafiri, Tatu Mohamed, Pili Juma, Mwatumu Mto and Mama Nyembo. "Those are the ones we were with." She went on to credit TANU, again, for educating women and providing them with leadership positions. As for women's contributions to TANU, Bi Aziza talked about active attendance at meetings, cooking food, and hosting leaders. "For example, most of our leaders came to my place. We used to do this and participate in meetings, in elections; and women could sit in the meetings from beginning to end. The men could not ask us where we had been. No."

Leader of an *ngoma* group, "Walumba Siti," Bi Aziza, a Muslim, expressed the view that religion and the struggle for independence were different things. "Because one is struggling for your heart so that you can go to heaven, to God, and politics is here on earth."[30]

As for contemporary problems, Bi Aziza felt that rural women had the most difficulty and hardest work to do—certainly their struggle was harder than hers in town. "Really, my life is good. Because if I had a bad life, I would have withered and grown very old with the age I have now. I wouldn't even be able to do anything. But I still have enough strength [to work]." When she began to add that in the past, if your husband mistreated you you had no where to go, the secretary intervened again. "And then, during that time [before independence], there were no implements to assist the [farming] woman. You had to do all your work with your hands; you had to thrash, grind, with your hands. But now, although they have problems in the villages, look, they have machines, isn't that true Mama Lucas? Isn't there a difference [even] in the villages?" Bi Aziza agreed, but added that many women did not live close enough to the machines. She had, however, gotten the point. "It is much better now. Even some women are opening up their own shops, running their own lives."

Although she had no children of her own, Bi Aziza had cared for her brothers' children. She returned to the topic of greater independence for women.

For us old people, things have really gone up. Things have changed. I can't wait for the husband to bring me anything anymore. God blessed me and I got a small kiosk here but it needs renovation. It was a good building in the past, but now I want a modern one.

---

30   The UWT secretary added that TANU insisted strongly that religion should not matter, which was why "people couldn't notice" if religious groups helped or hindered the independence struggle. "Of course," she continued, shifting the focus to her own generation, "we were students at that time. Our headmistress and our teachers were mostly indifferent to TANU. Sometimes we were not allowed to listen to the radio or speeches. Later, we learned that they were preventing us in the name of UTP. We didn't notice this because they were Catholics."

Tunu Nyembo[31]

My name is Tunu. Mrs. Tunu Nyembo. I am a Zaramo from Dar es Salaam; but I was born here in Mwanza, Rufiji Road, in 1928. My father, Selemani, was a mason. He built the houses at Bwiru Secondary School. My mother, Fatuma, was a farmer. I had three sisters and three brothers who have all died.

When I was a child, my life wasn't too hard because as I've said, my father was a mason. I went to religious school until I got my first period. I was twenty-one years old when Mr. Nyembo married me. We moved to Dar es Salaam for a while and later returned here.

Initially, my husband was a tailor; then he became the first secretary of TANU. I just farmed. I was involved in TAA, as a representative; that was around 1950 here in Mwanza.

I heard of TANU for the first time in 1954 here in Mwanza. Initially, there was some activity in 1952, if I remember correctly. This man came to give cards in secret, and the cards were given from my house because he was staying there. The cards were two shillings each. This continued until my husband was accused by the government. They were caught—my husband, Munanka and Agustini. Munanka and Agustini were jailed; my husband was fined.

Even with all this, I carried on.... If you were caught with a card you could be punished and anything could be done to you. It went on like that until Mwalimu went to UNO. When he came back in 1956 we were given power. I think it was 1956; but I might be wrong because it has been a long time.... Later, we were brought together for independence and the flag went up in 1961. It was 1961, wasn't it?

Colonialism was not all bad, but everyone wants the same rights. We wanted to be independent and have our rights. I thought freedom would bring equality to the Tanzanians. Equality as you see it now, we women can get work in offices, some become ministers; we can do whatever men do.

Some of us had studied religion and when adult education started, we learned how to read. Previously, we could only be told and we would sign with our thumb. You put ink on your thumb and then press the paper. But now we hold a pencil and sign our names.

At that time, women were given positions in TANU. Some were representatives, some became ministers. We voted, we mixed with the men and advised each other. I think that was important. We women also did things for ourselves. We opened our stores; we made our child care centers.

Women were strong at that time.... Many of them have died. Those who are still alive are Mama Ntungi, Zuhuru Musa, Agnes Sahani, Aziz Lucas, Pili Juma, Chiku Mzee, and others like Shera Waraga, Mwamvua Kibonge, Mwajuma Msafiri. These are the ones we worked with.

Besides my involvement with TANU at that time, I had my *ngoma* group and until now, I am chairman of "Rumba City." We received all the important people who came and we were invited to all national ceremonies. We also performed at weddings.

I am a Muslim. Religion didn't harm the fight for independence. Christians and Muslims—we were all the same. We all worked together. As for

---

[31] Interview with Tunu Nyembo, Mtaa wa Makongoro, Isamilo, November 21, 1988.

me, life is good now except there is pain as age sets in. Since independence, I've just been doing business. We have had cooperative shops. We come together in groups of twenty, thirty, and forty. When we do well, we divide the profits and continue. But when you get older, you get problems. Your feet ache; sometimes your eyes don't work right. So this stops you from doing business.

I don't have any children. I had one; it died.

Let me sing you a song that our group performs:

> Reading and writing is the shield of an African
> When the colonist gets here, seeds will shake
> When he sees Nyerere has managed Tanzania
> Women, let us go read and write
> The shield of an African
> The shield of an African
> When the colonialist gets here, seeds will shake
> When the colonialist gets here, seeds will shake
> When he sees Nyerere has managed Tanzania.

Halima Ntungi[32]

My name is Halima Ntungi. I was born in Mwanza. I don't know what year I was born and in those days, parents didn't send their children to school. At the time of the first war, I was already born. I am Sukuma. My father, Ntungi, was a chief. My mother, Nzilani, was a farmer. I had brothers and sisters, but I am the only one remaining.

When I was very young, my mother left to marry someone else and I was brought up by my grandmother. After the war, she came back and took me to live with her until I got married here to a prison guard, Hassani, when I was eighteen. I had two children with him, and we travelled to Dar es Salaam and Tanga before coming back here. I continued to live here after I left my husband. I built this house with my own hands.

I joined TANU when it was called TAA. And I am still in CCM. When the president [Nyerere] came to Mwanza in 1958, I received my TANU card from his hand. I was very excited by the news of his arrival. I had seen all the suffering that happened during colonial times. The colonialists were torturing our elders and it pained me. I knew it was better to have independence. With independence we would be human also; we could govern ourselves and be independent.

Colonialism was bad. There was no peace. For example, you couldn't own anything without being asked where you got it. And I am a human being who works! You couldn't walk freely. Wherever you went, you were asked where you were going. There were a lot of problems. I thought independence would bring the things we have: everyone has his space; you govern yourself independently; you are able to use your possessions freely without any worries.

For women, participating in TANU was like being married. Before that, you aren't really a woman yet. What I mean is that in joining TANU you get to decide issues together, have equal access to work. Now we work in

---

32   Interview with Halima Ntungi, Mtaa wa Mkanyenye, Mbugani, November 22, 1988.

the same places with our men. The wife works, and the husband works. During colonialism a woman only had work in the kitchen....

Women did very important work for the party. We bought more party cards than men! And we voted. I was a leader of the Women's Section and I was elected to the advisory committee of the region. I was also on the advisory committee of the district. For six years, I was TANU branch chairman; then I became a councillor for four years. Then I became the chairman of UWT for two years—the chairman of the district. Now I am a representative of the CCM for the region....

I have also been dancing *lelemama* since I was a child. I am the chairman of an *ngoma* group called "Wisdom Rose." It is still here. I have one child; the other one died. And seven grandchildren—three girls and four boys. Let me share two songs with you:

> Tax for us is coming, aaa
> Cattle tax, leave us
> Knock knock, Mr. Governor. We are coming, aaa
> Cattle tax, leave us
> We are asking help from all Africans
> Our property is cattle
> White people help, we the whole of Africa
> Our property is cattle
> We are asking for help to be forgiven, ee-aaa
> Cattle tax leave us

> Take.... weeee
> to ask the government
> take ...
> we praise the government.

It has been a long time, and in those days we had our own choir. The Youth Leaguers used to be young. Now they've all lost all their teeth!

> Tanganyika, my country, I love it very much
> Tanganyika, my country, I love it very much
> With its goats and its cows, and all that is in it is ours.
> This is our party that speaks for us
> Tanganyika, what Africa, our property
> Please, Afrikeni, stop it, rejoice in it
> Let's do our work with one purpose.

> We give thanks, we praise the government
> We give thanks, we praise the government
> Lord protect it, to leave our cows
> Lord protect it, to leave our cows.

Mwajuma Msafiri[33]

Mwajuma Msafiri was born in Dar es Salaam in 1933 and referred to herself as a Bwadi from Kigoma, Lake Tanganyika. Her father, Msafiri, was a German

---

[33] Interview with Mwajuma Msafiri, Uhuru Street, Mbugani, Mwanza, November 22, 1988.

guard and her mother, Tausi, a farmer. Bi Mwajuma had four brothers and two sisters, one of whom died. She attended Koranic school for about two years at which point, she says, "I had learned enough about praying. Once you knew about your religion and what it did, then it was enough." At the age of thirteen, Bi Mwajuma was married to Mohammed Said, a businessman. They moved to Bukoba where her work was to "cook, embroider cloth, and plait palm leaves." Then they moved back to Dar es Salaam until 1959, when they moved to Mwanza.

Bi Mwajuma first heard about TANU while she still lived in Dar es Salaam. But in 1954, she says, she was not yet eighteen (a discrepancy with her stated birth date) and was therefore too young to get a card even though she wanted to buy one.

I heard about TANU when the president came to Dar es Salaam in 1954. A person called Debe Moja—his name was Athumani Omari. Debe Moja—there were people who carried loads and we called them Debe Moja [*debe moja* in Swahili, means one four-gallon tin]—was getting water, so he called me and told me to come and see someone who has come to give TANU cards. He told me that the president would be passing by on Sunday, so he would come to get me to see him. So he passed by because my house was not far from the road to Msimbazi.

The president had public meetings at Mnazi Moja and we would go. I never stayed behind. We would always go, right up until the organizations for women and for parents were formed. When they wanted women to join the party, Titi Mohamed was found. She is the one who united the women of Tanzania.

Women really gave the most to fight the colonist. "We tied two kangas at the waist very tight," you see, until we got our independence. A lot of us joined and fought, along with making joyful and approving noises [*vifijo na vigelegele*] until we got independence. We took out TANU cards, UWT cards, parent association cards.

Women joined the TANU Youth League. Even now, there is this lady from the TANU Youth League. She passed here, but her condition is not too good. They used to wear those green uniforms when they were in TANU Youth League. And when the president came, they would be there to receive him; they were like what police are now....

There were more women in TANU because they liked the party ... more than the men. Some men were still refusing to get cards because the colonialists would fire them from their work. They were scared of being fired; but the women were not scared. They would get the card and go hide it.

Colonialism was not good. Life was not good; people were not free; we could not even get schools. The colonialist didn't care about schools for [African] children or about development. I tell you, the colonialist just wanted it all for himself.... In those days, there were no women working in offices, not even one. Only men worked there and then only if they had studied to Standard IV or Standard VIII. Then they could work in an office—wearing shorts, not trousers like "the master."

But now, women are ministers, we are in hospitals, we go to Europe, we go everywhere.... We see ourselves as complete Tanzanians. Before independence, women had to stay home.... So by the time she has a child, she is already old. When she is married, she is already old; she does not have any understanding of the world; she just sits around. She goes to the man and stays in. The man works, maybe only earning six shillings. So life is hard, because that's how life under colonialism was.

When I came to Mwanza from Dar es Salaam in 1959, I found many strong women. Mama Sahani, Mama Ntungi, Tatu Mzee, Chiku Mzee. I found Mama Ntungi working a lot with TANU; I found Mama Waraga and another lady called Mama Salama in TANU Youth League. I found Rukia Kassim in TANU Youth League; also Aziza binti Rajabu, who is now dead. I tell you, a lot of women. Mama Rahima who is also dead was with TANU Youth League. And another one, Binti Faraji, she too is dead. I am naming those who worked; those who worked every day....

I worked with the party and then with UWT. I worked with the parent section and until today, I am still working. I was chosen here in this TANU branch, then I was on the advisory committee for the subdistrict; then I was chosen to be in the district and then I was the vice-chairman of the district UWT. Now I am the chairman.

I am Muslim, but religion had nothing to do with independence.... Religion and the party did not touch each other, even a little bit....

My life since independence has been good. We continue our development, to move forward. But ... we have problems because the economic situation is not good. That is about the development of the country; when it is good, then life will continue to change.

Pili Juma[34]

Pili Juma, who identified herself as Manyema and who was fifty-six in 1988, was born in Mwanza town. Her father, Juma Mirambo, a mason and builder, died when Pili was seven years old, leaving her mother, Aziza, to care for four children. Bi Pili went to Mwanza town school and when she finished, to Tabora Girls School where she completed Standard VIII in 1948. When she was twenty-one, she got married to Ali Mohammed and remained in Kirumba, Mwanza. Her husband worked as a government mechanic.

Bi Pili first heard about TANU "here and there" in 1954 but did not understand much about it since she was essentially staying inside and her husband did not want her to participate in any political organizations.

I heard about it from the husbands of my friends when they passed by talking, while we were sitting. They would talk, and you would hear. I got very excited by the news and my heart felt longing. Why shouldn't I know about this? It meant that I had the heart to want to know what TANU's purpose was.

"At the time, colonialism was bullying us too much," Bi Pili continued. Elders were whipped and tied with rope, and she herself was harrassed by men in the colonial police force when she went to school. Like many other women activists, Bi Pili pointed out that women could never get jobs for pay before independence and that they had few rights. "But TANU decided that all humans are equal—all become equal."

---

[34] Interview with Pili Juma, Kirumba, Mwanza, November 21, 1988.

Pili Juma echoed the view that women were really the ones who brought freedom to Tanganyika. "They tied two kangas at the waist very tight." They did what
had to be done and gave everything to achieve freedom.

Women were in front fighting verbally and physically until *Uhuru*. Men
were behind.... I was a Youth Leaguer, and secondly, I was the secretary of
the party for fifteen years. Of the women who were strong in Mwanza at
that time, the first was this woman who came in—Agnes Sahani. And then
the second was Makongoro binti Selemani; then Tunu Nyembo, Halima
Ntungi and a lot of others. Zuhura Mussa. These are the ones in the book
of freedom. And Binti Msafiri, Mwajuma Msafiri and Chausiku Mzee. All
of them were working with TANU.
    They worked to unite women.... They would go "tempt" other women
to join. That was their most important and biggest job. As for me, I belonged to the parents' association and to the TANU choir. I'm a Muslim
and I can tell you that there was no conflict over religion at the time of
mobilizing for freedom. We all united and worked together. Islam and
Christinity were one thing; freedom was another. That was our goal; we
never fought about religion.

Pili Juma also echoed the thoughts of many other women who distinguished
between the importance of having independence and the ability to make political
decisions, and the economic problems facing Tanzania—problems that were causing hardship.

My life since *Uhuru*? Which life? Me, I've got freedom. I am free. I don't
have any worries in my country. But yes, life is getting more difficult. I
worked in the party for fifteen years, then I had health problems. I stopped.
I just sit around. So right now, I don't work. I'm only farming. Women
have problems because life is hard now. Even me, here, it is hard. Things
are harder to get, expensive; there isn't enough money. So you sometimes
see a woman with children without a father. You find that she has problems what to do with the children. Others are unable to go to school because there is no money for school fees. So they just stay without doing
anything.
    Women's problem is life in general. It is mostly bringing up children
and that gives us a problem, because when you have a child it is yours
until it grows up. Is it sick? Where did it sleep? What will it eat? It is a
mother's problem.... Life has become very hard. Hard times are a recent
thing—very recent.

At this point, a listener stressed, "But economically only. Politically, we don't have
problems." By this time, however, Pili Juma was beginning to think about the connection between politics and economics. "Yes," she said, "this is true. But isn't it the economic problems that have to be solved to develop the country? Without the economy,
can a country be a country? The economy is bringing problems into life."
    Bi Pili had two children and six grandchildren. One grandchild had recently
been "taken by God." She returned to the problem of children:

I'm adding this thing about life. Life has become very hard. We are unable
to give our children education now. Schools want everything from parents and you find that parents don't have it. So the child just sits. School
fees have become expensive; you find that you don't have it. So you just

find that you are troubled, anxious. Sometimes you have grandchildren—
no mother, no father. So you stay with them, even though you are an old
person. You want to send them to school but you don't have school fees
so they just stay. They should help us women. They should give us education; something that will enable us to develop. That is what I am asking
for. I don't have any more to say.

So now Mama [Susan Geiger] is the one who is going to go fight for us
there. The women of Tanzania are very poor. They are asking for help.
You should send us a lot of aid to develop women—only that. You should
ask on our behalf, so that we can be humans. Go ask for us there in the
big nations. Ask them to bring help. We are still a young nation. Give us
help in education. Take them [the children] and give them education. Then
bring them back here to teach those of us who are ignorant. That is what
we are asking for.

Mwamvua Kibonge[35]

Mwamvua Kibonge was also born in Mwanza District, at Bukumbi village, Usagara.
She grew up at Rwegasare with two sisters and three brothers. Bi Mwamvua's
mother, Zena, sold rice flour fritters (*vitumbua*), and farmed. Her father, Kibonge,
was Manyema. He was an *askari* or (soldier) for the Germans, and then quit to go
into business for himself, first as a butcher, then as a shop owner where he sold
salt and bought and resold hides and skins. After that, he was appointed chief at
Bukumbi.

Bi Mwamvua remembers her childhood as good. There was plenty of food.
Her only schooling was religious. She helped her mother with domestic work—
making and selling fried dough (*mandazi*), farming, grinding and collecting water.
She was thirteen when she was married to her first husband in Mwanza, with whom
she stayed for three years: "Unfortunately, I was very young. I couldn't tolerate
him. He worked in Geita."

Bi Mwamvua joined TAA in 1952 or 1953. When TANU began in Mwanza,
people didn't buy cards on the street; they bought them in the mosques or churches.
And, she reports:

> We were going from house to house— "*Hodi, karibu* [greetings for enter-
> ing a house], we want to be independent. TANU is coming. We want to be
> self-reliant. Here is a card. It is two shillings." Then he would give you
> two shillings. If it was on the street you would greet the person and then
> you slap hands. You have to be somewhat secret.
>
> Under colonialism, you could enter the office [of a European] and find
> yourself trembling. You were trembling because you would be asked,
> "What do you want here? Whom have you come to see here?" And you
> would sweat. But now, when you enter an office, it is, "*Ndugu, karibu*"
> [come in, brother/sister]. You are welcomed, and if possible, your prob-
> lem is solved. And particularly Mwalimu and other leaders—all empha-
> size we should be treated well. Of course, there may be a problem with
> implementation, but to be frank, we have developed.

---

35   Interview with Mwamvua Kibonge, Sukuma Street, Mwanza, November 22, 1988.

Bi Mwamvua remembers that when Nyerere came to Mwanza on his way to Butiama, he said that with independence, women would one day be people. He wore short pants and a white shirt. He left cards. "The late Yusufu took the cards and gave some to Munanka and I was given about seventeen. Then Mwalimu left for Butiama." Bi Mwamvua didn't see him when he returned, but one of her contributions to the struggle and to TANU was to create plays—guerrilla theater—that were performed at the community theater.

> These plays were about how we welcomed Mwalimu. How he came to plead for independence. How the DC expelled him, and then I met him. He was there in the garden. He sat down, very thoughtful, and then I asked him how he was and he said he was fine. Then I asked him what has happened and he said he was expelled by the DC who told him he couldn't get independence. He said, "An African cannot get independence. He cannot." So Nyerere clapped hands and then he touched his head. I was here. I saw him. So I took these ideas and put them in a play....
> People who watched these plays contributed ten cents and we got a lot of money in those days. And we gave Mwalimu a lot of presents to help him. My play was a sign of development. Well, I made this play and then I made some remembrance of the way we welcomed him; the way we had problems; and the way the party was born.... From that date I have my card.
> We did all that. And we also welcomed leaders—Islamic sheiks and priests and other leaders of TANU and government. We put off the light for one minute. Then we put Nyerere's picture and the picture of another person—I can't remember, he is now deceased—up. We were all excited and then we cried. We made a play even for the RC (regional commissioner). Using the same door Mwalimu used, we read a speech and then I talked about this door saying that Nyerere used the same door to sell TANU cards. Admission was five shillings and food was available. We got Shs.1,400/ from that event ... it was earmarked for a TANU building. When Nyerere came, the door opened and our children played traditional *ngomas* and we talked with our chairman and then I gave him Shs.500/.
> Our efforts were many. I worked for TANU until the house of my late mother was destroyed. The rains came and the roof was taken away. Then I went to Sengerema District. The local leaders said they were going to help....

Zuhura Mussa[36]

Born at Nantare Samwe village in Kwimba District, Zuhura Mussa thought she was about sixty years old when we met in November 1988. Bi Zuhura's father, Mussa, was a mason and her mother, Mwibombi Kahalaga, a farmer. Both were Sukuma. Bi Zuhura had no siblings and did not attend school. When she was "a big girl"—she could not say how old—she married a chief and moved to Ruguru Ntilima, past Maswa in Shinyanga Province, where she farmed and undertook the

---

[36]   Interview with Zuhura Musa, Mwanza, November 21, 1988.

usual household chores. Bi Zuhura left her husband, probably in the late 1940s or early '50s, and came to Mwanza where she joined the TAA.[37]

> I was a member of TAA, then it was banned; some time passed then TANU was formed. I became one of the first members [in my area]. Kisenge was our first secretary, and Bhoke Munanka and [Richard] Wambura were our representatives. I became a TANU chairman and representative for the whole province, including Shinyanga and Mwanza. I was one of the people who was really involved.... I travelled to Dar es Salaam to represent the province.

As Zuhura Mussa and other Mwanza activists interviewed made clear, local TAA leaders were far better known as nationalists in Mwanza than was Nyerere in the mid-1950s; the banning of TANU made it difficult for him to establish his specific credentials in the early years. According to an extract from a Tanganyika Intelligence Report of August 1956, when Nyerere visited Lake Province, he got a big welcome in his home town of Musoma; but only 100 Africans greeted his arrival in Mwanza.[38] All this was to change over the next two years. Just as Lake Province provided TANU with associations and leaders already committed to and espousing nationalist principles, so the Province provided, in the Geita rebellion of 1958, a pivotal blow to the colonial administration and corresponding victory for TANU as *the* major movement, and Nyerere as its undisputed leader.

The Geita Rebellion

Details of the crisis in Geita, which erupted over government attempts to impose multiracial councils on the "tribally" mixed and largely immigrant population of Geita, are thoroughly documented elsewhere[39] and will only be outlined here. Precisely because of the relative lack of depth of chiefly rule in Geita, two particularly authoritarian local administrators, Provincial Commissioner S.A. Walden and Neville French, the Geita district commissioner, decided that it was an ideal area for experimentation with multiracial councils. However, Paul Bomani, then a member of the Legislative Council, questioned whether Geita people had in fact consented to the councils, informed French that he intended to visit Geita, and requested that Nyerere be allowed to speak. French refused the speech, but he could not prevent Bomani and Nyerere from visiting the area, which they did in April 1958.

Nyerere's visit generated great interest, and thousands of people flocked to see him and to buy TANU cards. Although he could not speak and there were no public meetings, Nyerere's visit "acted as a catalyst to the pattern of discontent which was rapidly developing in Geita."[40] Subsequent *barazas* (public meetings) where French tried to force the idea of the new multiracial council quickly provoked questions and protest. In response, the administration arrested vocal opponents of the scheme, tightened controls, and banned TANU from Geita District. The results were predictable: civil disobedience increased and arrests mounted.

---

[37] It is not clear whether they were formally divorced.

[38] Extract. 125, EAF 46/7/01. Activities of the Tanganyika African National Union (PRO).

[39] The following summary is based largely on Maguire, *Toward "Uhuru,"* 196–234.

[40] Ibid., 215.

When the DC refused popular demands for the dismissal of chiefs, the abolition of the multiracial council, and the release of political prisoners, thousands of protestors decided to march on the PC's office in Mwanza in July 1958.

The PC insisted that the huge crowd had to leave the sports field where they had gathered, and that complaints had to be forwarded to Dar es Salaam. The crowd collected money to send its own delegation to Dar but refused to budge from the grounds, where they remained five days until they were ultimately driven off by tear gas and truncheons. Pili Juma, who was part of the demonstration, recalls that:

> We were all assembled from different areas at the field: Ukerewe, Geita, Kwimba—all the districts assembled.... And then tear gas bombs were thrown at us by the police. We scattered but we didn't give up. At night, we went into the hills; groups talking, finishing our discussion of the issues. The police looked but they couldn't find us.[41]

Trouble, arrests and disturbances continued in the district; French left in late August, and a confidential report was drawn up by the new DC, J. T. A. Pearce. September saw TANU's overwhelming Legislative Council election success throughout the country, and Mwanza hosted the founding conference of PAFMECA. Acts of civil disobedience multiplied and all forms of government regulation were increasingly opposed. By October, the government was forced to permit TANU to open branches in Lake Province, and on October 12, 1958, a TANU headquarters in Mwanza opened "almost exactly four years after the original ban on the party had been imposed."[42]

Zuhura Mussa referred to the events sketched here as "a protracted war," and explained the government's surrender to TANU thus:

> At a big public meeting in the field, these days called Nyamagana, the DC rose and asked members of TANU to raise their hands. All the people showed their party cards. So he found himself with no other alternative. The respresentative who had been brought to survey the membership became angry and insisted that TANU be unbanned. And it was unbanned.[43]

At the end of November 1958, Nyerere, accompanied by Bomani, Kisenge, John Rupia (TANU vice-president, from Shinyanga), and Bibi Titi Mohamed addressed 10,000 people in Mwanza for the first time since TANU's reopening. Everywhere the TANU leaders went, thousands of people came to see them. By the end of the year, there were 140 branches and sub-branches, and never enough membership cards for those who wanted them.

Chausiku Mzee[44]

Chausiku Mzee was born in Magu—she does not know the year—to Chief Mgerema, who died when Bi Chausiku was very young, and Mariamu, a daughter of Chief

---

41   Interview with Pili Juma, Mwanza, November 21, 1988.
42   Maguire, *Toward "Uhuru,"* 250.
43   Interview with Zuhuru Mussa, Mwanza, November 21, 1988.
44   Interview with Chausiku Mzee, Mwanza, November 22, 1988.

Mnyamongolo. Both parents were Sukuma, and Bi Chausiku had two sisters and five brothers, one of whom, Musa Mgerema, succeeded her father as chief. She went to school for four years but left when she was "still a child" to be married to an Arab, Mohammed bin Nassoro, now deceased. After divorcing, she was married to Alfari Hassani, with whom she moved to Mwanza, built a house, and "started politics." "When I got divorced from my [second] husband, I continued with my beer business and built this house."

Like many of the women interviewed in Mwanza, Bi Chausiku was politically active long before knowing much about Nyerere. Meetings had to be held in secret outside of Mwanza, and she remembers that an Indian who in 1988 continued to own cotton ginneries gave them a car for transport "before TANU owned a car." "The Indians who owned Tanganyika Bus also—they're the ones who provided us with transport for our political activities."

As with all activists who participated, Geita and the Mwanza march and demonstration stand out in Bi Chausiku's memory:

> We were beaten at our field, Nyamagana. We cooked porridge right there, we were teargassed and all of us were jailed. After that, we were able to open a District TANU branch in Geita. We then went to Maswa, Ngudu, and on to Shinyanga and Tabora—even Bukoba.... But the DC used to scatter us. In the end we held our meetings far away [in the bush]. The police were sent after us, together with government officials. But we responded by using nonviolent resistance....
>
> My husband Alfari was a Youth League leader, in charge of the young men. Our first office was at Makangoro. We began our politics there. Titi [Bibi Titi Mohamed] used to stay at my house, and Mzee Nyerere at Mzee Bomani's. We went on until we got internal government.

Bi Chausiku stressed the ultimate importance of the peaceful changeover to independence. "We came to an agreement with them [the British] and they granted us independence. They bid us farewell peacefully. We didn't spill each other's blood." When the governor left, "we escorted him, we gave him a military salute and he gave us one.... We returned with our president; we swept the State House in Dar es Salaam, we installed our president and we started UWT."

Bi Chausiku credits UWT with helping women achieve greater equality with their husbands. She had this to say about her own difficulties reconciling marriage and political involvement:

> I was the chairperson of the women's organization in this region. In the end my husband bothered me and I returned to Geita District. My husband used to frustrate me; sometimes he refused me permission to lead tours and so on. So I stopped.... Our problems were mainly with men— jealous ones. Sometimes you might be chosen to go on a tour to Musoma or Dar es Salaam; and then your husband makes a fuss. I stopped leadership work because of my husband. He used to force me off planes and trains while the leaders looked on. At the same time, he had signed [that he would let me travel] in the presence of the president. I thought, "Why argue?" So I just retired. I just left it because I used to return home and be beaten.

Bi Chausiku explained that she entered politics when she was very young, adding that she is still involved. "Up to now I'm still a politician because politics hasn't left me behind. There are old and new leaders. We are together. They haven't dropped me, and I haven't joined any other party." Shera Waraga,[45] who was born in Kayenje, Mwanza District (now Magu) in 1928 added that it was the children of her generation (she has five children and twelve grandchildren) who had gotten responsibilities— "promotions and so forth. They are moving forward. We old people—we are just sitting and depending on our children."

"Waridi Bustani"

The day before I left Mwanza to return to Moshi, I was invited to the house of a *lelemama* leader whose group, "Waridi Bustani" (Rose of the Garden) was assembling. After some of us had shared food in the sitting room, we joined many other women gathering in the passageway of the Swahili house. The UWT leader, Martha Makatani, who was certainly the youngest of the women gathered—in her mid-thirties—established her presence as national leader of the women of Mwanza during the course of the evening. For their part, the *ngoma* group of some twenty-five women seemed delighted to have her with them. She had, they told me, never joined them in this way before. The evening began with several songs, the first of which was a song of welcome in which prayers and good luck were offered for us, for the country, for "Chairman Nyerere," and for "Brother Mwinyi,"[46] the ministers, the members of parliament and "our councillors." "Justice! Justice! Justice! Oyee!! [clapping and ululations] The women salute you. "Waridi Bustani," that's our name. Our name is happiness."

> My fellow women, let us look ahead
> Let us not fight among ourselves
> Education is good, party members
>
> Education is good
> Education is good, oyee!!
> Old people, get education
> so that you can progress
> Get education, old people
> so that you can progress
>
> Oh, bitter talk will come and
> quarrel, bring trouble, oh, bitter talk
> bitter talk will come and quarrel
> bring trouble.
>
> Education is good, education is good. oyee!
> Get education, old folks
> So that you can progress!!

---

[45]   Interview with Shera Waraga, Mwanza, November 22, 1988.

[46]   President of Tanzania in 1988.

We rejoice in Tanzania
For the representatives we've elected [repeat]
Chairman of the party, his vice and his deputy

Tanzania, we rejoice for our leaders
the councillors
We rejoice for electing our party chairman
Unopposed
With his vice-chairman, and his deputy

What happiness! Parents, what happiness [repeat]
Let's cheer our representatives

The year '61, independence for Tanzania
'62, the republic
The youth we cheered [repeat]

'64, the Union of Tanganyika and Zanzibar
The youth, we cheered!
'64, well done, brother Nyerere
'62, independent republic
The youth, we rejoiced! [repeat]

The five young suitors, where are you?
Now we are grownups [repeat]

Now we are grown up
We have gaps in our teeth
The hair has remained
The manner of walking has changed
God has blessed us [repeat]

Following these and several other songs, the *ngoma* leader asked the women of "Waridi Bustani," "Are you warmed up?" "We are warmed up!" [followed by laughter, ululations and clapping]. Mrs. Makatani was then asked to speak, and the women began to clap and drum. When they had quieted, Mrs. Makatani offered her own song, about the daily work of women, and how neither women nor men can sleep while the struggle continues. The audience responded enthusiastically to Mrs. Makatani's reminder of how women had proved themselves in the struggle for independence.

Mama #1: And yesterday, I told you that we acquired the cards in plenty. It is we, the women who elected the president of Tanzania.

Makatani: My mothers who are present here, many over here fought in the struggle for independence. Some of whom were divorced by their husbands, are here.

Women: They are here.

Makatani: Even the nation recognized that in order for us to move ahead, we could not forget the women. We were given our organization, the UWT, which is foundering. But this foundering may be because of the weakness of some people. But we have an organization which can help us. Because if you have questions, if you wish to express your own views, you call upon one another, you come and talk it over—true or false?

Women: True.

Makatani: And that's what the party has done. Therefore, my dear mothers, without wasting time, I thank you very much. You have shown this lady [Susan] the determination you had during the struggle for independence. You searched for it with your cards, you struggled with your songs, your different groups, and in different ways, the work you did.

The women request that you [Susan] report that Tanzanian women are steadfast when you go home. Here you can see the women in this town in their respective activities. Here in the villages the women play their drums and sing their songs; they are singing their political songs about the way we were struggling during the fight for independence. Now they are singing songs of development, for building their country and for improving their party.

Now, when the women sing, they sing the truth. As you know, this is the real time. And you do it, yes. They are crying for the country of Mozambique. So when you go back, please give a reply to my dear mothers. I hope you have registered their faces well.

And I would like to thank you for your good ideas. After staying here in Tabora, you have taught our children. Sometimes they work. They work for us, their parents. But you had a record. When you read the history you saw ... umm. Where are the women of Tanzania? I think you had a good idea; the way you saw women and their affairs. When you read the history of the independence struggle, you didn't see women. And that's why I brought her here, as a woman. My dear mothers are very hospitable and when you are through, give them feedback.

My dear mothers, I thank you. Whenever you are called, please turn up on time, without grumbling. My dear mothers, thank you. Me, I know you. Whenever we call you for processions, you come out in full. Whenever we call upon you to be hospitable, you turn out.

Thank you very much, my dear mothers.

Mama #2: Are you okay?   *Women*: Yes, we are!

Mama #2: Are you okay?   *Women*: Yes, we are!

Mama #2: And our friend, please convey our greetings to Americans.

Women: eh, eh.

Mama #2: I am standing here to thank you on behalf of my children, who are here. And you have seen them. I am very thankful. When you get there, don't forget us, please remember us. And come back to Mwanza and see us.

Susan: Yes, I will remember you, and I thank you very much.

> The women of Tanzania
> We have liberated ourselves
> What is our shield?
> It is you, who are our shield.
>
> I say, I have liberated myself
> Nyerere is our father
> And Mwinyi is our father

Kawawa is our father
Sofia is our mother.

I say, I have liberated myself
Mwayungi is our mother
Halima is our mother
And Nyesi is our mother
Makatani is our mother.[47]

I say, I have liberated myself.... ahh [ululations]

Oyee!! Oyee!! Fellow women!
In 1964 our party [meaning UWT] was born
Oyee!! Oyee!! Fellow women, oyee!!
In 1964, our party was born [repeat twice].

And thanks we give to our chairman
And his deputy
The medicine they gave us
We will use it with wisdom [repeat]

Where are you today, dear women?
Up, up, high up!
Up, up, high up!
Women, we are high up in Tanzania, Oyee!! [repeat]

The women of "Waridi Bustani" who invited me to listen to them perform their songs in Mwanza, provided a glimpse into the style, lyrics, and intent of their political music. The themes were uncomplicated and important: struggling hard, supporting leaders, reaching out to others, cooperating and putting differences aside. In the Geita rebellion and Mwanza march of 1958, a large and diverse segment of the African population of Lake Province offered both the TANU national leadership and the British administration massive evidence of the direction and force of popular, transtribal anti-colonial determination. Women participated actively in these efforts, while their *ngoma*, and plays like the one written by Mwamvua Kibonge, recalled events in the struggle and celebrated the people, the country, the leaders. Governor Twining's alternatives to African-initiated demands for national independence—multiracial councils, the convention of chiefs, the UTP—lay exposed for what they were: belated schemes to maintain control over political change in Tanganyika. Elsewhere in the country, the nationalist messages delivered by TANU supporters, while less dramatic, were no less clear. Moreover, the imprint of women's nationalist consciousness and modes of expression on TANU was undeniable, and their integration into TANU organizational structures at the local level readily apparent.

Performing Nationalism

By 1955, the nationalist movement was offering, along with the politics of freedom, forms of engagement, entertainment, and spectacle, the attractiveness of which was itself annoying to administrative officers. Here, there was no possibility of charg-

---

[47] In this stanza, the women are referring to their local political leaders as mothers.

ing TANU with the ritual violence associated in the colonial mind with Mau Mau to the north. Indeed, administrators frequently seemed caught between wanting to dismiss TANU's popular appeal by characterizing people's (and particularly women's) enthusiasm as superficially responsive to the attractions of mass spectacle on the one hand, and fearing that the appeal of organized enthusiasm was dangerously significant on the other.

Evidence of the latter view became apparent as TANU gained membership and strength. In 1957, in response to the popularity of displaying TANU support and membership through clothing, the administration issued a public order making it a violation for any person to wear "a uniform or distinctive dress which signifies association with any political organization or the promotion of any political object" in a public place or to a public meeting. The penalty for contravention was a fine of up to one thousand shillings or up to six months' imprisonment, or both.[48]

Meanwhile, TANU was benefiting enormously from the appeal of uniformed members of the party's women's section and of the TANU choirs and Youth League (TANUYL), both of which had many women members.[49] They were identified and identifiable to visiting TANU leaders, to people gathering to see and hear these leaders for the first time, and to colonial officials who wished they were not there. Like the women's section, a TANU youth section was specified in the party's 1954 constitution; but also like the women's section, the Youth League, eventually formed in 1956,[50] owed its vitality and activities to its members, who became the self-appointed guardians and greeters of TANU dignitaries, and the TANU "police" in charge of crowd control.

The DCs now found themselves saddled with responsibility for preventing nationalist "entertainment," banning "distinctive dress which signifies...association with your political organization," and reminding local TANU officers that permission to organize an assembly or procession included the stipulation that no drum could be beaten before or after a meeting and that no meeting could be held near any local court.[51]

Similar reminders about drums and uniforms flowed from the district officers and police while infractions persisted. In November 1958, the assistant superintendent of police in Kigoma District complained that several party members had recently been seen "wearing distinctive dress signifying association with TANU" and referring "particularly ... to the green dresses worn by lady members at the Kigoma Railway station on the 15th November." Reminding the TANU district chairman of the order prohibiting uniforms, he went on to

---

[48]   R. W. Smith, DC, Kigoma, to Dist. Sec., TANU, Ujiji, 20 Mar. 1958, Ref. No. A6/5/32, TNA; Tanganyika African Association (TAA), Kigoma, citing Government Notice No. 20 of 11 Jan. 1957, "Political uniforms prohibition," Sections 2 and 3, A6/5, TNA.

[49]   Whether they wore a uniform of green shirts and dark pants or green blouses and dark skirts; green dresses; TANUYL sashes or arm bands; or matching *kanga* and a green swatch, these were the party faithful.

[50]   Iliffe, *Modern History*, 532.

[51]   R. W. Smith, DC Kigoma, to Dist. Sec., TANU, Ujiji, 20 March 1958, Ref. No. A6/5/32, TNA; N. D. Morant, Commanding Officer, Police, Kigoma District, to R. H. Missozi, Branch Sec., TANU, Mwangongo, 1 July 1958, Ref. No. A 24/9/84, A6/5 Kigoma, TNA. It is worth recalling that women in Ujiji and Kigoma had a history of political activism through organized performance; see McCurdy, "The 1932 'War.'"

point out lamely that the Kigoma Railway Station catered to the general public, and that:

> the assembly of large crowds interferes with the right of free access of the public and also causes obstruction to traffic.
>
> Would you please in future confine your reception or farewell committees to between 20 or 30 persons. Should you so desire, a larger demonstration of affection or loyalty can easily be arranged at some pre-arranged or more suitable venue on application to this office.
>
> I believe it to be correct that a similar point was recently put to your president and other Members of your Central Committee and they accepted it.[52]

This polite official was quite right: the commissioner of police, Dar es Salaam, had written to the TANU president on March 19, 1958, drawing his attention to the government order prohibiting "uniforms." He pointed out that the TANUYL sashes worn by stewards at a TANU meeting held at the airport on February 16 could well be interpreted as a breach of that order. He suggested that when party officials needed some form of identification at future gatherings, they should be identified by some more discreet symbol, such as a blue armband.[53]

The struggle continued. In January 1959, "some 100" TANU members went to the Kigoma Railway Station to say goodbye to two TANU visitors, Mr. G. Mlay and Miss Anna Gwasa, in direct defiance of previous orders.[54]

In addition to trying to limit the size of TANU groups and banning the signification of support through dress, the administration insisted that permission to use a loud speaker or megaphone and to sing songs be requested, and that the words of songs sung at TANU meetings be submitted in advance.[55] Miserly concessions were sometimes made. At a meeting of the Kigoma DO with TANU committee members, the TANU chairman requested that the police waive the rule requiring the words of every song to be submitted before each meeting, on the grounds that the repertoire was very small and the songs were always the same.[56] And in September 1959, W.J.W. Bowering, the DC Kigoma, wrote to the TANU district chairman that it wasn't necessary to give fourteen days' notice for using a megaphone or for permission to sing songs, and that monthly subscriptions could be collected in public. Unfortunately, it was not possible to waive the order concerning prior submission of copies of songs to be sung at meetings:

> However, if the songs are the same each time as the Committee assert it would suffice to give a complete copy of all the songs signed by the Chair-

---

[52] Asst. Super of Police, Kigoma District, to Dist. Chairman, TANU, Ujiji, 21 November 1958, Ref. No. S/14, A6/5, Kigoma, TNA.

[53] Commissioner of Police, Dar es Salaam, to President, TANU, Dar es Salaam, 19 March 1958. Ref. No. S/15/3/185. A6/5 Kigoma, TNA.

[54] Officer I/C Police, Kigoma District to Dist. Chairman, TANU, Ujiji, 5 Jan. 1959, Ref. No. S/14, A6/5 Kigoma, TNA.

[55] S. G. Pierce to Kashindye, Dist. Sec., TANU, Ref. No. KIS/A.24/24/41, 25 June 1959, re: TANU meeting to be held at Usagara ground, Ujiji, Kigoma District, 29 June 1959. A6/5 Kigoma, TNA.

[56] Notes of a meeting with TANU Committee, 9/9/59, A6/5 TNA.

man or Secretary. The songs should be numbered and future applications could read for example: "TANU Youth League singing songs 1, 2, 3, and 5."[57]

Women activists in Moshi and Mwanza frequently mentioned their deep involvement in the original TANU Youth League, formed in 1956, and the TANU "choirs."[58] It was through these groups as well as through their *ngoma* organizations that women *performed* popular nationalism and nationalist sentiment, composing and singing the nationalist songs and plays they developed and wrote.[59] These performances created TANU just as they expressed and constructed Tanganyika nationalism.

The comments of women activists interviewed in Dar es Salaam, Moshi, and Mwanza underline the fact that the performance of nationalism, like the selling of TANU cards, was largely women's work. Moreover, it was fundamental to nationalist formation in Tanganyika. British administrators were especially frustrated by their inability to curb women's skill and enthusiasm for organizing visible, colorful, and exciting signification of popular support for TANU.

Clearly, the TANU central leadership was not responsible for the various performances and significations of nationalist political culture that were put to the service of party mobilization and membership; yet performance and signification produced nationalism in Tanzania as surely as Nyerere's speeches. Moreover, TANU and later CCM leaders understood its importance, and Nyerere came to rely on its reproduction throughout his career. Like many popular expressions of nationalism, the wearing of identical dress to signify membership and support were appropriated by Nyerere and the post-independence TANU government bureaucracy and put to the service of the one-party state.

---

[57] W. J. Bowering, DC Kigoma, to Dist. Chairman, TANU, 23 September 1959, re: 9.9.59 meeting and police officer's reply concerning Youth League songs, copy No. KIG/A/8/2, S.G. Pierce, Officer I/C Police, Kigoma District, to DC Kigoma, 18 September 1959, A6/5 TNA.

[58] Iliffe suggests that the Youth League "contained a disproportionately large number of young men who had failed to enter middle or secondary school" and caused "numerous disciplinary problems" (Iliffe, *Modern History*, 532). Perhaps this was true in later years, or was true for some areas; but it hardly seems congruous with the active participation of numerous women, and it seems likely as well that vigorous militancy was sometimes characterized as a disciplinary problem.

[59] Johannes Fabian sees performance and sites of performance as integral to the expression of processes of power negotiation and oppression. See his *Power and Performance* (Madison, 1990).

8

Bibi Titi Mohamed: Independence and After

The formal process of colonial divestiture became a foregone conclusion following TANU victories in the Legislative Council elections of 1958–59, and again in the 1960 election ushering in "responsible government" (with a majority of elected rather than appointed council members). At the celebration of Tanganyika's independence from Britain on the night of December 9, 1961, Bibi Titi Mohamed shared the platform with Julius Nyerere, soon to be prime minister, and the other dignitaries and guests. Noting that Nyerere was the "only [political] survivor from TANU's original central committee of 1954,"[1] Iliffe goes on to make the related observation that first captured my attention in 1983: that Nyerere and Bibi Titi were probably the only leaders known throughout the country at the time of independence.[2] Bibi Titi herself did not describe this momentous occasion to me—an occasion marked by massive celebrations throughout the country; but Lucy Lameck, who also participated in the major event in Dar es Salaam remembered:

> [This celebration] was something completely different. I couldn't sleep the whole day, we were dancing, we were dancing all over the street. Just to see that flag come down and ours go up. It was just incredible. Fantastic. You just don't have that kind of feeling again. It was a moment in history; you don't see it twice. You see, it is incredible. You should have been at the stadium to hear the thunderous storms; and the women there were, you know, really shouting and crying, tears coming to their eyes ... unbelievable![3]

Although political independence was a primary goal for Bibi Titi, as for all the women activists of the 1950s, the nationalism women invested in TANU did not end with the achievement of state power. Hence, this book is not simply about the struggle for independence, but about the continuation of women's political culture of nationalism in the postcolonial years. In the early 1960s, Bibi Titi was able to

---

[1]   Iliffe, *Modern History*, 571–72.

[2]   Ibid., 572.

[3]   Interview with Lucy Lameck, Upanga (Dar es Salaam), November 12, 1984.

advance her broad nationalist vision as a leader of pan-African women's organizing. But in the years that followed, she found it difficult to lead a depoliticized national women's movement, and ran afoul of TANU's increasingly centralized and authoritarian one-party state. In this final segment of her life history, Bibi Titi recounts her political career, concerns and the difficulties that plagued that career following independence.

We women organized until we achieved our independence. My first trip outside the country was to India, in 1958, December. I left here and spent a night in Bombay—me and Tecla Gumbo. On the 6th, we left and we returned home on the 27th of January, 1959. And there were lots of other trips. Before I went to Guinea, I visited England, Denmark, China and Russia. I went to America later [in 1963].

I am the one who convinced African women to form the All Africa Women's Congress in 1962. It was I who organized the All African Women's Conference—who convinced the women in Guinea. I went to Guinea in February or March 1962, to attend a meeting. I was invited by Diallo Abdullahi, the secretary general of the All Africa People Conference [AAPC].... They came here in 1960. The committee was here in 1960 or 1961. I had a big party for the women's organization when they arrived. Besides this [AAPC] there was PAFMECA [Pan-African Movement for East and Central Africa]. The OAU had not been formed yet. Even the All Africa Women's Conference was not formed. But it started before the OAU.

I am the one who went to convince the women in Guinea, because Diallo had seen how I had organized the party and had prepared for the members and how enthusiastic they were. He was impressed. When they left, there was a West and Northern African Women's Conference. They invited us. I went with two Namibians. One was known as Mama Jomo. I have forgotten the name of the other woman. This woman's husband was from Namibia and she was from America—a Black American. We were invited in 1962, as observers. While I was there, I met a Kenyan. She had come to Cairo—that woman. We met there at that conference. Kenya had not achieved its independence at that time.

At the conference, we discussed women's problems—education, development, child care, and how to participate in politics. Even though we were participating, what is it we were going to do? What were we going to gain? What authority will we have after independence? The women discussed these issues. I told them that these problems were everywhere in Africa, not just in the West and North.

It was necessary to organize an All Africa women's meeting. Some of these problems affected everyone and others [some countries] hadn't achieved their independence. Nyasaland, Rhodesia, Congo-Zaire: they were still oppressed, even though Congo achieved its independence in 1960. Women were still oppressed and others were not independent. "Though we from Tanganyika have a voice, we are not sure where it ends—when the man will take over. Now we must have African unity, for the struggle for education, child care— we have to be together in one Africa, so we can be heard all over" [Bibi Titi's recollection of what she said at the conference].

Diallo said I had spoken the truth. That such a conference should be held. We agreed, and the chairman, a woman named Fatuma from Egypt, said that the meeting should be in Cairo. I said,

It is impossible. This meeting should be held in Tanganyika. It is near to Nyasaland [now Malawi]—people could come, even in boats, who haven't achieved independence.... We cannot provide tickets to Cairo. But [if the meeting is in Tanganyika] they can hide in the forests and come by various routes, because it is closer. When we form an organization we have to consider the situation of other Africans. If we go to Cairo, they won't see us. It will be the same thing—only Tanganyika will be able to come.... But even Namibians could come to a meeting held in Tanganyika....

Mama Jomo also stressed this, and that men would also help us. Fatuma agreed because women from Nyasaland and everywhere could come. This convinced her. So in June 1962, the All Africa Women's Conference was held here. It was formed in this country. There wasn't any such conference before this first annual general meeting. At the time, Bwana Mkubwa [Nyerere] had resigned as prime minister [to reorganize TANU], leaving it to [Rashidi] Kawawa [to serve as prime minister].

When they [the conference delegates] came here the meeting took a long time so we could not take them to different areas. The most we could do was take them to Morogoro, and we had an [auto] accident while going there. The driver and three women died. One from Kenya, and two from here—the daughter of Abdulrahman and Kijakazi—who were members of the Youth League. The delegate from Kenya was accompanied by Margaret [daughter of Jomo] Kenyatta. They were just going on an unofficial trip after our conference to see part of our country.

The leader of the All Africa Women's Conference was Hawa Keita from Mali. I was a committee member. There was a Black [American] woman— a woman from Liberia. She was a member, but the one from Guinea was secretary. She was called—I've forgotten, but the people concerned can tell you.[4] She was in that position until I was in prison and afterwards. She was expelled from office recently [1988].

On November 2, 1962, His Excellency [Nyerere] said that all the women's groups [in Tanganyika] should be dissolved—the YWCA, Tanganyika Council of Women, UMCA—to merge into one national women's organization, Umoja wa Wanawake wa Tanganyika [UWT]. "If you are developed and educated [he said], then you should educate these women."

UWT was different from the Women's Section of TANU.[5] First, the Women's Section didn't have a president. There were secretaries. The Youth League and the Women's Section and the Elders—all had secretaries. When the elections for secretary of the [national, or headquarter branches] Youth Leagues and the Women's Section took place in 1959, I was in Europe. So Lucy [Lameck] was elected. But the people refused, saying that Titi should

---

4 Bibi Titi is probably referring to Jeanne Martan Siese, who according to Dr. Margaret Snyder, "spent a lot of time in jail" and "must be remembered!" (Interview with Margaret Snyder, founder of UNIFEM, the United Nations Development Fund for Women who has been involved with the women's organizations of Africa since the early 1960s, Kampala, Uganda, January 27, 1996).

5 Established by TANU as an umbrella for all existing, registered women's organizations, UWT replaced the former Tanganyika Council of Women, then headed by Nyerere's wife, Maria, rather than the Women's Section of TANU. Because many women's groups (such as church-based or village groups, dance societies, and mutual aid groups) were not registered, they remained outside the UWT, at least initially. See Swantz, *Women in Development*, 159–60.

have the position, and if Lucy wanted, she should be under Titi. So they made me secretary in 1959. But that was the difference. UWT has a ... national president of the Union. The Women's Section [head] didn't have that title.

The UWT attracted all kinds of women, educated ones too. But then, the educated ones were worried about me. Some said that I did not like educated women because I thought maybe they could take my position.[6] I called a meeting at Jubilee Hall to reassure them. I told them: "I don't know anything. I am not educated like you. Now I want you educated ones to help in this country. When I lead you I also want you to lead me in those things I don't know. Let us guide each other. You are educated but I know things you don't know. And you, my colleagues, are learned about things I don't know. The benefit to this country is your education. You have been sent to school. You have been told that when you educate a woman in a family, you have educated a whole family. Now you should educate the whole country. This country is waiting for you. I only work for you."

So I reassured these women. Even if you ask Martha Bulengo [an educated UWT leader, still politically active in 1984], she will tell you so. We held a meeting there and then and elected a committee and divided the work amongst us. Work on handicrafts was started. During TANU, it wasn't there. They brought them together and taught women things like cleanliness in the house, cookery, child care—things that were not initially part of the women's section. Things like adult education and educating fellow women. Embroidery and basket-making were all taught. These were not done in the women's section of TANU. We had no time [for such things]. It was the Tanganyika Council of Women that did these things [before independence].

I remained president of UWT until 10 June 1967. Before I left, I talked with the other women to see who could be a suitable leader when I retired. Mrs. [Kanasia] Mtenga [TANU activist from Moshi] who was vice president wanted to be president. Lucy Lameck also wanted it. And so did Mrs. Maria Nyerere. *But Lucy couldn't do it because of her behavior[7]; and Mrs. Mtenga was too much of a European. She would have made demands in the villages and wouldn't sit on the mat with other women. As for Mrs. Nyerere, Nyerere didn't want his wife to run.*

Now being the way they were, and the fact that UWT had attracted women from the rural areas and from urban areas.... I advised them to elect Sophia [wife of Rashidi Kawawa]. I had already talked to her. She

---

[6]   The tensions between educated women brought in to provide technical expertise to UWT, and Bibi Titi, were immediately apparent. Margaret Snyder, who worked with the UWT in 1964, suggested that there was a tension between the approach of women like Martha Bulengo, who were trying to "professionalize" UWT, and Bibi Titi's "very earthy approach." Bibi Titi, commented Dr. Snyder, was not "strong" on technical matters; she was "very much the political person. Titi wanted to keep UWT as a TANU women's wing, emphasizing the mobilization of women for political purposes.... But there was a pull to get UWT involved in income generation projects, and so forth." Interview with Margaret Snyder.

[7]   I did not press Bibi Titi to explain what she meant concerning Lucy Lameck's "behavior," although I suspect that she was referring to rumors concerning her "reputation." Lucy Lameck was unmarried—that alone made her the object of gossip. Moreover, like many male colleagues, she enjoyed beer and other alcoholic drinks. Although neither of these factors prevented her from winning elections in her home district of Kilimanjaro, they were apparently regarded as impediments to her representing other adult women.

refused but I asked her not to refuse. I encouraged Sophia and she was elected chairman for Dar es Salaam region. "You must do this to help your country, and to help your husband too. Because in an organization if there is a weakness somewhere, the whole organization has problems." She agreed.

As a member of parliament,[8] I had to fight for equality, knowing that my fellow women had made a big contribution to TANU. Had it not been for them, it would have been impossible to be independent because the men were afraid. Some of them joined because they saw that their mothers and sisters had joined. I am sorry to say this, but now that we are independent, we should try harder to develop—to make our lives better. Women must also be educated, must be employed in the government. What was necessary for men to get ahead was also necessary for women. Although I, as their leader, was uneducated, those who were educated should be employed. They shouldn't be denied that right. And girls should go to school and be educated as far as they can.

As junior minister for community development, those were my responsibilities. I used to fight for the development of women in the rural areas and to advocate good child care—good, balanced nutrition, educating the children—because women were not insisting that their children go to school. They used to tell their children to assist them in the *shamba* work, and this prevented them from continuing school. That was basically my concern—that was my department, because my ministry had two departments—culture and community. I was on the community side and my colleague, Mwami Teresa Ntare,[9] was concerned with culture.

Independence meant a lot. Our children had a chance in school. They could get an education. We could also develop ourselves. How did development happen with the Indians? They were allowed to borrow money from the British. Once we were independent we could borrow money for agriculture, housing, and business. Our children could go to school and do other things. But before independence we were like slaves. The Indians' progress was a result of help from the British after World War II. The British trusted the Indians more. European banks loaned money to the Indians [but not to us].

After independence we were given loans to build houses. I myself had three houses after independence. The bankers went looking for people in their cars. Whether you had money or not, you were given a loan. They were encouraging us. But before independence, there was no such encouragement.

Among the male leaders, the one who really supported the idea of women's equality was Nyerere himself. He had seen the crowds of

---

[8]   From Rufiji District.

[9]   Born in 1928 into the ruling Tutsi family and educated at Tabora Girls' Secondary School, Teresa Ntare succeeded her father as chief (*mwami*) of Kasulu (Buha) in 1946. A progressive farmer whose husband led the Kasulu Coffee Cooperative Society in the 1950s, Mwami Ntare was one of the most powerful chiefs in the territory. During our interview at her home in Magomeni (Dar es Salaam) on November 21, 1992, Mwami Ntare spoke of encouraging women in Buha to grow coffee, and of ordering that the royal drum be sounded to summon sixty thousand people to hear a speech by Nyerere. Both she and her sister, Anna Gwassa, were active TANU supporters from the late 1950s. Mwami Ntare became legislative councillor for Kasulu in 1960. Junior minister for youth and culture from 1962 to 1965, she was the first member of Parliament for Kasulu constituency in Kigoma Region. Interview, and *Daily News*, May 25, 1993, reporting on Mwami Ntare's death.

women, and even when we said in Parliament that men should be punished for impregnating girls, Nyerere stood up to back us. The others in Parliament boycotted me and Lucy. So when we wanted to pass the legislation,[10] they refused. Among the few women—about seven or eight—were me, Lucy and the Swedish lady [Barbro Johansson] and a certain lady who was married to a Goan who was a settler in Amboni, Tanga. The men were angry with us. It was Nyerere who said that the bill should pass. Women should not be mistreated like this. If a man made a schoolgirl pregnant by luring her with his money which he had attained due to his age, he should be fined, imprisoned, or made to maintain the child until it grew up.

Frankly, the biggest support came from Nyerere. He was very helpful to women. The men were very angry and some of them opposed me very much. I made enemies of some of the men. The men complained that Titi was making their wives proud. I had no problems with women.

We used to go to many different meetings. Even to Britain, America, France. [What I discovered is that women] have the same problems. The whole world has them. I went to Copenhagen to attend a world meeting on women's problems. I went to Washington D.C. in 1963 for the same reason. The white women were complaining about not having any authority. We were told that women have problems every month and at the same time, want to hold a job. So all women are faced with problems. In the beginning we thought that these were African problems and that other nations were developed.... The most oppressed are the Arabs. They are always confined in the house—and also the Indians.

At this point in the interview, at Kanyama Chiume's request, Bibi Titi gave a lengthy account of her experiences during the army mutiny of January 1964.[11] The mutiny of 2,000 members of the Tanganyika Rifles, coming soon after the Zanzibar Revolution, shook the government and the population. With Nyerere initially in hiding, Kambona was the first to address the people with reassurances that calm had been restored.

Bibi Titi recounted two days of fear and confusion, during which she was verbally abused while attempting to find out what was happening to other government officials and in the streets. At one point, the cars in which she and several other members of government were traveling were stopped, and those who identified themselves were beaten. As Bibi Titi tried to walk away, she was recognized and beaten in front of her husband, who denied knowing her, saying he had just met her on the road and agreed to give her a lift to the TANU office.

Although considerations of length prohibit me from including this section of Bibi Titi's narrative, two matters mentioned in her account were subsequently to affect her life. The first has to do with the fact that Kambona, her good friend and political colleague, became the voice of the government at a time when Nyerere's whereabouts were unknown; the second concerns her husband's refusal to acknowledge their relationship in order to avoid being beaten.

---

[10] The Amendment to the Affiliation Act allowed unmarried women to claim child support from men who impregated them, so long as they could prove the identity of the father.

[11] For a detailed account of the mutiny, see Bienen, *Tanzania*, 363–81. Bibi Titi's full account is available from the author.

When Bibi Titi finished her account of the mutiny, Mr. Chiume and I asked her to tell us why she had lost her parliamentary seat in the elections of 1965, the first general election since independence, and the first to be conducted under the new constitution making Tanzania a formal one-party republic. Initially, sixteen women candidates were put forward, eight of whom were selected by the party. Bibi Titi lost in her home district, Rufiji-Utete,[12] to A. M. Mtauka, who had studed overseas and served as TANU secretary in the area. The vote was 7,343 to 18,145. In studies of this election, several reasons have been advanced for Bibi Titi's defeat. Born in Dar es Salaam, she was said to be out of touch with her constituency, spending too much time in Dar. In addition, she was said to be less tactful than she might have been, and to direct her appeal primarily to women. Busy with UWT, TANU, and government duties, she was also said to have devoted too little time to "fence-mending."[13] Bibi Titi continued:

> I don't know why I lost the 1965 general election. That is, I don't know that there was any one particular reason. But it might have been due to one of my actions. I was junior minister for community development then. And I was given a lady from Community Development to take around to my constituency. I thought she was just coming along to see how the development program was being carried out. I had no idea she was actually there for other purposes. Everywhere we went, she behaved like a spy who was with me to collect information. And then, just before the election, the area commissioner of the district, whose name was Abdula Kassim Ugama—a man from that district who unfortunately died in Tandika— was transferred.
>
> They [people who sent the "spy"] had noticed that Ugama backed me strongly in that area. So they transferred him, and in his place brought Mr. Kaswende, the brother of the one in the police. He was sent there because there was a great problem [in that area] from the very beginning. There had never been a church in that [predominantly Muslim] area, either during the German or the British periods; but after independence, the priests from Kipatini Mission in Kilwa requested a place to build a church in the district. As a result, the people of Rufiji sent a delegation to Dar es Salaam. When the delegation came to Dar es Salaam, they came to see me as their representative. I said, "What is your problem?" They replied, "We didn't actually come to see you.... What we want you to do is to make an appointment for us to see the president."
>
> What they said was that "since the time of our birth no church has been built in our area. Why is it that you are now trying to bring a church to our area? If a church is to come, it shouldn't come so fast. It should be a slow process. Otherwise it will bring misunderstanding in the district— great resentment that may spill over to other areas. Let's do this thing slowly by talking to the people in the district for a bit longer. [If we don't] it will be bad and now that we are independent, we shouldn't have troubles of this type. Others have ruled this country: Germans for thirty years, the

---

[12] Although born in Dar es Salaam, Bibi Titi's parents were from Rufiji. Hence, Rufiji was her "home district."

[13] See Lionel Cliffe, ed. *One Party Democracy: The 1965 General Elections* (Nairobi, 1967), 365, 261; see also Bienen, *Tanzania*, 382–405.

Photo 9: Bibi Titi protesting her election defeat November, 1965. Credit: *East African Reporter.*

British for forty, and they never did this. To ask to do this after only four years of independence is asking for a lot of trouble."

I sent the message to the president. They met him and the president replied, "What can I do? As the president of the country, I cannot interfere in religious matters. These people have the freedom to do what they want as long as they don't break the law." That was Nyerere's reply.

So a collusion developed between teachers at Kipatimo [Kipatini] and some government officials. They ganged together with my enemies and they spread rumors that the people of Rufiji were foolish because they didn't realize exactly where Titi stands. As a result of these rumors and the reasons given above, I lost the general election. They said I was the one who instigated the people's opposition to building a church in the district. I never did such a thing. Such a thing—not allowing other people to have their own faith—is not something that is tolerated in my district. Even our religion doesn't say this. If a man comes to your village, which is all Muslims, and says, "We have become Christians and we want to build a church here," you have no right to refuse. Even our religion says this, because they [Christians] are also worshipping [one] God.

But they were mixing—confusing—religion and ignorance. When they asked me to take their request and I took it, it appeared that I was a bad person. For the people of Rufiji were asking, "Why is Titi agreeing with them? Why did she refuse to have the church built? Why is she keeping quiet? She must be the one who pushed the idea."

I don't know if it was also the stand of Kaswende's relative that led to my defeat. I'm not sure. I'm really not sure. But that's how it was. I am not sure because I knew this man had been brought purposely to create confusion as far as my election was concerned. One evening about seven p.m. when we were going to a place called Mtanza in Rufiji, I was leaving the house of the chairman of that place when I heard one teacher telling my opponent that whatever happened, he was going to win the election. He should have no fear at all. "Whatever happens and despite the enthusiasm with which the crowd receives this woman, you will triumph."

I went back inside the house and told the chairman what this teacher, who was an election returns officer, was saying. The chairman wanted to take action by reporting to the delegate [TANU person from another area who would oversee the election]. I said, "Leave it alone. I don't want to argue." I am the one who stopped the chairman from taking action; but as a result, I lost the election.

[After 1965] conflicts began to emerge between regional commissioners [RCs] and TANU secretaries all over the country. There was confusion between them as to who was responsible for what, and in many cases, collisions occurred, not just over politics, but over the execution of their duties, where they were interfering with each other.

At that time, Kambona was the minister of rural development. Kambona said he had told members of the cabinet and national executive that there were conflicts between regional commissioners and area secretaries and that it was therefore important to hold a seminar so that each could be told his responsibility. From what I know about the matter, this question then went to the Central Committee, for as you know, reports go to headquarters periodically—that there was conflict between TANU secretaries and regional commissioners and that this conflict wasn't confined to one or two areas. It was everywhere.... "We must spell out what each one is required to do and the limitations of the responsibilities. Today we have been asked to hold this meeting for RCs and TANU secretaries. They should meet in Tabora where the minister should have a seminar and address them to define the responsibilities for each one of them. Then, they should go from there to Arusha for a meeting of the National Executive. We will ask them to hold their meeting in Tabora while we members of the National Executive are in Arusha."

This is what we understood in the Central Committee. We understood that we were leaving Kambona to address the RCs and regional party secretaries and going straight from there to Arusha to join the rest of the members of the National Executive. During this meeting of the Central Committee, the president, vice-president, secretary general, and all members of the National Executive were there. However, before we got to Arusha, we began reading in the paper about the Arusha Declaration.[14]

I was traveling in the same plane with Mr. Werner Kilian Kapinga, who was in the cooperative movement. Later on, he was in COSATA [Cooperative Societies of Tanganyika]. He asked me, "Did you read the paper?" I replied, "I have heard and I have seen." "When did the Arusha Declaration arrive? Anyone who is in a leadership position cannot have this and that? When did we discuss this? When did we talk?" Kapinga said, "I will oppose this vigorously, as my name implies" [*pinga* means to object or obstruct]. I said, "We should either be told or we should ask how this came about." I said this to Mr. Kapinga.[15]

At that time there were sixty-three members in the National Executive together with the president. Sixty of us were delegates, including those of the Central Committee, and the other three were the president, vice-president, and secretary general.[16] How could sixty-three of us change the laws governing the life of the people and just tell them this shall not be that, and that shall not be this—the 15 million or so people? "Well, we will go and ask in the meeting."

And we went there and found that things were hot. Each one of us was saying something else. I also said something: "This law is bad. What is intended here is to put each other down. We asked the people when it was the question of a one-party state. We should go about the country and ask, as we asked them on [that question], because this new law interferes with customs and traditions of the people of this country. We must therefore go to the custodians of those customs and traditions and ask them about proposed changes. We must get each one of them to say what he feels about it. We should bring those reactions to another meeting of the National Executive and then make a decision as we did with respect to the one-party state."

---

[14]   *The Arusha Declaration* and TANU's *Policy on Socialism and Self-Reliance* were the most important statements of policy formulated under Nyerere's leadership, and shaped party ideology and practice for the next twenty years. As Bienen points out, all of the themes—"socialism, nationalization, rural development, an end to elitism, new educational directions, independence in foreign policy—are permeated by an insistence on development through self-reliance" (Bienen, *Tanzania*, 406–47, esp. 408). That these policies, whether successful or not, required substantial and continuous infusions of foreign assistance created the conditions for the economic crisis of the mid-1980s.

[15]   Lionel Cliffe concluded that it was very difficult to determine the circumstances leading to the Arusha Declaration. But his statement that "There was certainly no sustained analysis and discussion involving the Party in general in the lead-up to the Arusha meeting in 1967," confirms the concerns expressed here by Bibi Titi and Mr. Kapinga. Lionel Cliffe, "Political Struggles Around the Adoption and Implementation of the Arusha Declaration," in *Re-Thinking the Arusha Declaration*, ed. Hartmann, 106.

[16]   According to a 1992 government publication, the TANU National Executive Council had 70 members in 1967, 9 percent of whom were women, while the Central Committee had 11 members, all men. See The United Republic of Tanzania, *Women and Men in Tanzania*, Bureau of Statistics (Dar es Salaam, 1992), 56.

But apparently, the issue had already been decided. One man, Ibrahim Changas [regional commissioner, Singida], stood up and pointed at me and said I was a lying woman and accused me of having built ten houses already. Then one young man from Musoma ... said, "This woman has already got houses. That is why it is not surprising she is rejecting this proposal. What are we to ask the people? What are these people to be asked? Is it not you people here [who are to be asked]? How many of you people have houses in the village?"[17]

Before he became regional commissioner, Changas was the area commissioner for Musoma. He was promoted to the rank of regional commissioner and posted to Singida before Peter Kisumo. These people bitterly opposed what I had said. After the national executive meeting, a huge meeting was held at Arusha. The president himself addressed this meeting and he told them this [the Arusha Declaration] was now the law of the country.

That is all I know about this issue. When it was clear that some of us were not satisfied, trouble started to creep into the country. And into the Central Committee. To speak frankly, not only did trouble creep into the Central Committee but some of us began to resign.[18] Bitter words began to emerge—words that could not be tolerated.[19] And we felt that things were becoming impossible. Those of us who could tolerate [the Arusha Declaration] remained in the Central Committee. Those of us who were unable to tolerate it—we quit. And that is all.

After we left, then came the allegations about overthrowing the government—the idea that this was our intent. Frankly speaking, I knew nothing. I really didn't know anything. I did associate with Oscar [Kambona] until he left the country.[20] And he was better informed than I since he had a number of security men under his wing—among them people like Akena—who made him run away. They told him, "You will be arrested." This is what I heard. And they added that if he was arrested, he would be

---

[17] Several scholars have attempted to explain why Tanzania's ruling class was willing to agree to a "leadership code" that placed prohibitions on private accumulation. Susanne D. Mueller notes that TANU leaders were not at all united in their acceptance (as Bibi Titi's commentary in fact confirms) but were willing to sacrifice economic opportunity for political legitimacy. There were also accomodations made. For example, leaders could transfer property ownership to a trust in the name of their children; and they could employ labor, so long as the workers they employed were not full-time and permanent. In other words, leaders who owned farms could employ casual labor. See Susanne D. Mueller, "The Historical Origins of Tanzania's Ruling Class," African Studies Center Working Papers, No. 35, Boston University, 1980, 18–19.

[18] As Mueller notes, "the option of open political opposition was not really there" (Ibid., 19). Cliffe observes that this conflict "must have sent out great shock waves, but ... is scarcely acknowledged in the public record, either in official statements or in commentaries and scholarly analyses." Cliffe, "Political Struggles," 107.

[19] Mueller explains, "The all-out attacks on 'exploiters' and 'capitalists' ... were neither 'socialist' nor mere mystification. They were the result of real material contradictions between the need for revenues ... [and] opportunities for petit-bourgeois accumulation in the 1960s" (Mueller, "The Historical Origins," 19). In protesting the "leadership code," Bibi Titi was therefore among the "exploiters" and "capitalists."

[20] After 1965, Oscar Kambona was moved to the Ministry of Regional Administration and Rural Development—an obvious demotion from his position as minister of foreign affairs. By the time he was expelled from TANU (along with eight other MPs) in October 1968, he had already gone into exile. He then began to attack Nyerere as a dictator, and was "in turn charged with having taken funds out of the country, with having been one of the worst offenders as a capitalist accumulator, and with plotting against Nyerere." Bienen, *Tanzania*, 437.

poisoned and die. We were told this by people like Gray Likungu Mattaka [Kambona's cousin] with whom we were arrested. And he told us when we got to the police station and were having a meal that Kambona was told that if he were arrested and sent to jail he was going to be poisoned and would die. That is why he ran away.

Kambona himself tried to persuade me right from the beginning that we should leave the country. But I told him bluntly that I couldn't [leave] because I didn't see that we had done anything wrong. I asked him why I should be arrested. Was I to be arrested because I resigned from the leadership? I had resigned peacefully. I didn't steal anything. I didn't rob anybody of anything. I didn't do anything wrong. I didn't abuse anyone; nor did I abuse the government or the party. Why, therefore, was I to be arrested? I asked him. I had just resigned and I was staying at home. He told me there would be a day when I would have to leave. I said: "OK, but I don't see why I should leave the country. I have an old mother. I also have a grown up daughter although she is with her husband. But my mother is so old—she is ninety-five. I feel I cannot leave her. She doesn't know what this is about. If I leave her, she will complain. She doesn't know politics. In fact, she will think I just decided to run away from her. If I have to be arrested, let it be. Let her see for herself that I am arrested. Let me be killed. But I would like her to know and to see with her own eyes that I have been killed."

From my place [where Bibi Titi is living again, after 1988] we could see many people cooking food for those involved in the construction going on there [across the road]. In the neighborhood there was a lot of security. A scooter would pass, then a Peugeot, then a Volkswagen. They would check out who was coming in [the house]—where they came from, how many there were, and what time they arrived.

My husband was told to divorce me because I was to be arrested soon. "You'll find yourself in a lot of difficulty if you continue with this woman," he was told. Then, one day I received a letter from Verji [a lawyer] telling me that I was behind on two monthly installments on my house, and that either I had to pay immediately or an attachment would be put on my house. I went to Verji and asked him if they could really put an attachment on my house just because of two installments. He replied that he was just following instructions—that he had received a letter from Jubilee Insurance in Nairobi to that effect. "I think it would be better for you to go and see Sir Eboo [of Jubilee Insurance] and offer to pay the arrears in ten monthly installments. I am just a lawyer. I don't have the final say. I can't give you the final decision on this issue. You'd better go to Nairobi yourself."

I therefore decided to go to Nairobi. On my way, I found myself in the same plane with a big security man. I thought he was just going on normal duties; I wasn't aware that he was following me. When I got to Nairobi, Margaret Kenyatta, whom I had previously phoned, came to meet me at the airport. After staying for two days, I went to see Sir Eboo on the third day. He welcomed me to his office and told me that he had received the message about my visit. It appears that they had telephoned him from Dar es Salaam about the question of my house. When I got into his office, he apologized that Mr. Tom Mboya,[21] who had a previous appointment,

---

[21] Tom Mboya, an important trade unionist and nationalist leader in Kenya, who in 1968 was head of the Ministry of Planning and Development. He was later assassinated.

was due there any time. I explained that because of some problems I had not been able to pay those two installments. And I suggested that I pay the arrears in ten equal installments over and above my normal monthly installments. He said that he accepted the proposal and showed me the letter he was writing to the representative in Dar es Salaam, and asked me to come later to collect a copy of it.

Suddenly, Tom Mboya came in. When the secretary had told Sir Eboo of Mboya's presence, he asked me whether I wanted to meet him. And I said yes and Tom came and was surprised to see me. He asked why I had come to Kenya without looking him up. Tom had similar problems to discuss with Sir Eboo.

At this time, Tom was not on good terms with Mzee Kenyatta. I was staying with Margaret Kenyatta so I couldn't telephone him from that house. Tom asked where I was staying and why I wasn't staying with him. I apologized to him because I was staying with Margaret. He replied that if that's where I was staying, never mind. "But when are you going back?" I said, "Tomorrow. I've settled what I've come for." "It means we won't see each other" [he said]. And I said, "I think we won't." So we shook hands and I left.

The day I returned to Dar es Salaam, I found that the security man was again with me on the same plane. It appears he had thought I had run away from the country. Or that I would be meeting Kambona in Kenya. I had been followed.[22]

On my second day back home, my husband went to have a bath. After his bath, he sat on the bed and I went to have a bath. I came back to find him crying on the bed. "Why are you crying? What is the trouble?" He replied, "Didn't you know that I divorced you today?" I asked why. "For no reason. I've just decided to do so." I pressed him to tell me why. "Why are we to be divorced? What wrong have I done you? What are my mistakes? I thought you knew why I went to Nairobi, and the problem that took me there. I didn't even stay three days. What are we quarreling about? What is it that made you decide to just divorce me? Is it because I told you that I resigned from leadership? Is that why you are divorcing me?"

He replied that he had been told he would not be able to get a job because I have so many houses to rent. "If I want a job in the government, I won't be able to get one because I have a wife who is renting houses. Would you agree if I told you to sell your houses? I can't ask you to do that. Or do you think you would be able to do that sort of thing?" I said, "Don't you think we should have discussed this first before you suddenly decided to divorce me?" What I didn't realize then was that he had been told that I would be arrested. He emphasized that he wasn't going to advise me about anything and that day was the end of us. He left.

Six months later I was arrested and detained [in October, 1969].[23] I stayed in jail for two years and two months. First they took me to Central Police Station. From there I went to Ukonga [prison on Pugu Road]. From Ukonga

---

[22] During the trial in which Bibi Titi and others were accused of treason, the prosecution charged that she went to Nairobi in order to get money that was sent by Kambona to pay participants in the alleged coup, and in order to communicate with him (*Nationalist*, June 25, 1970).

[23] Bibi Titi was arrested and held under the Preventive Detention Act, along with five others. These five were Michael Kamaliza, former trade union leader and cabinet minister, and four officers of the Tanzania Peoples Defence Force: J. Herman, E. D. Lifa (Chipaka), E. P. Millinga, and A. Kyara (*Nationalist*, October 13 & 27, 1969).

I went to Keko [the largest remand prison in the country, suburban Dar es Salaam] and one morning I was taken from there to Zanzibar. Then from Zanzibar, we came back to Dar es Salaam.

I really don't know why I was taken from one place to another. It seems to have been their system. How they operated. I went to Zanzibar at four a.m. on the second day of my arrest. I stayed there for one week and then I was removed from there during the night.[24] I was sent to Mr. Karume [first vice president] who told me that Mr. Nyerere wanted me returned to Dar es Salaam. Munanka [minister of state in the president's office] came to collect me. We slept there. In the morning both of us flew to Dar es Salaam and we went to see President Nyerere at the State House. I was a prisoner and I was taken to the security building.

Nyerere said he didn't know anything. "You go with them; we shall later know what to do. You know it is not my job, Bibi Titi. You've been arrested by the government but we shall want to know what happens." I was just taken straight to him [Nyerere] and from there I was taken to the security building where we were roughly handled and tortured a lot to tell them what they regarded as the truth.[25] From there we were taken to Keko again. And from Keko I was transferred to Dodoma [Central Tanzania]. I stayed at Dodoma Prison. I went in October and I stayed there until February [1972] when I was released. I went back to my home in Temeke only to discover that all three of my houses had been confiscated.

[Because she had said very little about her time in prison during our initial interviews in 1984, Mr. Chiume and I asked Bibi Titi if she could tell us more about her time in prison when we met again in 1988.]

Jail is jail. It is bad. It can never be good. The life of any prisoner is never good. Do you think that as long as Mandela in South Africa is in jail there is anything good? Never! Jail is jail. I was alone in a cell. I was entitled to second-class food, consisting of rice, meat, and beans. I don't know what the first-class diet was. Third-class was *ugali* [stiff maize porridge], beans, *mchicha* [spinach-like greens], and once a week, rice. I didn't do any work. I wasn't even allowed to go outside. I used to get the newspaper through the kindness of a certain prison officer. I wasn't entitled to it. And I used to get letters. My mother and my daughter used to come to visit me; even my other relatives used to come. Whoever wanted to see me could see me.

But the first cell I was put into—when they took me from this house [her house in Upanga]—in that cell, there had been a certain lunatic called Pasizioze—a Haya. She had defecated for two days and all the dirt was still there. She had burnt her house back home for which she had been arrested. She was from Bukoba. She was mad. And I found that in the cell in which I was put there was two days of feces from this woman. Mind you, after coming from this home of mine!

I left this house [in Upanga] at eleven p.m. on the 10th of October [1969]. And I never came back again until the 31st of August this year [1988].

---

[24]   According to trial documents, Bibi Titi wrote a letter requesting to be transferred back to Dar es Salaam from Central Prison in Zanzibar because she was not receiving adequate medical treatment there (*Nationalist*, July 23, 1970).

[25]   Bibi Titi's claims to have been tortured to exact a confession were dismissed by the chief justice, Mr. George, who stated that "there were no swellings, no humiliations, her breasts were not pulled nor was she left naked" (*Nationalist*, September 2, 1970).

[After my release from prison] I just used to come to check my furniture. I had tenants. They had rented both the house and the furniture. One young man, an Asian who was killed in front of the Oyster Bay Hotel whose name was Nizzar, helped my daughter after I had been arrested. He was killed by his fellow Asians in front of the Oyster Bay Hotel in 1971. He was the one who convinced my daughter that it would be better to rent this house because my mother was crying every day, and go to Temeke and stay there because my mother would be close to her relatives.

This house was confiscated after it had already been rented. Even when I was around here myself, I rented the upper portion to a man called Johannes who was director general of Ethiopian Airlines, I think. Whatever, he was their boss. He stayed upstairs. Here, downstairs, there was the first secretary of the Burundi Embassy. They also wanted to arrest this man in this house, on the orders of their government. He was the first person to be arrested. They came with all the show of force and followed him. I got out of the house and asked what was happening here. They replied, "We want Emanuel. Emanuel Ngiri." And I told them he lived upstairs. They went there quietly and then disappeared. I followed up and found that the man had already run away. He had been tipped off to do so. And then I asked his wife what exactly had happened. She replied that Michombero had already given the order that her husband should be arrested. He alleged that he had been organizing groups of people from Burundi to go back and overthrow the government. He therefore wanted him arrested and deported to Burundi. This was the result of fabrications by our ambassador, Mr. Mangona.

But the Tanzanian government had actually helped us. It tipped off Emanuel to run away. He was told, "We are bringing police to arrest you at such and such a time. You get out of the house and run away." When they got there, he had already left. They had told him to disappear. That was in the very same year—1969. I think it was in May or June. I was arrested during the night—at midnight in the month of October.

[We asked whether Bibi Titi had to agree to any conditions when she was released from prison in 1972.] When I was released from jail, it was without conditions.... At first I was detained and then I was put in remand for six months. After that I was jailed. I stayed as a prisoner for six months. The whole period comes to two years and two months. I was not given any conditions. I was just released and pardoned by the president.

[We asked her if her release came as a surprise.] I wasn't surprised to be released. I didn't expect it, yet I wasn't surprised. I didn't expect to be released in such a short time. I thought I'd be in jail for three or five years, and then after that I would be released. And yet, when I was suddenly released I wasn't surprised.

He [the president] never called to see me. The only time I saw him was when I went to demand that my house be given back. I went to see him just to demand that.

I committed no crime. I saw myself as a person who had been wrongly imprisoned. I didn't know what crime I had committed. And since I didn't know what I had done, I didn't know what offence I had committed, I wasn't surprised to be released. I thought that perhaps they themselves, after further investigation, had concluded that there was no cause for me to be in jail, and therefore decided I should be released. If I had committed any big crime and then had been forgiven or I had—as it was alleged—

conspired with soldiers to overthrow the government, or that I had known about something like that, I would have been surprised that such a person who had committed such a great crime would be released so quickly. But I didn't participate in any such conspiracy. I just found myself arrested as a result of false allegations by other people; and I knew it was just false allegations by my enemies which brought me into prison. I was not worried about the questions I was asked in court[26] because I knew that I had done nothing wrong.

Some of the people I was arrested with stayed in jail for a long time—nearly eleven years. The Chipaka brothers came out only recently. Perhaps only four years ago. They stayed a long time in jail. Mattaka [Kambona's cousin] had committed no crime. He was found not guilty. That very same Matlaka who was supposed to be our leader in the mutiny was found not guilty. That very leader was found not guilty. It is therefore surprising that we were imprisoned. And Kamaliza was found not guilty. He came out after the appeal along with Colonel Chacha. I lost the appeal.[27]

After I got out of jail I just sold *mafuta* [paraffin oil]. That was the only business I was involved in. I gave it up after a while. Life was not good to me. Life was very difficult. But I was patient. I put up with my situation. How could life be good when my houses had been confiscated? I had no job. How can life be good under those circumstances? Life was very difficult, but I remained patient. When one of my houses was returned, I rented it—the one on Haile Selassie Street. I rented it for 3,000 shillings a month. At that time that was not a bad deal. And that was what I used [to live on]. I was staying in a Swahili area in a house where expenses were not very great. For example, we swept the yard in turns. While that was enough there, it is not enough where I am staying here.

I got the first house back in 1976. I was very much helped by Tabitha Siwale [minister of lands]. There were many ministers of lands whom I had approached on this question but they didn't even mention my request to Nyerere. I will always remember that young girl for the rest of my life. She helped me tremendously. When Siwale became minister for lands, she was able to confront Nyerere and kept on pushing him until I got that house back.

Why did she keep on urging? How come Mzee [the old man, referring to Nyerere] kept refusing? Our law says that if a person has two houses,

---

[26] The entire court case is covered in a series of articles in the *Nationalist* beginning on May 8, 1970, through the verdicts given in February 1971 and appeals in May 1971. A useful index of articles is available in the national library, Dar es Salaam.

[27] The charges against the accused of conspiring to overthrow the government and kill Nyerere were primarily based on the testimony of chief state witness and informer, Potlako Leballo, a South African whose association with the Pan Africanist Congress was supposed to carry with it the promise of involving "freedom fighters" in the coup. Oscar Kambona was described as the "brains" and nerve center of the conspiracy, and was number one among the eight formally accused. From exile in Britain, he pronounced the trial a "show trial" and stated that he only wished to form an effective opposition to Nyerere, who was "establishing a regime of personal power" (*Nationalist*, May 14, 1970). After proceedings which lasted from May 1970 to February 1971, Bibi Titi, journalist Gray Likungu Mattaka, and two brothers, John and Elia Chipaka, were convicted of treason. Michael Kamaliza, and William Chacha, Colonel in the Tanzanian People's Defence Forces, were acquitted of treason but convicted of misprision of treason, and Alfred Millinga, a lieutenant in the Tanzanian People's Defence Forces, was acquitted on all counts (*Nationalist*, January 31, 1971). Bibi Titi, Mattaka, and the Chipaka brothers were all given life sentences. Chacha and Kamaliza received ten years each, but won acquittal on appeal (*Nationalist*, February 10, 1971).

you confiscate one and leave the other. "Now we have confiscated three houses. We must give her back one." She fought bravely—that young woman—until I got the house back. But the men were afraid to approach Nyerere to tell him to return Titi's house to her. They were frightened.

As for my involvement in politics now [1988], I go to functions when I am invited, but I am not involved on a permanent basis. The sort of help I give is that when they ask me to say a word or two, I do so. For example, when we went for the tree-planting campaign in Shinyanga, it was arranged that I would participate. I went to the army area to plant trees in 1987. I said one or two words to thank them [people who had participated]; but I don't participate as actively as I used to in the past. I am a member of UWT and also of CCM.

Although women themselves say they have not progressed, I who know them since the early days feel that women's lot has improved tremendously because our government is helping women. They are giving us all sorts of help. The problem is with the [women's] leadership, not with the general population of women.

There is progress, Alhamdulilahi! [Praise Be to God] If you visit hostels, there are women. The only kind of job that many women haven't participated in is the kind which requires great strength. Most don't want that because their bones are different from men's. It is different with Chinese women [referring to her visit to China]. I personally wouldn't want to persuade a woman to be like that; but teachers, doctors, directors, administrators—women are suited for such jobs.

In her enthusiasm for the establishment of the All Africa Women's Conference, Bibi Titi expresses her commitment to a pan-African women's organization, which would enable African women to sustain a post-independence political presence and voice. In her view, she achieved an especially important victory when she convinced other representatives to hold the second All Africa Women's Conference meeting in Tanganyika, where women from countries not yet independent could participate more easily. The deaths of conference participants in a road accident while on a field trip to Morogoro overshadowed this meeting.

During the early 1960s, women leaders from Uganda, Tanganyika, and Kenya also met for several East African Seminars initially organized by Margaret Kenyatta. At the seminar held April 11–18, 1964, in Nairobi, Bibi Titi, then a member of Parliament and president of UWT, gave one of the major speeches. She gave it in Swahili, because, she said, Swahili was East Africa's common language, and foreigners needed to know that Swahili was valued and to know that when they visited, they were in Africa.[28] "We in East Africa are promoting foreign things—clothes, languages, way of life," she scolded, "so that even the foreigners despise us now. They have us feeling that they are the only ones with good things to offer, and that we have nothing."[29]

---

[28] Although Bibi Titi had strong political reasons for promoting Swahili as an African *lingua franca* beyond the nation's borders, it is also well-known that she was never comfortable speaking English, even after taking a course through the British Council after independence. See Hon. Bibi Titi Mohamed, M.P., "Women in Politics," in Report of East African Women's Seminar, Kenya Institute of Administration, April 11–18, 1964, 52. I wish to thank Aili Tripp for providing me with a copy of this document.

[29] Ibid.

It was in this vein that Bibi Titi proceeded, linking her views on the importance of African dress, culture, language, and perspective in what today might be called the language of "empowerment." So few of her speeches survive that I cite this one (in translation from the Swahili) at length to provide a sense of Bibi Titi's post-independence nationalism.

> Don't feel that Bibi Titi is here to fill you up with politics—but let me tell you that there is nothing you can do that does not include politics. Politics is being taught in every way and in everything: in medicine, in teaching, in agriculture, even in culture.... Our government says that government servants should not indulge in politics and yet government itself is politics.... The teacher is told not to get into politics, and yet she has to teach the children the policy of the government. How can she do this without getting into politics? This is an astonishing idea that must come to an end in East Africa.
>
> [About remembering where you come from now that you are a "modern" person] ... but when you were five years old where were you living? And what were you before you attained your present status? Everyone in the city has come from the village.... You feel that the stool that your grandmother sat on is too dirty for you. It's not bad to look after yourself, but remember not to look down upon your parents. Do not despise those who made you what you are. That is the influence of colonialism. This we must leave aside.
>
> Foreign cultures will not benefit us now. What we need is to polish our own culture. We have chased away foreigners but their deeds still remain....
>
> [Noting that West African women wear their African clothes proudly, and similarly women in India, but after the opening ceremony of the seminar, the East African women were all in Western dress] We do not refuse to put on Western dress but we would like occasionally to have Westerners copy us. If they like Africa, then they should like some things of Africa. Perhaps they like Africa because they have big *shambas* [farms] or there is big trade; that is not proper liking of Africa. To like Africa is to like the people and their traditions....
>
> I don't want the seminar to be just words. We in the seminar have come as teachers who will go back and teach people in the villages what has been going on in the seminar.... If we are going to make decisions, our governments must recognize our decisions....
>
> [Stressing that all the male leaders of Africa had mothers who contributed to their development as leaders, Bibi Titi noted that there were no women in the Parliaments of Uganda or Kenya and said this was shameful. That in Tanganyika there were six elected and two nominated women in the parliament, and two under-secretaries and an area commissioner. Moreover, there were women at every level of TANU, from village to the National Executive.]
>
> I am not satisfied to see you, my friends in East Africa, not playing any part in the govenment or in the political parties. This is your own fault; you are not joining parties. In Tanganyika the women did this long ago— the women struggled just as much as the men. Some women have been left by their husbands, some have been beaten up, some have been abused—but we didn't mind. Some homes have been broken up because the mother was out most of the time conducting meetings in the villages— but we didn't mind. That is why the government has recognized us. If we

had just sat down and shouted "Why are we not in the government," nobody would have listened to us.... But do you think you will be elected
just sitting in your house and shouting "Won't you choose me"? They
won't elect you because they don't know you.[30]

It was, of course, one thing to insist that "everything is politics" and another
to infuse the UWT or the East African Women's Seminars with a clear sense of the
political nature of their undertakings. To remind seminar participants, or the
younger, educated women of the UWT that TANU women had sometimes chosen
political activity over husbands and even children did not offer an image or model
that translated well in the post-independence period. To "help other women," yes;
but now was also a time, it was assumed, for women to enjoy the presumed fruits
of self-rule as well.

Bibi Titi's lack of formal education was an obvious source of tension within
the UWT. While she commanded respect and admiration for her central role in the
independence struggle and as a leader who would and could sit down with "ordinary" women, it was the younger, educated women who believed they had important things to teach these same women. There was no easy transition, then, from
politics to "women's development," and politics remained Bibi Titi's forte.

Bibi Titi's personal account of the army mutiny of 1964 suggests that, at least
in 1988, she was less attuned to the potential damage to Nyerere's leadership and
the way in which Kambona's role might have seemed threatening than to the particulars of her own experience. From the time of the Zanzibar Revolution and subsequent army mutiny on the mainland, Nyerere tightened his control over all ele-
ments of society. Not only was there less consultation in general in Tanzania after
1964, but the very bodies that might have expressed a collective rather than individual view were increasingly outlawed or circumscribed.

Bibi Titi was not alone among TANU's leading incumbents to lose in the the
country's first national elections of 1965. As Bienen notes, "All told, 22 out of 31
TANU officeholders were unsuccessful; and 16 out of 31 MPs lost."[31] But losing the
1965 election was clearly a blow to Bibi Titi and an indication to TANU and the
government that politicians, regardless of their past national records, were expected
to serve their constituencies. A reading of Bibi Titi's negative response to the Arusha
Declaration and Leadership Code as one of simple self-interest ignores her genuine concern over the lack of consultation (as distinct from acclamation) that pro-
pelled the country into the mode of "socialism and self-reliance." Moreover, the
consequences of a "one-house policy" were decidedly different for a woman with
little education and no prospects for employment in the formal sector once out of
office than they were for an educated politician with post-political opportunities in
the private or international sector—a man whose capital had been invested elsewhere. The burden of the leadership code fell unequally, then, on political leaders
with fewer prospects, however enthusiastically the charges of "capitalist accumulator" sounded throughout the country.

---

[30]   Ibid., 52–54.

[31]   Bienen, *Tanzania*, 394. Bienen further notes that junior ministers like Bibi Titi were hit hardest by a
popular "throw-the-varmints-out" sentiment because "they had all the liabilities of being out of touch
and antagonizing people by their relative wealth." Ten of the fourteen junior ministers lost their seats
(ibid., 394).

Following the Arusha Declaration, Bibi Titi was clearly tainted by her long-time friendship with Oscar Kambona, who left the country to begin a political offensive against Nyerere's policies from a position of relative safety. In Tanzania's first treason case, Bibi Titi, "alias Mama Mkuu [Big Mama], alias Mwamba Mkuu [huge rock], alias Mkuu, alias Mwamba, alias Anti [auntie]" was charged with seven others[32] of conspiring between July 1968 and September 1969, to "overthrow the government by unlawful means...."[33]

At this trial, Bibi Titi's opposition to the Arusha Declaration, her resignation from the leadership of the UWT in June 1967, and her friendship with Kambona became evidence of "political frustration" that caused her to join a Kambona-led and -financed conspiracy to overthrow the government by force. The "third accused," Bibi Titi was specifically charged with instigating, counselling, and persuading "one person to recruit people to assassinate President Nyerere."[34] True to form, Bibi Titi entered her plea of "not guilty" in Swahili, while all the others (with the exception of Colonel Chacha) denied their guilt in English.[35]

The prosecution's prime witness, Potlako Leballo, recounted secret meetings with Bibi Titi during which she allegedly told him of widespread discontent in the country and of a coup plan, "Operation Ufagio."[36] When she finally took the witness stand on October 19, 1970, Bibi Titi acknowledged that until her arrest on October 10, 1969, she had participated in the "constitutional reform campaign" that Kambona began after resigning from government and his post as TANU secretary-general, and had communicated with Kambona in London regarding other individuals concerned with changing the constitution. She vigorously denied, however, that she had ever advocated force to overthrow the government, that she had any knowledge of a plot to overthrow Nyerere, or that she had ever solicited Leballo to recruit South African "freedom fighters" to kill the president. She cited her twelve-year friendly working relationship with and admiration for Nyerere, and pointed out that except for Kambona, she didn't even know any of the other accused very well.[37] Her response to charges of secret meetings, subversive correspondence, and money from Kambona, along with questions about her own state of indebtedness regarding her houses, involved five days of court testimony, during which she reiterated that security men had obtained a false statement about her guilt by beating her, abusing her, and threatening to kill her.[38]

In cross-examining Bibi Titi, Attorney General Mark Bomani pursued a gendered line of questioning that revealed the ease with which women's right to

---

[32]   The others, with their positions and ages at the time of the trial were as follows: Oscar Salathiel Kenneth Kambona, 43, former minister for regional administration, self-exiled in the United Kingdom; Gray Likungu Mattaka, 34, a journalist; John Dustan Lifa Chipaka, 38, former official of the Workers' Development Corporation of NUTA; Michael Marshall Mowbray Kamaliza, 40, former secretary-general of NUTA and minister of labor; Elia Dustan Lifa Chipaka, 32, captain in the Tanzania People's Defence Forces; William Makori Chacha, 46, colonel in the Tanzania People's Defence Forces, and Alfred Phillip Millinga, 27, a lieutenant in the Tanzania People's Defence Forces (*Nationalist*, May 8 and May 11, 1970).

[33]   Ibid., May 8, 1970.

[34]   *Nationalist*, June 1, 1970

[35]   *Nationalist*, June 9, 1970.

[36]   Ibid. *Ufagio* refers to a small bundle of twigs used for sweeping.

[37]   *Nationalist*, October 20 and 21, 1970.

[38]   *Nationalist*, October 24, 1970.

equality, presumably advanced with TANU's independence victory, could be "forgotten." After asking Bibi Titi to explain why she refused to leave politics when her first husband said he would divorce her if she didn't, Bomani chided: "So you were not prepared to bow down to your husband?" "You seem to be a very tough woman." "I don't know," Bibi Titi replied. "Tough women don't want to get married. I want to. Anyway, I am not tough."[39] Later, when pressing Bibi Titi about why she ever trusted Leballo regarding letters to Kambona and how money was being spent [whether for constitutional reform activities or a coup], Bomani asked, "Excuse me, was there any sexual attraction on your part to Mr. Leballo which made you foolishly accept everything he told you." Bibi Titi said no.[40]

Page one headlines of the *Nationalist* of December 23, 1970, proclaimed "Titi A Forceful Personality." In his closing statement regarding Bibi Titi, Attorney General Bomani argued that Bibi Titi was very strong, and not "meek and pliable" as her defense lawyer tried to suggest. She had not hesitated to "ditch her husband when he stood [in] her way." Even the chief state witness, Leballo, "would not play with her."[41]

In February 1972, the month Bibi Titi came out of prison, a series of tabloid photographs entitled "Rise and Fall of Bibi Titi" captured the way in which her political narrative was constructed for a Tanzanian public. A picture captioned "Bibi Titi in Her Heyday" shows Bibi Titi and Nyerere, both looking young and smiling, dancing together western style at a "glittering ball." Another of Bibi Titi with both hands raised (apparently addressing a crowd that cannot be seen) is entitled "Power Was Her Undoing," while yet another entitled "And a Top Crowd-Puller" shows her, mouth wide open before a microphone as "tough, domineering, persuasive." A final picture of her with a basket in her hand at a handicraft exhibit becomes the opportunity to state that Bibi Titi could not resist "The Allure of Wealth" and to note cryptically, "Her own pleasures were not quite so simple. She found more satisfaction in creating wealth."[42]

Two years later, a reporter interviewed Bibi Titi, casting her personal and political history in the article text as well as photographs in the light of the "menial" (shredding coconut for curry) and "humble" (caring for her grandchildren and marketing) "roles" to which she was now seemingly reduced. At the time, she was living in her daughter's house with her daughter, six granchildren, and ninety-three-year-old mother. The "rise and fall narrative" produced by the reporter included Bibi Titi's "love life." After repeating the standard story of her divorces, the reporter quoted her as saying that she has had no more love affairs since leaving prison—that she has "parental love—my mother whom I love and care for—and I have my own daughter and grandchildren. At my age you don't need the love of a man so much. I get by as I am. It never bothers me not having a husband."[43]

By the late 1980s, it was no longer appropriate to comment on Bibi Titi's personal, marital, or sexual life since it now served the party's interest to resurrect her.

---

[39] *Nationalist*, October 27, 1970.

[40] *Nationalist*, October 29, 1970.

[41] *Nationalist*, December 23, 1970.

[42] *Drum Magazine* "Exclusive," *Trust*, February 1972.

[43] "My Amazing Life," an interview with Bibi Titi Mohamed, in *Trust*, August, 1974. (Reporter unidentified in my copy).

In December 1988, in an issue of the *Business Times* marking Tanzania's twenty-seventh year of independence, a list of some two dozen "Highlights"—notable events since December 1961—included the following reference to Bibi Titi: "1970—The treason trial involving Bibi Titi, a Party veteran, and others. She was later pardoned and rehabilitated." Once erased from TANU's noble history because she, in Nyerere's words, "slipped a little," Bibi Titi was now back in the public record as "rehabilitated."[44] By 1991 and Tanzania's celebration of three decades of independence, Bibi Titi appeared in a supplement of the government-owned newspaper, *Uhuru*, not simply as a rehabilitated woman, but as "A Heroine of Uhuru Struggle." In this story, as Ruth Meena points out, there is no mention of the fact that she was once accused and condemned for treason.[45] Although the title for Ruth Meena's 1992 article asks whether Bibi Titi is a "Traitor or Heroine of Uhuru?" and notes in the subheading that she has recently been declared "a heroine of *uhuru* (freedom) struggle,"[46] complete rehabilitation clearly seems to require the erasure of a significant period of Bibi Titi's and of TANU's nationalist history. More recently still, a major Dar es Salaam street, Umoja wa Wanawake Street, has been renamed Bibi Titi Mohamed Street.

---

[44] *Business Times*, 9 December 1988.

[45] Meena, "Bibi Titi," 46.

[46] Ibid.

9

Postscript: Nationalism in "Postcolonial" Tanzania

Bibi Titi wasn't educated. Of course few women were educated in the 1950s. I don't quite know how to put it, but Bibi Titi was a particular kind of woman—the kind who obviously no husband would put up with [because] she was riding around in a TANU Landrover with men for months on end. So she was courageous to go ahead and be political—something it wasn't possible for a woman to do. Now, there are many educated women in politics, and this is acceptable because they have drivers who bring them home at night.[1]

"Naming:" Bibi Titi Mohamed's Praise Poem

There were many women with courage in TANU
Like Bibi Judith Matola.
But many have died.
Judith Matola died in Mbeya.

Asha binti Waziri has also died, and Binti Saidi.
I knew them because they were on my committee.

Asha Ngoma is still alive.
Mwamvita is still alive but very old.
They were all in Dar es Salaam.

Tatu binti Mzee was my vice-chairman.
She is the same person as Tatu Mohamed.

Mwabufu has died.
Mtumwa Mzuri—they were from Tabora.
Maofi from Nzega....

As for Mama Hawa of Zanzibar,
She was just after something.

---

[1] Discussion with Lt. Col. Hiza, CCM Regional Secretary, Moshi, October 7, 1988.

I am telling you!
She just used to come to meetings.
She was a person to be told what to do.

But they travelled by themselves
all over the country.
Asha binti Mohamed in Musoma.
And Kijakazi Ferruzi in Dodoma.
Binti Sultani from Tanga,
She is dead.

At the moment, the wife of Shariff Maina,
Binti Kassimu, is here from Tanga.
To see her, ask Juma Mapachu.
He was in the organization in Dar es Salaam.

Vitabu Kondoa, she is also dead.
Moshi, bi Zena is dead.
Bi Mgeni Simba is dead.
Lucy Lameck is left.
We were together from the beginning.
But she left for education
and came back in the 1960s.

We went together to Copenhagen to a women's meeting.
We went together to China.
We are discoverers of China!
She was my interpreter.
I was supposed to go with Shemsanga.
But when she returned, she said
"You shouldn't go with Shemsanga.
We'll go together."

Hadija binti Swedi went from Morogoro.
Bibi Kibadaga from Songea also went.
She has resigned, but her daughter, Zaituni,
is still in the party.
She is married and a member of the NEC.

Binti Salehe Kibuyu!
Write, "Kibuyu binti Salehe."
She was an *ngoma* leader.
And Rehema binti Selemani was an *ngoma* leader.
They are both dead.

And then Binti Fundi Mkono.
There is Mwamvita Ramahdani, she is dead.

Hadija Kamba was not a leader.
Her leader was Binti Makubuli.
If this lady is still alive,
you should talk to her
Because she was "Mrumba."
In her group, this one was their leader.
"Mrumba" was a traditional dance

Of the Wanyamwezi,
And of the Wamanyema also.

Mwamvita Mnyamani is alive but very old.
She lives in Narung'ombe Street.
If you are coming from Lumumba Street
you turn left at the shop facing Lumumba.
The second or third house is hers.
First, go and find out if she is alive or dead.

Asha Tuwazeni, Asha binti Waziri, Saada binti Kipara.
Halima binti Hamisi—these were the first ones.
Halima binti Hamisi was a teacher.
She was teaching.

Anna Gwassa, Mwamvita Bundizi—she is dead.
Hawa Mafuta—she is dead.

Hadija Malaya Mambo—she is dead.
She lived in Buguruni.
That one was married to Mambo Mzinga.
But when she became a leader
she was already divorced.

Binti Madenge is dead.
Binti Mohammed Ndimi Mbovu, Mary Ibrahim.

Mama Pamba has left the names Masha Bilali [Kiongo].
Mwamvita, sister of Mr. Thabit,
who was CID [Intelligence].
It is known.
These came later, towards the end.

Mtumwa Kitete is dead. Miss Hawa of Mkunguni.
There is also one lady,
Mwanaharusi binti Fundi.
A leader, Mama Dezi, stays in Temeke Bonderi—
Mjimwema [Miji Mwema?]
Mwasubiri Ali, a leader.
Mama Sakina (Mchikichini).

I began this book with the retelling of that "extraordinary event" in October 1985 when Julius Nyerere took the occasion of the beginning of his own gradual withdrawal from the formal political life of Tanzania to publicly acknowledge Bibi Titi Mohamed's significant place in the nationalist movement. Thus began Bibi Titi's "rehabilitation." Beginnings and endings interconnect and cross paths at this moment. And it is this, perhaps, rather than "progress," that characterizes historical process (or history).

The notion of Bibi Titi Mohamed's rehabilitation fits a Tanzanian nationalist metanarrative of continuing achievement through claims to coherence and regularity. Ironically, it is a version of nationalism devoid of the complexity, nuance, or human content embodied in Benedict Anderson's insightful term, "imagined community." It is a nationalist story that allocates all but a few Tanzanians to the role of respondent or spectator. I begin this postscript with a specifically voiced but

widely accepted representation of Bibi Titi as a political actor—*not* as a woman—
and how having a driver (exemplifying both state privilege and the restitution of a
gendered protection) presumably makes it no longer oxymoronic to be a "woman
politician." Bibi Titi Mohamed's "praise poem" disrupts this master narrative with
insistent naming.

Women's invocation of names is a powerful commonplace in worlds and contexts as vastly different from each other as Dar es Salaam, Charleston, South Caro-
lina, and the cities of Argentina, El Salvador, and Guatamala.[2] In Charleston, Mamie
Garvan Fields insisted on what her sociologist granddaughter termed "god-awful
exhaustiveness," or the kind of "flawless memory" imposed by standards of "so-
ciability" that Karen Fields calls "the wedding list/church program sort of memory."
When Fields gave her grandmother a typescript of the Epilog to *Lemon Swamp and
Other Places* (Mamie Garvan Fields' life story, told to her granddaughter), her grandmother said it "absolutely would not do."

> It needed to mention Mrs. So and So, of Such and Such Street. It could not
> possibly be published without remembering Pastor This and That. Why,
> these are the people I have worked with for decades. They deserve the
> credit. These are the people who have been waiting to see my book, who
> put their names down to buy the first copies off the press. My rejoinder,
> that no one outside Charleston would care, did not count: The important
> audience was in Charleston. If the details got tedious to outsiders, well
> we couldn't help that. Gram's purpose assigned those details to what can-
> not, nay, *must not be remembered mistakenly* [my emphasis]. My purpose
> consigned them to just as obligatory forgetting.[3]

Elizabeth Tonkin offers a generalization that unites such acts of naming so
often performed by women:

> Women animate words, as they bring life into the world; the past is pur-
> posefully deployed so as to change the future and people are honoured
> and individualised by specifying their names and the past of these names.
> No wonder, then, that the language structures in which they speak can
> carry such oblique and complex placings of persons and of time....[4]

In Bibi Titi's case, the insistent remembering, the naming and the phrasing of
words are hers. I am responsible for calling her summoning, her insistence on naming women, a praise poem. In doing so, I am not arguing—though Bibi Titi undoubtedly would—that these women belong to the pantheon of African nationalist
heroes. The purpose of this book has not been to glorify "women's role," in the
usual nationalist parlance. On the other hand, I do propose that these women, and

---

[2]   The mothers of the disappeared of El Salvador, Guatemala, and Argentina paraded and posted pictures of loved ones taken from them by the militaries of these repressive state regimes, and sang and
shouted their names in acts of political struggle and will—a refusal to forget and an invocation of individual lives, a denial of the dominant state discourse of "terrorists," "subversives" and statistics, and an
assault on the anonymity to which the state hoped to assign the dead and disappeared. See Renny Golden,
The Hour of the Poor, The Hour of Women (New York, 1991), 108.

[3]   Karen E. Fields, "What One Cannot Remember Mistakenly," Memory and History Symposium, 25–26
February, 1988, Waco, Texas (unpublished paper), 5-7.

[4]   Elizabeth Tonkin, *Narrating Our Pasts: The Social Construction of Oral History*, (Cambridge, 1992),
65.

thousands of women and men not unlike them, not only directly challenge the metanarrative of Tanzanian nationalist history, but also its obverse, the profound disenchantment expressed in Basil Davidson's "authoritative grand story"[5] about the failure of African nationalism, *The Black Man's Burden*. The view that African nationalisms have "failed" is predicated on official and essentially liberal/heroic constructions of African anticolonial political movements subverted and dashed against postcolonial realities. Like Walter Rostow's stages of economic development,[6] African nationalism was supposed to be, according to the anticolonial scholars of the 1960s and '70s, a story of progress told in ever more triumphant political stages. Tanzanian women participants in TANU complicate this story, and suggest the importance of refusing the characterization of nationalist movement as "success" or "failure."

From the TANU Women's Section to the UWT, Revisited

The narrative of a largely unproblematic transition from a preindependence TANU women's section to a postindependence national women's organization as a party affiliate of TANU (UWT) constitutes the gendered component of the nationalist metanarrative. Writing about the UWT in the early 1980s, I participated in this narrative, noting, for example, that the "roots" of the UWT lay in the TANU Women's Section, and that its leadership and members were drawn from it.[7] At that time, I was critical of the UWT's failings, including what I saw as a top-down approach to women's problems, a concentration on economic projects of interest to women who were already relatively well off, and a neglect of the "poorest of the poor"—namely, rural women. Based on the theses of several Tanzanian students at the University of Dar es Salaam, I also concluded that the UWT was inhibited by inefficiency, inadequate funding, and too close an attachment to the party (Chama cha Mapinduzi, CCM, the "party of the revolution," by this time). From this work, and from interviews and conversations with Tanzanian women, I also agreed that the organization suffered from *fitina* (discord, misunderstanding, quarrelling, antagonism) among women—especially between rural and urban women, and educated and non-educated. I argued, however, that all of these problems were symptomatic of government unwillingness to "move from rhetoric to concrete action in addressing the issue of unequal gender relations in Tanzanian society" and to "confront the issue of women's subordination and lack of control over their own labor power in the rural family or household."[8]

Although I was clear at the time of my earlier research that the TANU Women's Section and UWT had different agendas, I did not look closely at the period of transition from one to the other—the period beginning with the establishment of the UWT as a TANU affiliate on November 2, 1962, just eleven months after the country's independence. When most of the women I interviewed for this study

---

[5] Pieter Boele van Hensbrock uses this phrase in "Cursing The Nation-State," a review of *The Black Man's Burden* in *Transition*, 61 (1993): 114.

[6] W. W. Rostow, *The Stages of Economic Growth, a Non-Communist Manifesto* (Cambridge, 1960).

[7] Rogers, "Efforts Toward Women's Development"; Geiger, "Umoja wa Wanawake."

[8] Geiger, "Umoja Wa Wanawake," 59.

narrated an unproblematic transition from pre-(TANU Women's Section) to postindependence (UWT) organizing and association on the basis of gender, I probed no further. For example, in Moshi, Zainabu Hatibu spoke of belonging to two of the TANU Youth League women's groups—she was in her late teens at the time—and later, of being the third woman in Kilimanjaro to buy a UWT card and the first woman in Moshi to be on the UWT local council. Mario Kinabo, among the best-known of Moshi's TANU women activists, was chairperson for a local UWT cooperative which ran three shops when we met in 1988. Similarly, Nsiana Njau became regional chairperson for the UWT when she retired from nursing in 1985; and Violet Njiro saw women's successful economic projects, often undertaken through UWT, as evidence of TANU's insistence that women and men were equal and should not be restricted in their ability to meet together for economic or other purposes.

As I noted in Chapter 6, Moshi women activists tended to be younger and better educated than their Dar es Salaam counterparts, and were therefore more likely to see UWT's project orientation as a logical and important extension of TANU's support of women's equality in all spheres. But I did not ask whether there might be contradictions between the roles of the Women's Section and UWT. As a result, the insights provided in the interview context were either somewhat unintentional, as in the tensions between what TANU activist Aziza Lucas of Mwanza wanted to tell me about and what the UWT secretary who accompanied me on the interview seemed to think were more appropriate topics; or personal, as a return to the comments of Kanasia Mtenga and Bibi Titi Mohamed will illustrate.

CCM party secretary at the time of our meeting in 1988, Kanasia Mtenga stated that as the UWT's first vice president in 1962, she was "virtually alone there" because Bibi Titi was "already in trouble." Thus, Mrs. Mtenga continued, she had to convince both men and women that a women's organization was still necessary—not to fight men, who were worried, but to help women improve themselves.

It is relevant to recall that Mrs. Mtenga came to TANU rather late (1959), having been a Tanganyika Council of Women member, and with the advantage of considerable education and experience as a governor-nominated councillor of the Moshi Township Council. Like many Tanzanians, Mrs. Mtenga believed that the significant distinction between the TANU Women's Section and the UWT was that the former concerned "politics," while the latter concerned "women's issues and problems."

For Bibi Titi, a major difference between the Women's Section and the UWT was exemplified by their respective leadership titles: the Women's Section's most important officer was a secretary, while the UWT had a president. As the UWT's first president, Bibi Titi was acutely aware of a problem of trust between educated and less educated women in the newly established organization and, in her narrative, emphasized her attempts to reassure educated women that she needed and wanted their participation.

As should now be clear, the UWT was neither an outgrowth of TANU women's activism nor a product of their imagining. The Constitutional Congress of the All Africa Women's Conference held in Dar es Salaam in July 1962 had stipulated in its draft constitution that this body sought "the emancipation and rehabilitation of women, so that they could 'participate in all creative activities in the social and political fields of Africa.'"[9] But it was Nyerere and his advisors who determined that women needed to "develop" and, more specifically, help other women to "develop," and that existing women's groups already dedicated to this purpose should be brought under a single, government-affiliated and controlled organization. As Marja-Liisa Swantz notes with a mixture of dismay and irony, suddenly at independence women became "an ignorant, backward part of [the] population ... targets and not actors and initiators in development." "Only after Independence," she adds, "did the problem of how to organise the women arise."[10]

Just as the UWT was Nyerere's idea of what women needed next, the newly created Ministry of Cooperative and Community Development drafted the UWT constitution with the help of foreign advisers.

> [In establishing the UWT], we looked at different constitutions from Nigeria, from Ghana and from two other countries to see what kind of structure we would need. We wanted an executive board at the top that wouldn't be controlled by the party; but at the same time we wanted our decision-making felt by the ministry. We wanted the ideas from the lower levels [the grassroots] to come to the UWT and then from the UWT those ideas could be channeled through the ministry for the purpose of coordination and implementation to become government policy.[11]

As an umbrella organization designed to incorporate other registered women's organizations, the UWT replaced not the TANU Women's Section but the former Tanganyika Council of Women, whose president at the time was Nyerere's wife, Maria. Swantz notes,

> At a preparatory meeting held in July 1962 to discuss the draft, only representatives from the TCW and YWCA were present, together with the male officers from the Ministry, one of them an expatriate. It led to the actual founding of the organisation in the following September, after the All Africa Women's Congress.[12]

Both the TCW and YWCA saw assistance to women and women's roles in classic Western gendered terms. The TCW, in particular, had been part of the colonial apparatus intended to slow and direct the nationalist movement. Tanganyikan women associated with the TCW did not need to know of its larger unrealized goal to absorb both its approach to defining women's needs and its antipolitical philosophy into the new organization. To be an "open umbrella," the UWT had to shelter in uneasy alliance and proximity groups that represented diverse interests and populations of women. Gone was the political consciousness-raising of the TANU Women's Section; gone was a focus on equality not just between women and men, but among women.

Margaret Snyder, who served as an advisor to the UWT in 1964, remembers these tensions. On the one hand, no one doubted Bibi Titi's authority as head of the organization. Bibi Titi wanted the UWT to remain faithful to the tasks of the TANU Women's Section, emphasizing the mobilization of women for political pur-

---

[9]   Swantz, *Women in Development*, 159.

[10]   Ibid.

[11]   Lameck Interview, November 12, 1984.

[12]   Ibid., 160.

Photo 10: UWT group making mats, Kigamboni, 1969. Courtesy of the Government Information Office of Tanzania.

poses.[13] She was, as Snyder put it, a very powerful person—a "commanding personality" and a "tough boss" with firm views, one of which was that the UWT was her organization. She was the decision-maker. She didn't participate in the everyday running of the office, but, like a chairman of the board, she was "the power. There was no question who was in command."[14] Her constituency—her following, and the bulk of active UWT members—were what Snyder calls "the Mamas."

> When you first saw them in their black *buibuis*, you would think, "Oh dear, poor things;" and then you would find out that they had a key to a house here and a pack of cigarettes there, and you looked at them quite differently. They were a certain age group. There was Mama Hawa, and Mama Daisy, who was a younger, uneducated woman who was a kind of bridge between the mamas and the younger, educated women.[15]

Programmatically, however, the UWT was in the capable hands of women intent on "professionalizing" the organization and bringing "technical expertise" to the issue of women's economic problems and needs. That this was where Nyerere wanted UWT energies focused was clear. Many of the younger and more highly educated women who became part of the organization's central leadership were assigned to it from other government institutions and ministries. Martha Bulengo

---

[13]   Interview with Margaret Snyder, January 27, 1996, Kampala, Uganda.

[14]   Ibid.

[15]   Ibid.

from the Ministry of Community Development, Christina Nsekela, Sara Nyarenda, and Leah Lupembe were among the most important new actors on behalf of women—seeking funds and logistical support for women's training and leadership seminars, nutrition projects, and income-generating schemes of various kinds. But according to Snyder, only a handful of educated women worked with UWT, and young educated girls "couldn't fathom how this movement fit with their aspirations, their interests and their needs."[16]

The minutes of the UWT conference in 1965 provide an important text on the "new," newly subordinate, and internally fractious place of organized women in independent Tanzania. Although TANU women activists of the 1950s referred to Nyerere as their "son," it was as *Baba wa Taifa*, "Father of the Nation," that Nyerere opened the conference with paternalist remarks befitting his new title. After reminding the delegates that the government had established UWT to unite all women whether they had been involved in politics or not, rich and poor, educated and non-educated, he told them to identify both internal and external enemies who sought to destroy unity, and to hold a peaceful election of UWT officers in which the choice of the electorate was accepted by all, including the defeated candidate.

Nyerere also chose that occasion to address the nation regarding Ian Smith's Unilateral Declaration of Independence in Southern Rhodesia, and to emphasize that as the country's foreign minister, he was the only legitimate spokesman on this critical matter.[17] Thus, in one speech, Nyerere asserted government control over the UWT and established its mission; echoed the paranoia (enemies within, enemies without) that would increasingly mark Tanzanian citizen behavior as each person worried about the political correctness of her own and others' political views; and reminded all Tanzanians that his was the voice of foreign policy.

While the delegates readily accepted the president's speech, they challenged the UWT secretary general's report with questions and complaints about the cost of UWT leaders' trips overseas and the failure of those leaders to report back to the regions. One delegate charged that letters intended for regional delegates were being hidden by the *wakubwa* (big people) and were not being sent promptly from UWT headquarters.[18]

Mrs. Nyerere, who had never played a role in the TANU Women's Section, but was now in the UWT leadership, questioned UWT expenses but also chastized critical delegates from Tabora. Why were regional leaders at loggerheads with UWT leaders? Who was at fault? She went on to charge that the women themselves did not care about their offices/work. As for overseas trips to meetings and conferences, Mrs. Nyerere insisted that not just any woman could go because of what was involved. Mrs. Kawawa, wife of vice-president Rashidi Kawawa, echoed Mrs. Nyerere: Only those educated members who spoke English could be sent abroad, although there were some trips where even non-English speakers had been sent.[19]

Bibi Titi entered the debate to state that sometimes the UWT received scholarships for which they could not get "the right people from the regions," and

---

[16]   Ibid.

[17]   Mkutano Mkuu wa *Umoja wa Wanawake wa Tanganyika*, 1965, TNA 540, CCD 23. Translated from the Swahili by Suleiman Ngware.

[18]   UWT Conference minutes, 2.

[19]   Ibid.

were therefore forced to pick candidates from Dar es Salaam. For certain conferences, she added, it was necessary to choose individuals who knew something about the topics; on the other hand, for ordinary tours abroad, the UWT had sent many different people. Some complaints about favoritism were therefore unfounded.

The discussion continued, with UWT leaders from Dar es Salaam simultaneously defending the choice of certain women for international trips and pointing out the difficulties of communicating results to all members; while regional delegates spoke of a lack of equal opportunities and an absence of information. Mrs. Nyerere explained that sometimes returnees from overseas were not given the opportunity to report to the UWT what they had learned abroad; but a delegate from Tanga asserted that it was wrong for those returning from overseas not to tell others what they had seen and learned.[20]

It is, of course, the exchange itself that exemplifies the multiple tensions and divisions emerging in the context of postcolonial, government-dominated women's organizing in Tanzania. Hierarchies of position, place, and levels of education held by leaders at the UWT headquarters in Dar es Salaam were expressed through greater access to rewards and privileges, especially trips abroad. While the "reasons" why only certain women (i.e., knowledgeable English speakers) could adequately participate in conferences were reiterated, tensions around travel as a means to acquire knowledge, and around the responsibility of those who benefited to share that knowledge on return, spoke to the rift between rural and urban, regional and central, less educated and more educated women. The charge on the part of regional delegates that letters (information) were being withheld and decisions made unfairly, spoke to a not unwarranted suspicion that the benefits of UWT membership and leadership were not fairly distributed.[21]

Opening the second day of the conference, Minister for Community Development Mgonja, spoke to the women in terms equally symptomatic of women's depoliticization and the assertion of bureacratic state control. Whereas the TANU Women's Section had rallied women to join the struggle to create the nation, Mr. Mgonja told the delegates that by taking care of children, they were caring for the whole nation.[22] Emphasizing the importance of unity, he praised women for their support during the independence struggle. Now, however, it was their "gardening, poultry keeping, construction of wells, [and] tree planting," as well as their "hospitality and participation in adult education," that were praiseworthy. Echoing the concern that prompted Nyerere to establish a Ministry of National Culture and Youth as one of his first acts as president in 1962,[23] Mr. Mgonja warned the UWT delegates that African culture had to be promoted and saved because the colonialists had despised it as savage and backward, substituting their own culture in its stead.

---

20   Ibid., 3.

21   Emblematic of the situation was the fact that while UWT leaders from the central office were identified by name (i.e., Mrs. Nyerere, Mrs. Mgeni Saidi, Mrs. Mtenga, Ms. Mary Ibrahim, Ms. Lupembe, Mrs. Kawawa, Bibi Titi Mohamed), all other conference participants were identified only as "Tabora delegates," the "Lindi delegate," a "delegate from Kasulu."

22   Conference minutes, 3.

23   Julius Nyerere, *Freedom and Unity/Uhuru na Umoja* (London, 1967), 186.

Like Nyerere himself, Mgonja seemed to be ignoring the fact that women's dance groups had been instrumental in nationalist mobilizing, that women's "crafts" were alive and well, or that Swahili had also made possible the extensive communication of TANU's agenda. Now "traditional dances, language, and crafts" had to be promoted.

While there was a certain truth to Mgonja's remarks (albeit a strange parallel as well, to Huxley's interest in "rural jollification") most Tanganyikans, and especially most women, would have been surprised to learn that their "culture" needed revitalization. Like many postcolonial state-focused visions, this one reflected the experience of the educated and aspiring middle class, a group that no doubt saw the contradictions in their Western styles and aspirations, and felt ambivalent regarding what they might be experiencing as cultural loss. In his inaugural address to Parliament, President Nyerere bemoaned the fact that "so many of us" learned to rumba, chachacha, twist, waltz and foxtrot, yet had never heard of "the *Gombe Sugu*, the *Mangala*, the *Konge*, *Nyamg'umumi*, *Kiduo*, or *Lele Mama*." "It is hard," Nyerere continued, "for any man to get much real excitement from dances and music which are not in his own blood."[24]

Delegate responses to Mr. Mgonja's speech reflected the UWT's financial dependence on the Ministry of Community Development and a lack of cooperation between the ministry and UWT officials. The UWT wanted the ministry to pay for women's seminars and for teachers. Mr. Mgonja told the delegates to prepare specific reports identifying areas needing help.[25]

The adoption of a new UWT constitution provoked little discussion. Yet several articles are noteworthy for what they tell us about the organization. One article, for example, denied membership to thieves, instigators, and those who spoke negatively against the UWT, while another denied participation in UWT conferences to men from organizations with no female representatives. An article concerning term limits affirmed presidential and vice-presidential terms of two years, but one year terms for UWT officers involved with rural women (leaders at the grassroots level), who should "work very hard so that they can be reelected after the first year."[26] Other articles barred foreigners from UWT membership unless they were already members, established UWT Branch Committees on the new cell (ten household) system that had been put in place by TANU, and specified that the UWT district chairman should not be the regional chairman at the same time.[27] Thus the UWT Constitution reflected the framers' acceptance of vigilance against enemies and evil people as a major organizational issue, the need for greater accountability at the regional but not the central level, and an attempt to force the selection of women representatives in organizations where none existed.

Needless to say, organizational and bureaucratic issues took precedence over statements of principle in the new constitution. At the same time, delegates received a booklet of UWT guidelines intended to assist UWT branches in the proper oganization of activities, the formation of committees, the organization

---

[24] Ibid.

[25] Conference minutes, 3.

[26] Conference minutes, Agenda Item No. 3, To Adopt New Constitution, articles a, c, d, p. 3.

[27] Articles f, k, and l of the UWT constitution, Ibid.

of meetings, adult education, child education and culture. There was no discussion of the cell system, since publication had preceded the introduction of that system.

During the afternoon session of the conference, November 16, 1965, Mrs. Sophia Kawawa read a statement from her husband calling for a peaceful meeting and peaceful elections. "Skirmishes break homes," warned Mrs. Kawawa on behalf of her husband, "so be very careful whom you vote for."[28] Mrs. Kawawa's central role in the UWT, like that of Mrs. Nyerere, signaled another significant shift from the TANU Women's section, where neither woman had been prominent despite the political status of their husbands prior to independence.

Oscar Kambona, who had been relieved by Nyerere of his Foreign Affairs portfolio and made minister for regional affairs, was the only speaker at the UWT conference who directly addressed the importance of the TANU Women's Section, albeit to take credit for it. Kambona opened the morning session on November 17 by reminding the delegates that he was responsible for getting hard-working leaders like Bibi Titi, Tatu Mzee, and others to work for TANU. Women needed to work for development, since no country could be considered modern and developed unless its women were developed. Falling in line with his colleagues, however, Kambona went on to assert that development had to be rural as well as urban, and that UWT leaders needed to "return to the villages" to plan activities—not just concentrate on urban areas, which seemed to be the case so far. For his part, Kambona promised to ensure that TANU regional secretaries cooperated with UWT leaders in any way they could.

In the election of UWT officers that followed, Mrs. Agnes Sahani, the delegate from Mwanza, proposed that Bibi Titi Mohamed should continue as president, whereupon the delegates stood up and applauded and danced for twenty minutes "celebrating her reelection." Under the circumstances, it took some time for the acting chairman, Mrs. Sophia Kawawa, to persuade the delegates to nominate someone to stand against Bibi Titi. After four individuals were named only to withdraw from contention, a vote for president was held with 94 delegates voting, 91 yes, and 3 spoiled ballots. Mrs. Kanasia Mtenga was renominated and as no one agreed to stand against her, she was similarly reelected for a second two-year term as vice president.

A speech by First Vice-President A.A. Karume (of Zanzibar) closed the official conference.[29] The concern of Nyerere's government to merge all mainland government affiliates and organizations with their island counterparts was reflected in the charge to the UWT to do the same. Three delegates from Zanzibar's Afro-Shirazi Party therefore attended the annual conference, and closer ties between the UWT and UWZ were emphasized by Mrs. Lupembe, who introduced Vice-President Karume. Praising UWT leaders for "their efforts in nation building," Karume appealed to women to work harder to help the weak and poor of all races, and to "take care of the children." He warned against racial and religious discrimination[30] and urged women to be self-reliant and diligent. Empha-

---

[28]   Conference, Kawawa's speech.

[29]   The islands of Zanzibar, twenty miles off the mainland coast, united with Tanganyika on April 25, 1964, following a bloody revolution in which the Zanzibari sultanate was overthrown.

[30]   Thousands of Asians fled Zanzibar, and many Arabs were killed during and following the revolution.

sizing that UWT and UWZ were "one"—the "difference only in name"—Karume closed by praising the delegates for re-electing Bibi Titi and was given a UWT badge and the first copy of the UWT newspaper.[31]

District agenda items suggest the distance travelled from the nationalist mobilizing undertaken by TANU women in the 1950s to the UWT's attempts to negotiate its role in a state "nation-building" enterprise which conceptualized women as objects of development and policing efforts, while addressing issues of gender inequality and oppression that plagued women regardless of class status, education, or location. Thus delegates discussed at length the importance of "national dress" and how it should be worn, especially during celebrations and conferences, concluding that short dresses, whether made of *kanga* or *kitenge*, should not be allowed. Beyond that, delegates agreed that the UWT could not interfere with an individual's choice of attire, except to suggest that dresses should not be tight.[32] The significance some women attached to policing women's attire emerged again when delegates from Geita called for a ban on all writing on *kangas* because of the abusive words sometimes used. In addition to supporting this ban, delegates voted to inform the Ministry of Commerce and COSATA of the UWT's declaration, and to urge that *kangas* be made larger and heavier. A second major issue concerned the prohibitive cost for some women of buying both TANU and UWT membership cards, and the requirement, in some places, of possessing a TANU card in order to buy a UWT card. The chairman ruled that women who wanted only UWT cards should be allowed to purchase them, but pointed out that it was important for UWT leaders to continue to try to convince women to join TANU. A shortage of UWT cards, delays in receipt, and the cost of transporting them were also discussed at length.

At the same time, attempts were made to address issues of gender discrimination, specifically whether or not the UWT could prevent husbands from expelling or divorcing their wives after the latter had borne many children. Delegates agreed that this was a painful issue and the conference strongly condemned the act. At the same time, they strongly condemned "women who are fond of snatching others' husbands, thus causing divorces." Having in this way effectively undermined the clarity of their initial concern, the delegates agreed that the UWT could not, in any case, legislate concerning the issue. Instead, they tabled a motion to call on the government to enact a law concerning children and divorced wives, and to form a committee to examine marriage laws in the context of cultural and religious practice.[33] Delegates also "complained bit-

---

[31]   Conference minutes, 8.

[32]   Conference minutes, "Agenda from the District," 1. The patterned lengths of cloth with clearly defined borders known as *kanga* invariably have Swahili sayings on them, and are often worn and prized for what they "say" as well as their color and pattern. A *kitenge* (pl., *vitenge*) has neither the words nor borders characteristic of *kanga*.

[33]   It was not until 1971 that The Law of Marriage Act was passed, providing women with increased security "through legal registration of marriages and divorces, minimum age regulation (fifteen for women, eighteen for men), the power to declare the intention at the outset of keeping the marriage either monogamous or potentially polygamous and, in the latter case, the need for the consent of the first wife (wives) to be obtained by the husband before he can take another wife." (Swantz, *Women in Development*, 12).

terly" over the abuse and ill treatment of pregnant women and children by nurses, and voted to have UWT head office ask the Ministry of Health to take stern measures against "the culprits."

Amidst these issues relating directly to the perceived abuse of women, however, were others: the payment of a subsistence allowance to conference delegates and of 10 percent of the money collected to UWT fee collectors; the serious transportation problems in many districts (UWT could not afford its own vehicles and depended on TANU leaders, area commissioners, and community development officers for transportation); and the need to get the Ministries of Education and of Health to pay teachers and nurses who were volunteering to teach women. In addition, a motion was tabled asking the UWT head office to write to the central government asking them to find employment for illiterate women who desperately needed work.

Finally, delegates raised the problem of men treating women with contempt and insulting them in various ways. Perhaps not surprisingly given the postcolonial ethos of women's need to "develop," "change," and "work harder," dominant voices at the meeting conveyed the sense that women were somehow responsible for the way men behaved toward them, and that in order to "do away with this behavior" women had to "work harder, without getting tired or despairing in their quest to consolidate their unity."[34]

Here, then, were the attempts of a national women's organization, now subject to the politics of the nation state, to address the newly discovered problems of "women and development" in 1965. If they sounded like the problems Tanganyika's first European women social workers and club organizers sought to address in the late 1940s and early 1950s, it is because they were similar problems. Now, however, it was an independent African government determining what organized women should do and care about, and African women conveying the message to other women.

Despite these tensions, however, many women activists of the 1950s managed to make the transition to postcolonial realms of state politics and participation in one way or the other—via continuing activity in TANU at the local level, UWT activities and leadership, or the TANU Youth League. All remained committed to a nationalist vision that had been thoroughly fueled by the bright and hopeful fires of 1950s anticolonial idealism and for many women, was kept alive through ongoing involvement with each other.

The postindependence political life history of Lucy Lameck, whose earlier political career is recounted in Chapter 6, offers substantial insight into the commitment required to keep an acceptably politicized vision of and for women. Lucy Selina Lameck was not "typical" of the TANU activists who spearheaded the TANU Women's Section of the 1950s or of women in the post-independence UWT. She completed secondary school, trained as a nurse and acquired further education in Britain and the United States. She was more highly educated than the vast majority of women of her generation, and she was not Muslim. Both of these aspects of her identity faciliated her political career into the late 1980s. She died on March 21, 1992, of complications related to liver disease.

---

[34]   District Agenda, 2.

Lucy Lameck[35]

In 1962, I was lucky, he [Nyerere] ... recognized the contribution of the women in the party right from the beginning, and knew full well that the active participation of women was needed in the new development of the country. [So he] appointed [me] junior minister of community development and cooperatives, where I worked with women's groups and with cooperatives which were also geared towards women's economic activities. At that time, as you will remember, the cooperative movement in our country was the first and the strongest in the whole of Africa. And it was one of the most important economic units which was ... based on the social aspirations and values of our country ... and the community development aspect of it was dealing largely with questions of women and children.

So I was appointed a deputy minister at that time up to 1965, when I decided to run for election in my home area. Fortunately, although I met stiff opposition, I won with a very good margin.[36] In 1966 I was transferred to the Ministry of Health and Housing and I was there up to 1972. So actually, I served in my capacity as a deputy minister for ten years...when I was released from responsibility, and concentrated more on women's activities and on my constituency at home.

In 1970 I stood for election again, against another tough opponent. He was regional chairman, and regional party chairmen are very powerful people. He also stood against me in 1975. Unfortunately for him, I was still popular with the people, and...he lost. So from 1970 to 1975 I remained a back bencher.... I did not win the election in 1975,[37] but I won the election in 1980. And I am still a back bencher, I'm still interested in women's affairs. I still have a lot to do in my country, and we are still struggling and we are still doing what we think is correct....

Historically, Tanzanian women have been very strong politically in mobilizing and supporting the party. And that is why we can say what we want to say very strongly and be heard ... because it is historical, it is not just something which arrived today. And we did not start by wearing all sorts of expensive clothes and gold and whatever. We started as humble, simple peasant women, representative of the rural poor people of this country. This is where we differ very much from other parts of Africa....

But I would also add, Susan, that the attitude of the leadership contributed.... We did see, and we still feel that we had the right person [in Nyerere] to whom we could entrust our country. And we felt that there

---

[35] Lameck interview, November 12, 1984.

[36] According to Lionel Cliffe, Lameck ran the "toughest and best organised private campaign in the region" to win handily (26,902 to 1,616) and maintained her position as a junior minister as well. See Appendix IC in Cliffe, ed., *One Party Democracy*, 373–74.

[37] As a secondary school student, Theodora Bali remembers serving as a poll watcher in Weru Weru, Kilimanjaro, for the 1975 election. The wife of Lucy Lameck's opponent stood on her property, which happened to be very near the polling station, shouting to all who came to vote that Lucy Lameck was a prostitute. Because she was "just a girl," Theodora did not know what to do about this. When Lucy Lameck arrived at the polling station the two women began shouting vehemently at each other. Lucy Lameck was furious, but could not stop her opponent's wife because even though there was a rule against campaigning so close to a polling station on election day, the woman was on her own property and could therefore shout to her heart's content. Conversation, Theodora Bali, May 18, 1995.

Photo 11: Lucy Lameck, 1960. Courtesy of the *Daily News/Sunday News*, Dar es Salaam, Tanzania.

was honesty, and there would be room to breathe, there would be free-dom, there would be justice...no color bar, our children would go to school.... In our priorities, therefore, we had no legal tangles, who cooks for whom, who goes for what....

[I]f you ask me whether there was a woman who was thinking about a better salary, I doubt that very much.... Of course, women had particular problems and women who joined TANU...had problems.... Fair enough, Susan [women had specific problems], but what I'm trying to tell you is this: Now we are in a better position to fight those prejudices than we were before independence. Before independence whom could I talk to? Who would listen to me? I would not even sniff around near the House of Parliament. I couldn't even be near there, nobody would listen to me. Now that there has been an opportunity, there are a few women in Parliament and I hope there will be more and more....

In the remainder of our interview, Lucy Lameck spoke passionately about the need to continue the battle against customs and laws that prevented Tanzanian women from achieving equality with men in all spheres of society. But she believed that the struggle had to take place at all levels, with women's grassroots concerns expressed through the UWT and echoed by women in the party and in Parliament; and she further believed that the system whereby regional community development workers served as UWT secretaries facilitated this process. She also insisted that Tanzania was far ahead of most African countries with respect to legislation on behalf of, and support for women, and spoke of the significance of the research into women's problems being undertaken by women at the University of Dar es Salaam and other institutions. Only scientific data, she stressed, would convince men of the need for change.

She spoke of her high regard for rural Tanzanian women, emphasizing their intelligence, political awareness, and enthusiasm, and contrasting them with African women who seemed to think that wearing expensive clothes and gold was progressive. She praised Tanzania and the government for a commitment to mass education, rural health clinics, and rural development, all of which benefitted women. At the same time, she deplored the fact that at the time (1984), pregnant schoolgirls were being expelled from school while the teachers, classmates, and other men responsible went unpunished. Sex education, she added, was a difficult topic to introduce in the schools.

Lucy Lameck stated that women were often favored over men as employees in banks, hotels, the post office, and other places, because they were considered more honest and trustworthy. In fact, she considered the needs and problems of rural women to be the most pressing, and emphasized how difficult it was to solve them in such a poor country. Moreover, she was critical of the United States for failing to understand and acknowledge both Tanzania's desperate need for economic assistance *and* its right to make independent policy decisions.

Lucy Lameck's vision was of a multipurpose training institution for women in every district, geared to agricultural production and storage, appropriate technology to lighten women's work load (e.g., solar ovens, biogas), and maternal and child welfare. As for whether women thought they had a right to control what they produced, she said, "That is coming ... not as soon as we want it, but it is coming. Yes."

Narrative, Experience, and the Gendered Construction of Tanganyikan Nationalism

At the conclusion of his comprehensive history of Tanganyika to independence, John Iliffe offers a perceptive observation that captures the life stories propelling this book's narrative. "Tanganyikan nationalism was not simply about interests and their organisation. It was also about passions and their liberation."[38] Iliffe writes about "passions and their liberation" in the context of Nyerere's growing confidence in his supporters—a confidence that enabled him to see "the crowds' discipline, attentiveness, and gaiety ...[which] emboldened him to liberate emotions which others feared."[39] By investing Nyerere with the power to "liberate emotions" Iliffe shifts the source of nationalism from the women and men whose "discipline, attentiveness and gaiety" engendered it, to Nyerere, who molded that nationalism into TANU ideology, an independence struggle, and ultimately, an authoritarian one-party state.

Offering an additional insight, Iliffe notes that "most men" experienced nationalism in "everyday relationships."[40] Here, his reference is to male workers and labor actions; but his recognition of the importance of everyday relationships to the experience of nationalism is certainly echoed in this book. Women's relationships to one another, their ability to mobilize others through existing social organizations and networks and through newly created associations such as the Women's and Youth's Sections of TANU, constructed and expressed Tanganyikan nationalism.

Moreover, women's narratives or "political" life histories—inseparable from their associational relationships and from their experience—also expressed Tanganyikan nationalism. Based on memories which were themselves constituted out of the experience of nationalist mobilization and participation in TANU, especially during the 1950s, these narratives are obviously social constructions. Nationalism as an expression of collective sensibility, a quest for self-government and a unity of purpose is not, after all, subject to the test of scientific replication. So what, then can we say about memory as a valid "source" for nationalism? I can do no better than to return to the insights of Karen Fields:

> [M]emory "tainted" by interest is a dead-serious party to the creation of something true. The "mistakes" it may embody represent an imperfection only in light of the particular purposes scholarship has. Our scholarly effort to get the "real" past, not the true past required by a particular present, does not authorize us to disdain as simply mistaken this enormously consequential, creative, and everywhere visible operation of memory.[41]

In relying on TANU women's personal narratives (in this case, life histories), refusing a separation between experience and language and insisting on the productive quality of discourse, I have sought to reflect Joan Scott's view that the agency of TANU women was "created through situations and statuses conferred on them," and that their "experience is collective as well as individual." "Experience," concludes Scott, "is a subject's history. Language is the site of history's enactment. Historical explanation cannot, therefore, separate the two."[42]

---

38   Iliffe, *Modern History*, 537.

39   Ibid.

40   Ibid.

41   Fields, "What One Cannot Remember Mistakenly," 7.

42   Joan Scott, "The Evidence of Experience," *Critical Inquiry* 17 (Summer 1991), 193.

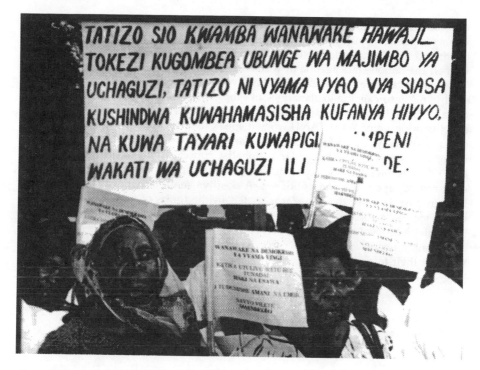

Photo 12: Women demonstrating in 1994 for a larger role in multiparty democracy. The text of the sign reads: "The problem isn't that women don't want to stand for parliamentary seats in their constituencies. Their political parties have failed to encourage them to do so and [have failed] to be ready to campaign for them during the elections so that they could win. We peacefully demand justice and rights so that we uphold/perpetuate peace and unity, and thus bring development." Courtesy of the Government Information Office of Tanzania. Translation: Nathan Chiume.

In this book, I have depicted TANU women's historical experience of nationalism in language expressed to me in the 1980s, albeit generally translated from Swahili. TANU women's agency as builders and performers of Tanganyikan nationalism was clearly shaped by and responsive to "situations and statuses conferred on them" in the context of TANU's need to mobilize an independence movement in the 1950s. But it was drawn, as well, from women's historical experience and lived realities that shaped TANU in turn and reflected a kind of nationalism rooted in Tanganyika's social and cultural history. Even in the late 1980s, TANU women's sense of nationalism seemed capable of withstanding extensive evidence of the failure of state and government policies, mismanagement, and corruption. Although women activists of the 1950s could not accomplish the tasks of the next generation or secure the emancipation of Tanzanian women in the 1990s, they spread nationalism and the ideas of equality and dignity though their own actions and through encouraging others to become political actors. With TANU's rhetoric to support them, they demonstrated that those ideas meant *women's* equality and dignity too. The processes of nationalist movement in Tanganyika were embodied in women's gendered understandings and actions—understandings and actions that continued to inform nationalism in the postcolonial state whether or not they informed the nation-state agenda or women's organizing.

Understandings gleaned from TANU women mobilizers and activists do not easily "fit" into existing explanations of "the rise of nationalism" found in traditional nationalist historiography. Nor do they fit the scholarly literature critical of that historiography. What TANU women speak to is what neither of these schools explain—namely, the persistence of the Tanzanian postcolonial state and a strong nationalist sentiment and popular nationalist consciousness present through the late 1980s despite extreme economic hardship and a high level of apathy or cynicism regarding politics and politicians. A positive sense of nationalism existed, at least in part, because this sense was rooted in the forms of popular mobilization expressed by "ordinary" Swahili women. Dignity, self-respect, equality regardless of ethnicity or level of education, pan-ethnic solidarity—these aspects of a nationalist consciousness continue to carry weight, although it is appropriate to ask whether their force will be felt when the older generation of activists is gone.

SOURCES

Interviews*

(Names followed by * indicate persons whose life histories were not directly incorporated into this book.)

Abdallah, Fatuma. Magomeni (Dar es Salaam), 26 September 1984
Ali, Asha. Magomeni (Dar es Salaam), 26 September 1984*
Ali, Mwasaburi. Dar es Salaam, 10 September 1984
Athmani, Tabu. Dodoma (Kanyama Chiume), December 1984*
DeMello, Christine. Moshi, 12 October 1988*
Ferouz, Salima. Magomeni, 26 September 1984
Feruzi, Kijakazi. Dodoma (Kanyama Chiume), December 1984*
Gupta, Elizabeth. Moshi, 20 October 1988
Gwassa, Anna. Kunduchi, 1 November 1984*
Hamisi, Halima. Dar es Salaam, 23 October 1984
Hatibu, Zainabu. Moshi, 13 October 1988
Kamba, Hadija. Buguruni (Dar es Salaam), 26 October 1984*
Juma, Pili. Mwanza, 21 November 1988
Kamba, Hadija. Dar es Salaam, 26 October 1984*
Kaundime, Bi. Dar es Salaam, 30 October 1984*
Kemp, Maida Springer. Pittsburgh, 19 February 1989*
Kinabo, Halima Selengia. Moshi, 7 October 1988
Kinabo, Mario. Pasua (Moshi), 8 October 1988
Kipara, Binti. Temeke (Dar es Salaam) 17 October 1984
Kibonge, Mashavu binti. Kariakoo (Dar es Salaam) 23 October 1984
Kibonge, Mwamvua. Mwanza, 22 November 1988
Lameck, Lucy. Upanga (Dar es Salaam) 12 November 1984
Ley, Blandina. Dar es Salaam, 21 November 1992*
Lucas, Aziza. Mwanza, 21 November 1988
Lyimo, Agnes. Moshi, 20 October 1988
Makatani, Martha. (Speech), 19 November 1988
Mbegu, Asha. Mwanayamala (Dar es Salaam), 2 August 1988*
Milando, Mbbuta. Dar es Salaam, 2 September 1984
Mnyamani, Mwamvita. Buguruni (Dar es Salaam), 26 October 1984
Mohamed, Bibi Titi. Temeke (Dar es Salaam), 10 September, 18 October, 23 November 1984;
    Upanga (Dar es Salaam), 4 September, 20 September 1988; 14 November 1992
Msafiri, Mwajuma. Mbugani (Mwanza), 22 November 1988
Mshamba, Natujwa Daniel. Kiboroloni (Moshi), 19 October 1988
Mtenga, Kanasia Tade. Moshi, 19 October, 16 December 1988
Mto, Mwatumu. Mwanza, 22 November 1988*

Muhundi Haji, Habiba (and others). Zanzibar (with Raya Ali), 5 October 1984*
Mussa, Zuhura. Mwanza, 21 November 1988
Mustafa, Sophia. Dar es Salaam, 2 November 1984*
Mzee, Chausiku. Mwanza, 22 November 1988
Mzee, Tatu binti. Kinondoni (Dar es Salaam), 18 October 1984
Ngoma, Asha. Temeke (Dar es Salaam), 17 October 1984
Njau, Nsiana Nathan. Moshi, 18 October 1988
Njiro, Violet. Moshi, 20 October 1988
Ntare, Teresa. Magomeni (Dar es Salaam), 21 November 1992
Ntungi, Halima. Mbugani (Mwanza), 22 November 1988
Nyembu, Tunu. Isamilo (Mwanza), 21 November 1988
Otieno, Wambui. Minneapolis, 22 September 1994
Sadala, Hatia. Mwanayamala (Dar es Salaam), 4 August 1988*
Sahani, Agnes. Mwanza, 19 November 1988
Salim, Mwamvita. Moshi, 13 October 1988
Snyder, Margaret. Kampala, 27 January 1996
Suleman, Fatna bint. Dodoma (Kanyama Chiume), December, 1984*
Swedi, Hadija. Morogoro, 7 September 1984
Waraga, Shera. Mwanza, 22 November 1988
Zawawi, Sharifa. New York, 20 May, 1988*

Archives

England

Public Records Office (PRO), London
Rhodes House (RH), Oxford

Tanzania

Tanzania National Archives (TNA), Dar es Salaam

Books and Articles

Anderson, Benedict. *Imagined Communities: Reflections on the Origins and Spread of Nationalism.* London, 1991.
Baalawy, A. E. "Nyerere and Muslim Tanzania." Pamphlet published by the Zanzibar Organization, Southsea, Hants (no date).
Barnes, Teresa. "The Fight for Control of African Women's Mobility in Colonial Zimbabwe, 1900–1939." *Signs* 17, 3 (1992): 576–608.
Barongo, E. B. M. *Mkiki wa Siasa Tanganyika.* Dar es Salaam, 1966.
Barry, Kathleen. "Biography and the Search for Women's Subjectivity." *Women's Studies International Forum* 12, 6 (1989): 561–77.
Behar, Ruth. *Translated Woman: Crossing the Border with Esperanza's Story.* Boston, 1993.
Bienen, Henry. *Tanzania: Party Transformation and Economic Development.* Princeton, 1970.
Bledsoe, Caroline. *Women and Marriage in Kpelle Society.* Stanford, 1980.
Bouatta, Cherifa, and Doria Cherifati-Merabtine. "The Social Representation of Women in Algeria's Islamist Movement." In *Identity Politics and Women: Cultural Reassertions and Feminisms in International Perspective*, ed. Valentine M. Moghadam. Boulder, 1994.

Bozzoli, Belinda. "Intellectuals, Audiences and Histories: South African Experiences, 1978–88." *Radical History Review* 46, 7 (1990): 207–63.

Bozzoli, Belinda, with the assistance of Mmantho Nkotsoe. *Women of Phokeng: Consciousness, Life Strategy, and Migrancy in South Africa, 1900–1983.* Portsmouth, 1991.

Brass, Paul R. *Ethnicity and Nationalism: Theory and Comparison.* Newbury Park, 1991.

Bryceson, Deborah Fahy. "A Century of Food Supply in Dar es Salaam." In *Feeding African Cities,* ed. Jane Guyer. Bloomington, 1987.

———. "The Proletarianization of Women in Tanzania." *Review of African Political Economy* 17 (1980): 4–27.

———. "Women's Proletarianization and the Family Wage in Tanzania." In *Women, Work and Ideology in the Third World,* ed. Haleh Afshar. London, 1985.

Bujra, Janet M. "Men at Work in the Tanzanian Home: How Did They Ever Learn?" In *African Encounters with Domesticity,* ed. Karen Tranberg Hansen, New Brunswick, 1992.

———. "'Urging Women to Redouble Their Efforts': Class, Gender, and Capitalist Transformation in Africa." In *Women and Class in Africa,* eds. Claire Robertson and Iris Berger. New York, 1986.

———. "Women 'Entrepreneurs' of Early Nairobi." *Canadian Journal of African Studies* 9, 2 (1975): 213–34.

Callinicos, Alex. *Making History: Agency, Structure and Change in Social Theory.* Cambridge, 1987.

Cartwright, John. *Political Leadership in Africa.* New York, 1983.

Chanock, Martin. *Law, Custom, and Social Order: The Colonial Experience in Malawi and Zambia.* Cambridge, 1985.

Chatterjee, Partha. "Colonialism, Nationalism and Colonized Women: The Contest in India." *American Ethnologist* 16 (1989): 622–33.

Chaudhuri, Nupur, and Margaret Strobel, eds. *Western Women and Imperialism: Complicity and Resistance.* Bloomington, 1992.

Chiume, M. W. Kanyama. *Kanyama Chiume.* London, 1982.

———. *Kwacha.* Nairobi, 1975.

Clark, Gracia. *Onions Are My Husband: Survival and Accumulation by West African Market Women.* Chicago, 1994.

Cliffe, Lionel, ed. *One Party Democracy: The 1965 Tanzania General Elections.* Nairobi, 1967.

Cloete, Rehna. *The Nylon Safari.* London, 1956.

Connor, Walker. "The Specter of Ethno-Nationalist Movements Today." *PAWSS Perspectives* 1, 3 (1991): 1–13.

Cooper, Frederick. "Urban Space, Industrial Time, and Wage Labor in Africa." In *Struggle for the City: Migrant Labor, Capital, and the State in Urban Africa,* ed. Frederick Cooper. Beverley Hills, 1983.

Coulson, Andrew. *Tanzania: A Political Economy.* Oxford, 1982.

Davidson, Basil. *The Black Man's Burden: Africa and the Curse of the Nation-State.* New York, 1992.

Denzer, LaRay. "Constance A. Cummings-John: Her Early Political Career in Freetown." *Tarikh* 7, 1 (1981): 20–32.

———. "Towards a Study of the History of West African Women's Participation in Nationalist Politics: The Early Phase, 1935–1950." *Africana Research Bulletin* 6, 4 (1976): 65–85.

———. "Women in Government Service in Colonial Nigeria, 1862–1945." *Boston University African Studies Working Papers* 136, Boston, 1989.

———. "Yoruba Women: A Historiographical Study." *International Journal of African Historical Studies* 27, 1 (1994): 1–39.

Duggan, William Redman, and John R. Civille. *Tanzania and Nyerere: A Study of Ujamaa and Nationhood.* New York, 1976.

Fabian, Johannes. *Power and Performance.* Madison, 1990.

Feierman, Steven. *Peasant Intellectuals: Anthropology and History in Tanzania*. Madison, 1990.
Geiger, Susan. "Efforts Towards Women's Development in Tanzania: Gender Rhetoric vs. Gender Realities." *Women and Politics* 2, 4 (1982): 23–41.
———. "Umoja wa Wanawake and the Needs of the Rural Poor." *African Studies Review* 25, 2/3 (1982): 45–65.
———. "Women and African Nationalism." *Journal of Women's History* 2, 1 (1990): 227–44.
———. "Women in Nationalist Struggle: TANU Activists in Dar es Salaam." *International Journal of African Historical Studies* 20, 1 (1987): 1–26.
Gengenbach, Heidi. "Truth-Telling and the Politics of Women's Life History Research in Africa: A Reply to Kirk Hoppe." *International Journal of African Historical Studies* 27, 3 (1994): 619–27.
Glassman, Jonathon. *Feasts and Riot: Revelry, Rebellion, and Popular Consciousness on the Swahili Coast, 1856–1888*. Portsmouth, 1995.
Gluck, Sherna Berger, and Daphne Patai, eds. *Women's Words: The Feminist Practice of Oral History*. New York, 1991.
Golden, Renny. *The Hour of the Poor, The Hour of Women*. New York, 1991.
Government of Tanganyika. "The 1957 Census of African Population." In *Readings on Economic Development and Administration in Tanzania*, ed. Hadley Smith. Dar es Salaam, 1966.
Halbwachs, Maurice. *The Collective Memory*. New York, 1980.
Hartmann, Jeannette, ed. *Re-Thinking the Arusha Declaration*. Copenhagen, 1991.
Hatch, John. *New From Africa*. London, 1956.
———. *Tanzania, A Profile*. New York, 1972.
———. *Two African Statesmen: Kaunda of Zambia and Nyerere of Tanzania*. Chicago, 1976.
Hobsbawm, E. J. *Nations and Nationalism Since 1780*. Cambridge, 1991.
———. "The New Threat to History." *New York Review of Books* XL, 21 (1993): 62–64.
Hoppe, Kirk. "Whose Life Is It, Anyway?: Issues of Representation in Life Narrative Texts of African Women." *International Journal of African Historical Studies* 26, 3 (1993): 623–36.
Hunt, Lynn A. *Eroticism and the Body Politic*. Baltimore, 1991.
Hunt, Nancy. "Domesticity and Colonialism in Belgian Africa: Usumbura's *Foyer Social*, 1946–1960." *Signs* 15, 3 (1990): 447–74.
Huxley, Elspeth. "The Lion Needs the Jungle." *Time and Tide*, 10 October 1952.
Hyden, Goran. *Beyond Ujamaa in Tanzania*. London, 1980.
Ifeka-Moller, Caroline. "Female Militancy and Colonial Revolt." In *Perceiving Women*, ed. Shirley Ardener. New York, 1977.
Iliffe, John. *A Modern History of Tanganyika*. Cambridge, 1979.
Jerman, Helena. "How I Feel To Be a Tanzanian: Political considerations, folk and analytical evaluations of Tanzanian identity." *Suomen Antropologi* 3, 93: 31–41.
Johnson, Cheryl. "Class and Gender: A Consideration of Yoruba Women during the Colonial Period." In *Women and Class in Africa*, eds. Claire Robertson and Iris Berger. New York, 1986.
———. "Grassroots Organizing: Women in Anti-Colonial Activity in Southwestern Nigeria." *African Studies Review* 25, 2 (1982): 137–57.
Kandoro, S. A. *Mwito Wa Uhuru*. Dar es Salaam, 1961.
Kimambo, I. N. *Mbiru: Popular Protest in Colonial Tanzania*. Historical Association of Tanzania, Paper No. 9. Nairobi, 1969.
Landberg, Pamela. "Widows and Divorced Women in Swahili Society." In *Widows in African Societies: Choices and Constraints*, ed. Betty Potash. Stanford, 1986.
Langess, L. L. *The Life History in Anthropological Science*. New York, 1965.
Larsson, Birgitta. *Conversion to Greater Freedom?: Women, Church and Social Change in North-Western Tanzania Under Colonial Rule*. Stockholm, 1991.

Leslie, J. A. K. *A Survey of Dar es Salaam*. London, 1963.

Liebenow, J. Gus. "Nyerere of Tanzania: The Legend and the Ledger." Universities Field Staff International Reports, 3 Africa/Middle East, 1987.

Listowel, Judith. *The Making of Tanganyika*. London, 1965.

Lonsdale, John. "The Emergence of African Nationalism." In *Emerging Themes of African History*, ed. T.O. Ranger. Nairobi, 1968.

Lovett, Margot. "Gender Relations, Class Formation, and the Colonial State in Africa." In *Women and the State in Africa*, eds. Jane L. Parpart and Kathleen A. Staudt. Boulder, 1989.

Maguire, G. Andrew. *Toward "Uhuru" in Tanzania: The Politics of Participation*. Cambridge, 1969.

Marks, Shula, ed. *Not Either an Experimental Doll: The Separate Worlds of Three South African Women*. Durban, 1987.

Mazrui, Ali. "Building Socialism Without a Vanguard Party." In *Re-Thinking the Arusha Declaration*, ed. Jeannette Hartmann. Copenhagen, 1991.

Mazumdar, Sucheta. "Moving Away from a Secular Vision? Women, Nation, and the Cultural Construction of Hindu India." In *Identity Politics and Women: Cultural Reassertions and Feminisms in International Perspective*, ed. Valentine M. Moghadam. Boulder, 1994.

———. "Women, Culture and Politics: Engendering the Hindu Nation." *South Asia Bulletin* 12, 2 (1992): 1–24.

Mba, Nina. *Nigerian Women Mobilized: Women's Political Activity in Southern Nigeria, 1900–1965*. Berkeley, 1982.

Mbilinyi, Marjorie. "African Education in the British Colonial Period." In *Tanzania Under Colonial Rule*, ed. M. Kaniki. London, 1980.

———. "'City' and 'Countryside' in Colonial Tanganyika." *Economic and Political Weekly* XX, 43, Review of Women's Studies, 26 October 1985, 83–96.

———. "'Runaway Wives' in Colonial Tanganyika: Forced Labour and Forced Marriage in Rungwe District, 1919–1961." *International Journal of the Sociology of Law* 16 (1988): 1–29.

———. "'This Is an Unforgettable Business': Colonial State Intervention in Urban Tanzania." In *Women and the State in Africa*, eds. Jane L. Parpart and Kathleen A. Staudt. Boulder, 1989.

McClintock, Anne. "'No Longer in a Future Heaven': Women and Nationalism in South Africa." *Transition* 51 (1991): 104–23.

McCurdy, Sheryl. "The 1932 'War' Between Rival Ujiji (Tanganyika) Associations: Understanding Women's Motivations for Inciting Political Protest." *Canadian Journal of African Studies* 30 (1996): 10-31.

Meena, Ruth. "Bibi Titi: Traitor or Heroine of *Uhuru*?" *Southern African Political and Economic Monthly*, April 1992.

Mosse, George L. *Nationalism and Sexuality: Middle-Class Morality and Sexual Norms in Modern Europe*. Madison, 1985.

Mirza, Sara, and Margaret Strobel, eds. *Three Swahili Women: Life Histories from Mombasa, Kenya*. Bloomington, 1989.

Molohan, M. J. B. *Detribalisation*. Dar es Salaam, 1957.

Mueller, Susanne D. "The Historical Origins of Tanzania's Ruling Class." African Studies Center Working Papers, 35, Boston University, 1980.

Mustafa, Sophia. *The Tanganyika Way*. Dar es Salaam, 1961.

Mwaga, D. Z., B. F. Mrina, and E. F. Lyimo. *Historia ya Chama cha TANU 1954 hadi 1977*. Dar es Salaam, 1981.

Nyerere, Julius. *Freedom and Socialism*. Dar es Salaam, 1968.

———. *Freedom and Unity/Uhuru na Umoja*. London, 1967.

O'Barr, Jean. "Pare Women: A Case of Political Involvement." *Rural Africana* 29 (1975–76): 121–34.

Obbo, Christine. "Stratification and the Lives of Women in Uganda." In *Women and Class in Africa*, eds. Claire Robertson and Iris Berger. New York, 1986.

Parker, Andrew, Mary Russo, Doris Sommer, and Patricia Yaeger, eds. *Nationalisms and Sexualities*. New York, 1992.

Parpart, Jane. "Sexuality and Power on the Zambian Copperbelt: 1926–1964." In *Patriarchy and Class: African Women at Home and in the Workforce*, eds. Sharon Stichter and Jane Parpart. Boulder, 1988.

Pedersen, Susan. "National Bodies, Unspeakable Acts: The Sexual Politics of Colonial Policy-Making." *Journal of Modern History* 63 (December 1991): 647–80.

Peter, Chris, and Sengodo Mvungi. "The State and the Student Struggles." In *The State and the Working People in Tanzania*, ed. Issa G. Shivji. Dakar, 1986.

Popular Memory Group, "Popular Memory: Theory, Politics, Method." In *Making Histories: Studies in History Writing and Politics*, eds. Richard Johnson, Gregor McLennan, Bill Schwartz, and David Sutton. Minneapolis, 1982.

Pratt, Cranford. *The Critical Phase in Tanzania, 1945–1968: Nyerere and the Emergence of a Socialist Strategy*. Cambridge, 1976.

Pratt, Mary Louise. *Imperial Eyes: Travel Writing and Transculturation*. New York, 1992.

Presley, Cora Ann. *Kikuyu Women, the Mau Mau Rebellion, and Social Change in Kenya*. Boulder, 1992.

Ranger, T. O. *Dance and Society in Eastern Africa, 1890–1970: The Beni Ngoma*. Berkeley, 1975.

Robinson, Pearl T. "Democratization: Understanding the Relationship Between Regime Change and the Culture of Politics." *African Studies Review* 37, 1 (1994): 39–67.

Robertson, Claire. "Women's Education and Class Formation in Africa, 1950–1980." In *Women and Class in Africa*, eds. Claire Robertson and Iris Berger. New York, 1986.

Rogers, Susan [Geiger]. "Anti-Colonial Protest in Africa: A Female Strategy Reconsidered." *Heresies* 9, 3 (1980): 22–25.

Romero, Patricia, ed. *Women's Voices on Africa: A Century of Travel Writings*. Princeton, 1992.

Rostow, W. W. *The Stages of Economic Growth, a Non-Communist Manifesto*. Cambridge, 1960.

Sabot, R. *Economic Development and Urban Migration: Tanzania 1900–1971*. Oxford, 1979.

Sacks, Karen Brodkin. "What's a Life Story Got to Do with It?" In *Interpreting Women's Lives: Feminist Theory and Personal Narratives*, ed. Personal Narratives Group. Bloomington, 1989.

Said, Mohamed. "In Praise of Ancestors." *Africa Events*, March/April 1988.

Said, Mohamed. "Founder of a Political Movement: Abdulwahid K. Sykes (1924–1968)." *Africa Events*, September 1988.

Samoff, Joel. *Tanzania: Local Politics and the Structure of Power*. Madison, 1974.

Schmidt, Elizabeth. "Patriarchy, Capitalism, and the Colonial State in Zimbabwe." *Signs* 16, 4 (1991): 732–56.

———. "Race, Sex and Domestic Labour: The Question of African Female Servants in Southern Rhodesia, 1900–1939." In *African Encounters with Domesticity*, ed. Karen Tranberg Hansen. New Brunswick, 1992.

Scott, Joan. "The Evidence of Experience." *Critical Inquiry* 17, 1991.

Shields, Nwanganga. "Women in the Urban Labor Markets of Africa: The Case of Tanzania." *World Bank Staff Papers*, 380, April 1980.

Shostak, Marjorie. *Nisa: The Life and Words of a !Kung Woman*. Cambridge, 1981.

Smith, William E. "A Reporter At Large. Transition." *New Yorker*, 3 March 1986.

Snyder, Margaret C. *Transforming Development: Women, Poverty and Politics*. New York, 1995.

Snyder, Margaret C. and Mary Tadesse eds., *African Women and Development: A History*. London: 1995.

Somers, Margaret R. "Narrativity, Narrative Identity, and Social Action: Rethinking English Working-Class Formation." *Social Science History* 16, 4 (1992): 591–630.

Spindel, Carol. *In the Shadow of the Sacred Grove*. New York, 1989.

Stahl, Kathleen M. *History of the Chagga People of Kilimanjaro*. The Hague, 1964.

Strobel, Margaret. *Muslim Women in Mombasa, 1890–1975*. New Haven, 1979.

Swantz, Marja-Liisa. *Women in Development: A Creative Role Denied?* New York, 1985.

Tanganyika. *Report for the Year 1953*. London, 1954.

Tanganyika. *Report for the Year 1955*. London, 1956.

Tanganyika. *Report for the Year 1956*. London, 1957.

Tanganyika. *Report on the Census of the Non-African Population, 1957*. Dar es Salaam, 1958.

Tanganyika. *Statistical Abstracts 1954*. Dar es Salaam, 1955.

Taylor, J. Clagett. *The Political Development of Tanganyika*. Stanford, 1963.

Temu, A. J. "The Rise and Triumph of Nationalism." In *A History of Tanzania*, eds. I. N. Kimambo and A. J. Temu. Nairobi, 1969.

Thomas, Caroline. *In Search of Security: The Third World in International Relations*. Boulder, 1987.

Tonkin, Elizabeth. *Narrating Our Pasts: The Social Construction of Oral History*. Cambridge, 1992.

Tordoff, William. *Government and Politics of Tanzania*. Nairobi, 1967.

Tripp, Aili Mari. *Changing the Rules: The Politics of Liberalization and the Urban Informal Economy in Tanzania*. Berkeley and Los Angeles, 1997.

Ulotu, Abubakar. *Historia ya TANU*. Dar es Salaam, 1971.

United Republic of Tanzania. *Women and Men in Tanzania*. Bureau of Statistics, Dar es Salaam, 1992.

Van Hensbrock, Pieter Boele. "Cursing The Nation-State." *Transition* 61, 1993.

Vaughan, Megan. *Curing Their Ills: Colonial Power and African Illness*. Stanford, 1991.

Walker, Cherryl. *Women and Resistance in South Africa*. London, 1982.

Wells, Julia. *We Now Demand! The History of Women's Resistance to Pass Laws in South Africa*. Johannesburg, 1993.

Werbner, Richard. *Tears of the Dead: The Social Biography of an African Family*. Washington, D.C., 1991.

White, Luise. "A Colonial State and an African Petty Bourgeoisie: Prostitution, Property, and Class Struggle in Nairobi, 1936–1940." In *Struggle for the City: Migrant Labor, Capital, and the State in Urban Africa*, ed. Frederick Cooper. Beverley Hills, 1983.

——. *The Comforts of Home: Prostitution in Colonial Nairobi*. Chicago, 1990.

——. "Prostitution, Identity and Class Consciousness During World War II." *Signs* 11, 2 (1986): 255–73.

Wipper, Audrey. "The Maendeleo ya Wanawake Movement in the Colonial Period: The Canadian Connection, Mau Mau, Embroidery and Agriculture." *Rural Africana* 29 (1975–76): 195–213.

——. "The Maendeleo ya Wanawake Organization: The Co-optation of Leadership." *African Studies Review* 18, 3 (1975): 99–119.

Wolf, Margery. *A Thrice Told Tale: Feminism, Postmodernism, and Ethnographic Responsibility*. Minneapolis, 1994.

Wright, Marcia. *Strategies of Slaves and Women: Life Stories from East/Central Africa*. New York, 1993.

Young, Crawford. "Nationalism, Ethnicity, and Class in Africa: A Retrospective." *Cahiers d'Etudes Africaines* 26, 103 (1986): 421–95.

Yuval-Davis, Nira. "Gender and Nation." *Ethnic and Racial Studies* 16, 4 (1993): 621–32.

Unpublished Theses, Papers, and Recordings

Amory, Deborah P. "Waswahili Ni Nani?: The Politics of Swahili Identity and Culture." Paper presented at the Annual Meeting of the African Studies Association, Baltimore, 1990.

Anthony, David Henry. "Culture and Society in a Town in Transition: A People's History of
    Dar es Salaam, 1865–1939." Ph.D. dissertation, University of Wisconsin, 1983.
Bujra, Janet M. "Pumwani: The Politics of Property." Social Science Research Council (U.K.),
    London, 1972 (mimeo).
Campbell, John. "Urbanization of Dar es Salaam." Seminar presentation, Women's Research
    and Documentation Project, University of Dar es Salaam, September 17, 1984.
Fair, Laura. "Pastimes and Politics: A Social History of Zanzibar's Ng'ambo Community 1890–
    1950." Ph.D. dissertation, University of Minnesota, 1994.
Glassman, Jonathon. "Social Rebellion and Swahili Culture: The Response to the German
    Conquest of the Northern Mrima." Ph.D. dissertation, University of Wisconsin, 1988.
Green, Allen. "A Socio-economic History of Moshi Town." Ph.D. dissertation, University of
    Dar es Salaam, 1979.
Kerner, Donna. "The Social Uses of Knowledge in Contemporary Tanzania." Ph.D. disserta-
    tion, City University of New York, 1988.
Luanda, N. N. "European Commercial Farming and Its Impact on the Meru and Arusha
    Peoples of Tanzania, 1920–1955." Ph.D. dissertation, Cambridge University, 1986.
McWilliam, Anita. "Is There Sexism in Kiswahili?" Occasional Paper No. 3, Women's Re-
    search and Documentation Project, February 1988.
Morgenthau, Henry. Interview with Bibi Titi Mohamed, 28 August 1965. OT 2162. 71–071–F.
    Indiana University.
Olenmark, Eva, and Ulla Westerberg. *Tanzania: Kariakoo, a Residential Area in Central Dar es
    Salaam.* Department of Architecture, University of Lund, Sweden.
Rogers, Susan (Geiger). "The Search for Political Focus on Kilimanjaro: A History of Chagga
    Politics, 1916–1952, with Special Reference to the Cooperative Movement and Indirect
    Rule." Ph.D. dissertation, University of Dar es Salaam, 1973.
Said, Mohamed. "Ally K. Sykes Remembers."
Shivji, Issa G. "Development of Wage-Labour and Labour Laws in Tanzania: Circa 1920–
    1964." Ph.D. dissertation, University of Dar es Salaam, 1982.
Trebon, Thomas J. "Development of the Pre-independence Educational System in Tanganyika,
    With Special Emphasis on the Role of Missionaries." Ph.D. dissertation, University of
    Denver, 1980.
Tripp, Aili Mari. "The Urban Informal Economy and the State in Tanzania." Ph.D. disserta-
    tion, Northwestern University, 1990.

INDEX